THE *MÒZǏ*

The *Mòzǐ* contains the collected writings of the followers of Mò Dí, an ethical, political, and religious activist and teacher who lived during the fifth century BC in the 'central states' that were later united to become the Chinese empire. Mò Dí and his followers initiated philosophical debate in China, introduced influential ethical, political, and logical theories, and were renowned for their outspoken opposition to military aggression and their expertise in defensive warfare. They played a prominent role in Chinese philosophical discourse for over two centuries.

CHRIS FRASER is Professor of Philosophy at the University of Hong Kong and the author of *The Philosophy of the Mòzǐ* (2016) and many dozen research articles on early Chinese ethics, politics, metaphysics, epistemology, philosophy of mind and action, and philosophy of language and logic, as reflected in Confucian, Mohist, and Daoist texts.

T0369594

OXFORD WORLD'S CLASSICS

*For over 100 years Oxford World's Classics have brought
readers closer to the world's great literature. Now with over
700 titles—from the 4,000-year-old myths of Mesopotamia to the
twentieth century's greatest novels—the series makes available
lesser-known as well as celebrated writing.*

*The pocket-sized hardbacks of the early years contained
introductions by Virginia Woolf, T. S. Eliot, Graham Greene,
and other literary figures which enriched the experience of reading.
Today the series is recognized for its fine scholarship and
reliability in texts that span world literature, drama and poetry,
religion, philosophy and politics. Each edition includes perceptive
commentary and essential background information to meet the
changing needs of readers.*

OXFORD WORLD'S CLASSICS

MÒZǏ

The Essential Mòzǐ
Ethical, Political, and Dialectical Writings

Translated with an Introduction and Notes by
CHRIS FRASER

OXFORD
UNIVERSITY PRESS

OXFORD
UNIVERSITY PRESS

Great Clarendon Street, Oxford, OX2 6DP,
United Kingdom

Oxford University Press is a department of the University of Oxford.
It furthers the University's objective of excellence in research, scholarship,
and education by publishing worldwide. Oxford is a registered trade mark of
Oxford University Press in the UK and in certain other countries

Published in the United States of America by Oxford University Press
198 Madison Avenue, New York, NY 10016, United States of America

British Library Cataloguing in Publication Data

Data available

Library of Congress Control Number: 2020933195

ISBN 978-0-19-884810-3

Printed and bound in Great Britain by
Clays Ltd, Elcograf S.p.A.

MIX
Paper | Supporting
responsible forestry
FSC® C018072

The manufacturer's authorised representative in the EU for product safety is
Oxford University Press España S.A. of el Parque Empresarial San Fernando de
Henares, Avenida de Castilla, 2 – 28830 Madrid (www.oup.es/en).

For those we lost

CONTENTS

Acknowledgements   ix

Introduction   x

Note on the Translation   xxiii

Select Bibliography   xxxii

Chronology   xxxvii

Maps   xxxviii

THE ESSENTIAL *MÒZǏ*

PART I: MISCELLANEOUS ESSAYS

Book 4: Models and Standards   5

Book 5: Seven Troubles   8

Book 6: Avoiding Excess   11

Book 7: Three Disputations   15

PART II: THE TRIADS

Books 8–10: Promoting the Worthy   19

Books 11–13: Identifying Upward   34

Books 14–16: Inclusive Care   50

Books 17–19: Condemning Aggression   64

Books 20–1: Moderation in Use   75

Book 25: Moderation in Burial   80

Books 26–8: Heaven's Intent   89

Book 31: Understanding Ghosts   108

Book 32: Condemning Music 116

Books 35–7: Condemning Fatalism 121

PART III: CONDEMNING THE ERUDITES

Book 39: Condemning the Erudites (II) 137

PART IV: THE DIALECTICS

Books 40–3: The Canons and Explanations 145

Book 44: The 'Greater Selection' 171

Book 45: The 'Lesser Selection' 176

PART V: THE DIALOGUES

Book 46: Gēng Zhù 183

Book 47: Valuing Righteousness 188

Book 48: Gōng Mèng 192

Book 49: The Questions of Lǔ 197

Book 50: Gōngshū 202

Explanatory Notes 205

Glossary 257

Appendix: The Chronology of the Triads 273

ACKNOWLEDGEMENTS

MANY of my teachers, colleagues, and students contributed in various ways to the interpretations presented in this book. I thank Chad Hansen for igniting my initial interest in the *Mòzǐ* many years ago; A. C. Graham for his monumental *Later Mohist Logic*, which helped to guide me and countless others through the Mohist dialectical writings; and Taeko Brooks, for showing us all a new way of looking at the Mohist triads. Conversations with Dan Robins, Ng Kai Chiu, Lee Kwok Wai, Loy Hui Chieh, Jane Geaney, Franklin Perkins, Carine Defoort, and Roman Malek shaped my reading of the *Mòzǐ* in various ways, and I am grateful to all of them. I thank Wang Huachao for spotting several errors in the translation. I am also indebted to the many students who have taken my courses on Mohism at the Chinese University of Hong Kong and on Chinese ethics at the University of Hong Kong, asked incisive questions about Mohist thought, and wrote thoughtful essays about it.

Part IV of the book is especially indebted to Lam Hong Ki, who was my research assistant and collaborator on a lengthy research project devoted to investigating textual problems in the Mohist canons. I also thank Dan Robins for offering detailed comments on several difficult passages. I gratefully acknowledge three grants that funded this project, two direct grants from the Arts and Languages Panel of the Chinese University Research and Technology Office in 2003–4 and a Competitive Earmarked Research Grant from the Research Grants Council of the University Grants Committee of Hong Kong in 2004–5.

I am also grateful to the Research Grants Council of the University Grants Committee of Hong Kong for a General Research Fund grant in 2016 that helped facilitate completion of the manuscript.

I thank the staff of Oxford University Press for all their assistance, especially Luciana O'Flaherty, Kizzy Taylor-Richelieu, and Peter Momtchiloff for their editorial guidance and Charles Lauder, Jr, for his painstaking copy-editing. I am deeply grateful to two anonymous readers for detailed critical comments on a draft of the translation, many of which have been incorporated into the final version.

Last, I thank my wife Flora Chi—a model of the practice of inclusive care—who patiently supported my work and shared her opinions on many Mohist locutions and possible English renderings.

INTRODUCTION

> Still, Mòzǐ was genuinely the finest in the world; seek his equal
> and you won't find it. Though withered and parched he would
> not give up—a man of talent.
>
> —*Zhuāngzǐ*, 'All Under Heaven'

THE *Mòzǐ* 墨子 is a foundational text in Chinese ethics, political theory, epistemology, logic, semantics, just war theory, economics, and science. One of the classical 'various masters' texts of the Chinese philosophical tradition, its systematic ethical and political theories constitute a milestone in the development of ancient philosophy, East or West. The Mohists were the first thinkers in the world to develop a consequentialist ethical theory, a brand of normative ethics that remains influential to this day. They may have been the earliest ethical thinkers to emphasize the notions of impartiality and equality. They were the first in the Chinese tradition to offer sustained, rigorous arguments for their views and the first to develop an explicit methodology of argumentation, based mainly on analogical judgement and reasoning, which influenced the rhetoric of all their contemporaries. Their writings deserve an English translation that allows readers to truly enter into and understand the Mohists' world of thought. Providing such an English version is the aim of the present volume.

The translation has a specifically philosophical focus. The terminology and selections have been tailored for readers interested in understanding and working with the text philosophically. Brief notes clarifying the gist of the text and calling attention to points of philosophical relevance have been included to help readers grasp and fit together the various elements of Mohist thought for themselves.

Historical Background

The writings in the *Mòzǐ* were composed and edited by an unknown number of anonymous followers of a charismatic moral teacher and social reformer named Mò Dí 墨翟, who came to be known as Mòzǐ, or 'Master Mò'.[1] Mòzǐ's followers and their movement were referred to as 'Mò zhě' 墨者, or the Mohists. The Mohists flourished during ancient China's Warring States era (481–221 BC), a long period of frequent war and turmoil during which seven major rival states—and many more smaller states—competed with each other for power and territory, the larger and more aggressive aspiring to conquer or subjugate all of the others under their rule. The Warring States period eventually came to a close between 230 and 221 BC, when the militaristic state of Qín conquered its six chief rivals one by one to unify the central states and found the Qín dynasty.

Despite—and perhaps partly because of—instability and upheaval caused by constant power struggles, shifting interstate alliances, and incessant military rivalry, the Warring States was a culturally, economically, and intellectually dynamic era later dubbed the period of the 'hundred schools' of thought. This is the era in which such philosophical classics as the Confucian *Analects* 論語, the *Mencius* 孟子, the *Xúnzǐ* 荀子, the *Dàodéjīng* 道德經, and the *Zhuāngzǐ* 莊子 were produced. Social, economic, and political changes presented new challenges for organizing and governing society that created opportunities for the *shì* 士 or 'officer' class—a middle class that included scholars, landowners, and military and civil service officers. Increased social mobility and the growing availability of education allowed talented commoners to climb the social ladder, move into the officer class, and perhaps find posts as government officials or advisors and retainers to powerful aristocrats.

Some of the *shì* rose to become roving policy advisors, who might be retained by the court of one or another of the 'various lords', semi-feudal princes or lords who governed cities and territories of various sizes. Exemplary, eloquent *shì* became renowned teachers and moral leaders, who attracted groups of students and adherents committed to their values, teachings, and way of life. The two most prominent of these were Confucius (d. 479 BC) and Mòzǐ, who was born very roughly around the time Confucius died. Confucius was associated with a cultural and ideological community or fellowship called the Rú 儒, or 'Erudites', men devoted to shared ethical, aesthetic, ritual, and political

---

[1] 'Mòzǐ' is pronounced roughly as a speaker of English might say 'mwo dz', with the vowel 'o' pronounced as in 'book'. 'Mò' is pronounced with a sharp falling tone, as might be indicated by an exclamation point in English.

ideals and practices they traced to the high culture of the Zhōu dynasty. Although not the founder of the Erudites, within a few decades after his death Confucius had become their most prominent figurehead.

The Mohists too formed an ideological community, one that eventually developed into a mixture of a religious fellowship, educational organization, social and moral reform movement, political advocacy group, and private militia. The founding father of this community, Mòzǐ himself likely flourished during the middle decades of the fifth century BC. He seems to have come from one of the small states near the geographical centre of the Warring States world, perhaps Lǔ 魯, also the home of Confucius, or possibly Téng 滕 or Sòng 宋. In one story (not translated here), an official in service to King Xiàn Huì of Chǔ (488–432 BC) refers to him as a 'lowly person', or commoner. The story provides rough clues to both his historical dates and his social status. He is widely thought to have originally been an artisan, perhaps a carpenter or wheelwright. The *Mòzǐ* frequently depicts him giving illustrations from the work of carpenters, wheelwrights, and other craftspeople. Indeed, the *Mòzǐ* is full of references to manual work, crafts, trade, farming and husbandry, warfare, and the welfare of the common people. These suggest that Mohism was a product of the emerging middle class of artisans, merchants, small landholders, and soldiers that grew in size and political influence during the Warring States era. By contrast with the literati and ritual priests who identified with the Erudites, the Mohists seem to have been mainly of non-elite social origin.

Consistent with their social background, the Mohists were deeply concerned about the welfare of commoners and the rural poor. They rejected the aristocratic ceremonial etiquette of the Zhōu high culture, including customs such as elaborate burials and ceremonial musical performances, which they regarded as wasteful and pointless. In place of this etiquette, they proposed that all conduct be guided by the standard of pursuing what increases the benefit of and reduces harm to 'all the world', including one's own and others' persons, kin, community, and state. The aristocracy were to reduce wasteful expenses to ensure that the hungry were fed, the cold were clothed, the weary got rest, and the disorderly were put in good order.

Mohism thrived from the fifth to the third centuries BC, the community of Mohist adherents branching into multiple contingents in different regions, each led by a local grandmaster. The Mohists formed disciplined organizations devoted to education, political advocacy, government service, and military service. Members who secured government posts were expected to donate part of their income to support the organization. Mohist groups seem to have been partly autonomous from state governments and could enforce their own laws. Early textual sources attest to their social and doctrinal influence, their fervent commitment to their ethical ideals, their frugal, disciplined lifestyle, and their military valour. Although they were anti-aggression activists who vigorously condemned unprovoked military attacks, the Mohists' doctrine of promoting the benefit of all led them to form renowned defence militias dedicated to protecting the innocent. At their peak, no other activist group or ethical movement was more prominent.[2]

Mohism gradually faded away during the Hàn dynasty (206 BC–AD 219), as multiple factors combined to diminish its appeal and influence. The stable, unified Hàn empire eliminated the social and political conditions that had fostered the Mohists' rise, attenuating their role as representatives of the middle class in small, endangered states and their utility as a social and military organization. By the Hàn, their most compelling ethical and political ideas—such as inclusive care and benefit for 'all under Heaven', the need for unified norms and a merit-based bureaucracy, and the importance of meeting the basic economic needs of all—had been widely adopted even by their opponents. Their remaining economic doctrines and their austere lifestyle were unpopular. The Mohists offered little to attract new adherents, especially compared with the Ruism and Daoism of the time. Eventually folk Daoism would incorporate Mòzǐ himself into its pantheon of immortals.

The Texts

A crucial point to understand before delving into the *Mòzǐ* is that—like all the early Chinese 'masters' texts—it is not a book by the person named in its title. None of the writings in the *Mòzǐ* purport to be from the hand of the historical Mò Dí. Nor does the *Mòzǐ* purport to be a historically reliable record or archive of Mò Dí's sayings

---

[2] This point is attested by Mencius (3B:9) and by Xúnzǐ, who devotes more critical attention to Mòzǐ than to any other rival thinker.

and actions. Some sections of the *Mòzǐ* may indeed transmit his statements, and a few probably transmit edited or reworked versions of his teachings. But he is not its author, in the modern sense of the person who composed the sentences and paragraphs in it. Indeed, the *Mòzǐ* has no author in this sense. Its numerous parts were most likely composed at different times, in different locations, by various unnamed Mohists and then edited, rewritten, and reorganized by other unnamed Mohists, most likely over a period of two centuries or more.

Nor is the *Mòzǐ* a discrete book or text in the modern sense. Rather, it is a collection of several dozen 'books'. The earliest bibliographical record to mention the *Mòzǐ* reports that it included seventy-one *piān* 篇 ('scrolls', 'books'). A *piān* was a bundle of thin bamboo or wood strips bound together with silk thread like a miniature wooden snow fence. The strips were read from right to left, each strip holding one column of script written vertically from top to bottom. The *piān* were stored by rolling them up to form scrolls. Seventy-one of these scrolls piled together would have filled several large bookshelves. No one would have considered them a single work or book, but rather the collected works of the Mohists or a library of Mohist books.

What's more, many of these individual books (*piān*) may themselves have been composite works produced by combining and editing shorter, originally distinct texts. The basic physical unit of writing in the Mohists' time often was not the *piān*, but a shorter section of bamboo strips called a *cè* 冊 ('sheaf'). Some *piān* in the *Mòzǐ* were probably formed by combining two or more pre-existing short texts, perhaps originally written on independent *cè*. The most obvious examples are the 'Dialogues', especially books 46–9, which consist of many short passages, some of which could have originated as separate texts and later been collected together. Book 39, 'Condemning the Erudites (II)', also consists of a series of short passages, which divide into two groups, the first seven criticizing the Erudites and some of their sayings, the next five relating disparaging anecdotes about Confucius. The two parts of the book and the passages within each part could have had diverse origins. Book 17, 'Condemning Aggression (I)', could have been created by combining what were originally two related but separate shorter texts, corresponding to §17.1 and §17.2. The two sections share the same anti-war theme, but nothing obviously ties them together as two parts of a longer, coherent essay.

Reading through the various books of the *Mòzĭ*, readers may notice numerous sections with formal or thematic features that display slight discontinuities from preceding or following sections. In some cases, these discontinuities might be due to the sections having a different origin from the material surrounding them. Without further data to work with, it is often difficult to confirm or disconfirm whether this is the case, however, or to formulate a convincing scenario about how any one book was formed. Some books appear to have been carefully edited by ancient Mohists so that they read fairly coherently even though their content may draw on disparate sources.

According to the *Hàn History*, the Hàn palace library possessed an edition of the *Mòzĭ* consisting of seventy-one books (*piān*), of which eighteen are now lost. The extant books fall into six groups, likely of different origin and perhaps the work of different Mohist factions.

1. Miscellaneous essays. The first group consists of seven short texts, including three essays summarizing Mohist doctrines on Heaven, political administration, economics, and defence (books 4–6); an anecdote about how people's environment colours their character, shared with *The Annals of Lǚ Bùwéi* and perhaps not Mohist in origin (book 3); a conversation about Mòzĭ's criticism of music (book 7); and a pair of essays expounding mainstream early Chinese views on self-cultivation and the value of worthy officers that have little relation to the rest of the Mohist corpus (books 1 and 2). This block of texts seems the latest part of the *Mòzĭ* and may be from the middle to the late third century BC or later.

2. The 'Triads'. Books 8–37 form the core of the *Mòzĭ*. This group consists of ten 'triads', or sets of three books expounding the Mohists' ten main doctrines. The books in each triad share the same title—most likely added by a later editor around or after the time that §49.14 in the Dialogues was written—followed by the Chinese words 'upper', 'middle', or 'lower', which are analogous to the Roman numerals 'I', 'II', and 'III' in English. Seven of these thirty texts are lost, leaving four of the ten triads incomplete. This block of books probably contains the earliest Mohist writings. Some of the books, or sections of them, may go back to Mò Dí's lifetime in the middle to late decades of the fifth century BC. The essays appear to be of varied date and origin, however, and linguistic, formal, and thematic evidence strongly suggests that they fall into

several chronologically distinct strata. One section of book 18 (§18.4), 'Condemning Aggression (II)', which seems a relatively early book, gives examples of 'earlier' and 'recent' states ruined through wars of aggression, all of which were conquered between 473 and 431 BC. These references suggest that this section might have been composed not too many years after 431 BC. A potential clue to the date of book 19, 'Condemning Aggression (III)', is that among examples of belligerent contemporaneous states (see §19.4) it mentions Yuè, which was absorbed by its enemy Chǔ in 334 BC. Book 28, 'Heaven's Intent (III)', also mentions the kings of Chǔ and Yuè (§28.2a), possibly implying that they were independent states at the time of writing. These clues suggest a very rough range of dates for the books in the Triads from the second half of the fifth century to the second half of the fourth century BC.[3] (For a discussion of the relative dates of the different books of the Triads, see the Appendix.)

3. 'Condemning the Erudites'. The third group are two books devoted to denouncing the Erudites, of which one is lost. The surviving book, book 39, 'Condemning the Erudites (II)', is unlike the Triads in that it presents no constructive doctrines. Its first half presents a series of rebuttals to the Erudites' views. Its second half is a collection of deprecatory anecdotes about Confucius. The style and content of the rebuttals are roughly congruent with those of the 'Dialogues', suggesting a similar date.

4. The 'Dialectics'. The fourth block consists of six books known as the later Mohist writings or the Mohist 'Dialectics'. These include two series of short 'canons' (books 40–1), two of slightly longer 'explanations' of the canons (books 42–3), a collection of fragments on ethics and semantics (book 44), and a short text on disputation and logic (book 45). These writings treat semantics, logic, epistemology, ethics, metaphysics, geometry, mechanics, optics, and economics. They are of the greatest philosophical and historical interest but unfortunately are also among the most difficult and corrupt texts in the entire classical Chinese literature.

[3] Other scholars have suggested dates ranging from the early fourth to the late third century BC. For a discussion of several alternative theories about the date of the Triads, see C. Defoort and N. Standaert (eds), _The Mozi as an Evolving Text_ (Leiden: Brill, 2013), 4–16.

These books are probably of a later date than the Triads. A reasonable conjecture, based on their implied intellectual milieu, is that they were composed between the late fourth and the second half of the third century BC.

5. The 'Dialogues'. The fifth group comprises four books (books 46–9) that present sayings attributed to Mòzǐ and brief conversations between him and various disciples, opponents, and rulers or officials, along with one book (book 50) relating an extended anecdote about Mòzǐ persuading the king of Chǔ to abandon plans for an attack on the much smaller, weaker state of Sòng. These books reflect a mature, thriving Mohist organization that trains students, recommends them for government posts, and dispatches them on military assignments. Mòzǐ is depicted engaging in spirited exchanges with interlocutors representing rival standpoints, including the Erudites and others. The writers are familiar with parts of the Confucian *Analects*. Discussions in the Dialogues imply knowledge of the full set of Mohist doctrines developed in the Triads, suggesting that they date from around or after the time the later portions of the Triads were composed. Given the scope of the Mohist organization they depict, their stylistic and doctrinal features, and the intellectual milieu implied by their discussions with opponents, a likely conjecture is that they date from the last several decades of the fourth century or the early decades of the third century BC. Since Mòzǐ's lifetime was probably decades or even a century earlier, many of the conversations they present may be embellished or fictional. These books could be the work of a different faction of Mohists from those who produced the Triads, or they might represent a change in the Mohists' preferred literary format as their movement evolved.

Book 50, 'Gōngshū', is different in format from the dialogue books and arguably does not fit with them. Its dating is uncertain and could potentially be quite late. Since it highlights Mòzǐ's reputation as a brilliant military tactician, possibly it was intended to function as an introduction to the military texts. One difficulty in determining where it belongs is that the text and title of the next book, book 51, are both lost.

6. The military manuals. The final block of twenty-one books is devoted to military engineering and tactics for defending besieged cities. Ten of these books are lost, without even the titles having been passed down. Others are badly corrupt. Many sections are

organized as replies by Mòzǐ to questions from a head disciple, Qín Gǔ Lí, referred to as 'Qínzǐ', or 'Master Qín'. This honorific suggests the texts may have been written by Qín's followers. These writings are of great value to the historical study of ancient Chinese warfare, but they are beyond the scope of this translation.

The entire set of seventy-one books may have been complete at the time Hàn dynasty editors collated the collection, and the eighteen missing books could have been misplaced as the text was transmitted through the centuries. Another, perhaps more likely possibility, however, is that the Hàn editors were working from old records, which led them to preserve the names and titles of lost books even though the books themselves were no longer extant. Still another scenario is that the 'lost' triad books might never have existed. Having in hand three books on six of the main doctrines, ancient editors might simply have assumed there were originally three for each and left spaces for them that were never filled. Without further evidence, it is difficult to determine which of these scenarios is the most plausible.

Overview of Mohist Thought

An effective way of developing an initial understanding of Mohist thought is to turn to passages where the Mohists themselves declare their core concerns. A helpful place to begin might be §32.1, which announces that the benevolent seek to promote the benefit of the world and so take promoting benefit as a standard to emulate: 'Does it benefit people? Then do it. Does it not benefit people? Then stop.' Hence, according to the text, benevolent rulers do not pursue sensual pleasures at the cost of expropriating the common people's resources for food and clothing. These brief remarks are deeply informative about Mohist ethics. The Mohists prize the virtue of benevolence, which they regard as committing us to furthering the benefit of all the world (including ourselves). They see action as guided by what they call a 'model' or 'standard'. We ask whether actions match the model: do they benefit people? If so, we proceed with them; if not, we don't. In particular, we avoid actions that sacrifice the basic needs of people in our community so that the elite can enjoy nonessential pleasures. The Mohists thus advocate a consequentialist criterion for evaluating actions. What is benevolent or right is what has good consequences—namely it benefits people. Among benefits, basic needs such as feeding and clothing the common people take priority over sensual enjoyment.

Another informative passage is §25.1. Again, benevolence is valorized, the text foregrounding the role model of the benevolent agent. (Here, as in §32.1, the specific benevolent agent referred to is probably an ideal ruler, rather than simply a morally admirable person.) The benevolent agent plans for the welfare of all the world in a way analogous to how a filially devoted son plans for the welfare of his parents. Both do their utmost to seek wealth, a large family or population, and good order on behalf of those they plan for. The Mohists thus esteem the virtue of filial devotion and see it as a model for the benevolent person's attitudes toward the world as a whole. They tie benevolent or filial treatment of others to the pursuit of three basic goods: material wealth, a flourishing population, and social order. These are the goods that constitute benefit, as they understand it. Intriguingly, all three goods are associated with social groups, not individuals.

A third passage, §16.1, fills in important details. It introduces two technical terms, 'exclusion', or excluding others from the scope of those one cares about and benefits, and 'inclusion', or including them. The explanation of exclusion spells out the harms that the benevolent person seeks to prevent: war, feuding, oppression, tyranny, fraud, class contempt, aggression toward others, and failure to live up to the relational virtues of generosity to subordinates, loyalty to superiors, kindness to one's children, and filial devotion to parents. The solution to these harms, the Mohists propose, is the attitude of inclusion, which they explain as 'being for others as for oneself'—being committed to others' welfare as we are to our own. This is the psychological side of their ethical ideal of promoting the benefit of all.

A second informative approach to getting a quick overview of Mohist doctrines is to briefly survey the themes of the ten Triads. The Mohists most likely developed their teachings gradually. One plausible hypothesis is that they started with the core themes of caring about others, rejecting aggression, and moderating the use of resources, then elaborated their political and religious doctrines, and then developed their admonitions against wasteful burials and music.[4] Eventually, as depicted in §49.14, they recognized that they had the

---

[4] This hypothesis is motivated by the chronological stratification of the Triads sketched in the Appendix.

materials to formulate a neat platform of ten doctrines, organized as five pairs. The titles of the ten do not directly reflect the core of Mohist thought—their commitment to guiding conduct and policy by the standard of benefiting all the world—but they do give a reasonably accurate synopsis of what the Mohists stood for.

'*Identifying Upward*' and '*Promoting the Worthy*'. The primary end of government is to bring about a stable social, economic, and political order by promulgating unified moral norms. This end is to be pursued through a moral education programme in which people are encouraged to 'identify upward' with exemplary political leaders by identifying with their values and emulating their good statements and conduct. Cooperation is rewarded and defiance punished. Government is to be structured as a centralized, bureaucratic state led by a virtuous monarch and managed by a hierarchy of appointed officials. Appointments should be made on the basis of competence and merit, without regard for candidates' social status, origin, or relation to the ruler.

'*Inclusive Care*' and '*Condemning Aggression*'. To promote the welfare of all, people must care about one another all-inclusively, being committed to the welfare of other persons, families, and communities as they are for their own, such that when interacting with one another they seek to benefit both sides. Military aggression is wrong for the same reasons that theft, robbery, and murder are: it harms others in pursuit of self-interest and so fails to promote the benefit of all.

'*Moderation in Use*' and '*Moderation in Burial*'. Wasteful luxury and useless expenses must be eliminated in order to better ensure that basic material needs are met for all. The elite custom of rich, elaborate burials and protracted mourning rituals must be moderated to better promote prosperity and social order.

'*Heaven's Intent*' and '*Understanding Ghosts*'. Since Heaven is the noblest, wisest moral agent in the cosmos, its intentions provide a reliable, objective model of righteousness. Heaven is the head of the cosmic sociopolitical hierarchy, so good order requires that its intentions be followed. Social order and moral conduct can be advanced by encouraging the understanding that ghosts and spirits—Heaven's agents—reward the good and punish the vicious.

'*Condemning Music*' and '*Condemning Fatalism*'. Extravagant, state-sponsored entertainment and luxuries for the ruling elite are wrong, since they waste resources that would benefit society more if used to feed and clothe the poor. Fatalism—the view that outcomes are predestined and effort is useless—must be rejected, since the ancient sage-kings denied it, people cannot observe it, and in practice it fails to promote the benefit of all.

One feature of Mohism that comes across clearly from this quick look at their doctrines is the practical, active orientation of their movement. Although Mohist doctrines rest on a well-developed theoretical foundation, their chief teachings read like a set of policy papers or a political platform. The Mohists saw themselves mainly as a moral, political, and religious advocacy movement devoted to realizing their vision of the morally right society and way of life.[5]

Reading the Mòzǐ

How should readers new to Mohism or Chinese philosophy approach the *Mòzǐ*? Rather than starting off by simply reading the text straight through, readers can consider picking and choosing sections or books depending on their interests. For example, to get a quick idea of the Mohists' fundamental concerns and patterns of thought, a reader might turn first to book 4, 'Models and Standards', and book 17, 'Condemning Aggression (I)'. For a more detailed overview, one could add book 11, 'Identifying Upward (I)', and book 15, 'Inclusive Care (II)'.

For readers interested in the origins of Mohism, book 14, 'Inclusive Care (I)', book 17, 'Condemning Aggression (I)', and book 20, 'Moderation in Use', seem likely to be the earliest writings in the corpus. Comparing books 8 and 9—two versions of 'Promoting the Worthy'—or books 11 and 12—two versions of 'Identifying Upward'—gives an idea of how Mohist thought developed in sophistication between its early and middle periods. The elaborate arguments and detailed treatment of objections and replies in book 16, 'Inclusive Care (III)', are an example of Mohist writers and editors aiming to make the clearest, most compelling and exhaustive case they can for their doctrines. Book 25, 'Moderation in Burial (III)',

---

[5] For a more extensive, easily accessible introduction to Mohist philosophy, see C. Fraser, 'Mohism', *Stanford Encyclopedia of Philosophy*, E. Zalta (ed.), https://plato. stanford.edu/entries/mohism/.

presents similarly thorough arguments. Books 9, 12, 16, 25, and 27, 'Heaven's Intent (II)', are examples of Mohist argumentation from a relatively mature stage of the movement's development.

Major statements of Mohist ethics can be found in books 4, 16, 25, and 32, 'Condemning Music'. The Mohist political theory is presented mainly in books 11 to 13 and 8 to 10. §12.7c and §9.5a are fine examples of how the Mohists sometimes express profound, far-reaching insights using deceptively simple rhetoric.

Early Mohist epistemology and argumentation are illustrated well by the opening sections of books 35, 36, and 37—the three versions of 'Condemning Fatalism'—and by books 15 and 16, two versions of 'Inclusive Care'. The later Mohist investigations in semantics, logic, epistemology, and other subjects are found in Part IV. Mohist theology is presented in books 26 to 28, the three versions of 'Heaven's Intent', book 31, 'Understanding Ghosts', and books 35 to 37, on fatalism. The Mohist just war theory is found in books 17 to 19, the three versions of 'Condemning Aggression' (especially §19.5), in books 49 and 50, and in §28.5.

Part V, the Dialogues, presents interesting, occasionally witty anecdotes and depictions of the Mohists' intellectual milieu at the height of their movement. Part III, with its attacks on the Erudites, probably dates to around the same period.

Readers will notice that Mohist rhetoric can be repetitive and long-winded, particularly when the arguments rely on laboriously enumerated lists of parallel examples. The texts probably read this way for several reasons. One is that the Mohists considered this rhetoric effective, as in their view it supports their conclusions forcefully and covers all relevant details. Another is that this style was suitable for public oratory. Some parts of the texts may have originated as speeches, intended for oral delivery and transmission. Still another reason arises from the manner in which some of the Triads, in particular, were composed. Different texts on the same or closely related doctrines appear to have been modelled on each other, and the same or similar passages were sometimes edited and reused repeatedly in different contexts. Readers should be prepared to skim and skip through such passages if they become too repetitive. At the same time, however, it is worth appreciating that the very features of Mohist rhetoric that sometimes fall short of contemporary conceptions of style and grace are invaluable in helping us understand how the Mohists thought, reasoned, and spoke.

NOTE ON THE TRANSLATION

THIS book presents an abridged translation of the ethical, political, and dialectical sections of the *Mòzĭ*, supplemented by commentary sufficient to allow readers of English to engage with Mohist philosophy and see for themselves how the Mohist worldview hangs together. The translation seeks to offer a clear, easily readable English text that reflects the flavour and philosophical terminology of the original Chinese. The goal is to enable students, general readers, and philosophers who do not read Classical Chinese to enter the Mohists' world of thought and develop a thorough understanding of their concerns, their contentions, and the grounds for their views. To facilitate these objectives, the translation keeps scholarly apparatus such as textual and historical notes to a minimum while providing extensive notes elucidating key terms and claims and their relation to other Mohist views. The book also aims to meet the need for a compact, accessible translation of *Mòzĭ* that reflects the progress made in philosophical interpretation of Mohist thought in recent decades.

The translation is a self-standing work but is intended to complement my earlier monograph on Mohist philosophy, *The Philosophy of the* Mòzĭ: *The First Consequentialists* (New York: Columbia University Press, 2016).

The translation and commentary presented here have three signal features: fidelity to the Chinese text, a philosophical emphasis, and a distinctive selection of material.

The translation seeks to accurately reflect the nuances of the Mohists' philosophical terminology, arguments, and style of thinking. Key terminology is translated consistently, so that readers can see how the same concepts, themes, and patterns of thought appear repeatedly and how they are linked through various conceptual associations and inferential relations. Significant details of the Mohists' concepts, reasoning, and doctrines can be obscured if a translation is insensitive to the distinctive terminology they use to express their thought.

To illustrate this point, let me give an extended example involving several Mohist technical terms. The Mohists often use a single word, *yán* 言—here rendered 'state' as a verb and 'statement' as a noun—to

refer to assertions, claims, teachings, doctrines, maxims, and guidelines. To understand Mohist philosophy, one must understand that
the Mohists regard assertions, teachings, maxims, and so forth all as
statements or declarations with the potential to guide conduct.

Statements fall among a variety of things—including measuring
tools, exemplars, role models, idealized descriptions, and rules—that
can function as what the Mohists call 'models' or 'standards' (*fǎ* 法).
Models are guidelines for action, speech, and thought. The Mohists'
most commonly used examples of models are the carpenter's set
square and the wheelwright's compass, which guide and check the
production of square corners and round wheels. Like the carpenter
and wheelwright, we apply models by emulating them or comparing
things to them. Suppose a *Mòzǐ* passage considers whether we should
take as our model the statements made by proponents of a certain
doctrine (as, for example, §25.2a does). If an English translation renders this question instead as one of whether, for example, we should
'follow their rules', readers will be unable to see how the discussion
fits into the Mohists' broader view of the role of statements and
models in guiding action, speech, and thought.

The Mohists understand perception, cognition, reasoning, and
action as grounded in how we draw distinctions (*biàn* 辨) between
similar and dissimilar kinds of things. Accordingly, they understand
the process of evaluating a statement as a matter of distinguishing
whether it is 'this/right' (*shì* 是) or 'not' (*fēi* 非). Models provide
criteria by which to draw such distinctions correctly. Suppose a *Mòzǐ*
passage proposes models to aid in distinguishing whether statements
are 'this/right' or 'not' (as, for example, §35.1 does). If a translation
presents the passage as instead proposing tests by which to examine
or analyse a theory, again the nuance will be lost, as will the conceptual connections between the passage and others touching on statements and models. Moreover, this wording risks injecting into the
translation implications that are absent from the original Chinese
text, because the inferential relations associated with English words
such as 'test', 'analyse', and 'theory' are significantly different from
those of the Mohists' 'model' (*fǎ*), 'distinguish' (*biàn*), and 'statement' (*yán*). Readers unaware of the implications of and conceptual
relations between these Mohist notions will struggle to understand
what exactly Mòzǐ is claiming when he declares, for example, that
'following Heaven's intention is a model of righteousness' (§27.3b).

Two aims of this translation, then, are to use English terms with associations and implications that correspond fairly well with those of the Mohists' Chinese terms and to use these terms consistently, supplementing them with annotations clarifying the details of Mohist usage in particular contexts. A related aim is to convey the sense of the Mohists' phrasing reasonably accurately—within the practical constraints of producing readable English—as the details of how they phrase a point may sometimes be pivotal to understanding what they are saying.

A further respect in which the translation aims for fidelity is by mirroring the painstaking way the Mohists build the case for their views, often using repetitive examples, redundant transitional words, and elaborate rhetorical questions. Mohist writers are so concerned to clarify the steps in their arguments and the relations between their ideas that they habitually use lengthy parallel phrases, clauses, and even paragraphs bound together with a profusion of transitional phrases and logical connectives. To accurately represent the character of their thought and rhetoric, when practical the translation replicates the organization of their sentences and paragraphs and preserves most of their redundant transitional words without attempting to smooth out the diction. By the standards of contemporary English, the result can sometimes be awkward, but the ungainly phrasing helps readers appreciate the patterns of Mohist thought and argumentation. In many cases, Mohist rhetoric may have originated from oral composition and been intended for oral delivery. Repeated chains of formulaic, parallel sentences facilitate recall for a speaker and can create a strong impact on an audience. While reading blocks of such rhetoric in the *Mòzǐ*—section §17.1, on unjust aggression, is an example—it is worth imagining the lines being delivered by a fiery public speaker indignant about the wrongs he is denouncing.

A second salient feature of the translation is its focus on philosophical interpretation rather than textual, philological, or historical issues. Although extensive textual scholarship has gone into preparing the translation, I have largely refrained from including textual and historical notes, aiming instead to keep the text relatively uncluttered and accessible. The translation includes mainly brief notes explaining significant terms and phrases and highlighting points relevant to philosophical interpretation, along with notes cross-referencing closely related passages in different parts of the *Mòzǐ*. A further feature is a Glossary giving brief interpretations of selected concepts.

There are two main reasons for this relatively streamlined approach. The first is that the main audience envisioned for the book is students, general readers, and philosophers, not specialists with Sinological training. For this audience, extensive textual and historical notes would only add unnecessary bulk. The second is that because the *Mòzǐ* was relatively neglected by scholars before the Qīng dynasty, it presents many more minor textual problems than other early philosophical texts. Addressing these explicitly would entail adding lengthy footnotes to nearly every paragraph. The purpose of the volume is not to present research on textual problems but only to incorporate the results of such research into the translation.

Fortunately, most textual questions outside of the dialectical writings have been adequately resolved by Qīng dynasty and twentieth-century scholars. Hence with few exceptions I generally pass over minor textual problems without comment and simply adopt what seems the most reasonable reading from one of the leading scholarly editions. In handling textual issues, I have relied mainly on the editions of Sūn Yíràng,[1] Wú Yùjiāng,[2] and Wáng Huànbiāo.[3] I have also consulted the modern vernacular editions of Lǐ Yúshú,[4] Wú Lónghuī,[5] and Lǐ Shēnglóng.[6] Unless otherwise specified, I have generally followed readings or emendations suggested by either Sūn or Wú and occasionally those of the other editors. Specialists who consult Sūn's and Wú's editions will easily be able to see the issues at stake and how I have attempted to resolve them. Readers of the Chinese text can conveniently consult corrections from Sūn's and Wú's editions in the online electronic text at the Chinese Text Project.[7]

---

[1] Sūn Yíràng 孫詒讓, 墨子閒詁 [*Interspersed Commentaries on* Mòzǐ] (Beijing: Zhonghua Book Company, 2001).

[2] Wú Yùjiāng 吳毓江, 墨子校注 [*Collated Annotations on* Mòzǐ] (Beijing: Zhonghua Book Company, 1993).

[3] Wáng Huànbiāo 王煥鑣, 墨子校釋 [*Collated and Explicated* Mòzǐ] (Hangzhou: Zhèjiāng Arts Publishing, 1984).

[4] Lǐ Yúshú 李漁叔, 墨子今註今譯 [Mòzǐ: *Contemporary Notes and Translation*] (Taipei: Commercial Press, 1974).

[5] Wú Lónghuī 吳龍輝, 墨子白話今譯 [*A Vernacular Contemporary Translation of* Mòzǐ] (Beijing: Zhōngguó Shūdiàn, 1992).

[6] Lǐ Shēnglóng 李生龍 and Lǐ Zhènxīng 李振興, 新譯墨子讀本 [*A Newly Translated* Mòzǐ *Reader*] (Taipei: Sanmin Book Company, 1996).

[7] See https://ctext.org/mozi. The Chinese Text Project is edited and managed by Dr Donald Sturgeon.

The exception to this policy of avoiding detailed discussion of textual issues is Part IV, the selections from the Mohist dialectical texts. The many complex textual problems in these extremely difficult sections make it uninformative to translate or discuss them without furnishing detailed notes explaining and justifying one's reading of the text. Accordingly, I have prepared a separate digital supplement to the translation of these sections that includes an introductory historical and methodological discussion, detailed textual notes, and the full Chinese text. This supplement is available online at http://www. mohistcanons.net.

The third prominent feature of the translation is that it presents an abridged version of the *Mòzǐ*, omitting material inessential to following the Mohists' arguments and reconstructing their doctrines. The aim is to present, in a concise package, the key portions of the *Mòzǐ* needed for English readers to understand its philosophy. Toward this end, I have abbreviated the text in three ways, two intended to enhance readability, the third to maintain a compact, accessible translation.

First, the translation omits numerous repetitive passages that recount purported historical events, ancient documents, and folk tales not needed to support the doctrinal claims at stake. The Mohists regularly seek to justify their doctrines by citing historical examples and purported ancient documents, typically relating deeds of the six ancient sage-kings. These examples and citations are of great significance to the Mohists themselves, as they invoke the prestige of wise, virtuous sage-kings and the authority of purported historical records in support of Mohist doctrines. To modern readers, however, they can be obscure and repetitive, since the text may cite several lengthy examples or documents one after another. In such contexts, I have generally included only one or two of the examples or documents, so that the overall pattern of the discussion is clear, and omitted the others. All of the argumentative content has been included, so the abridgement removes nothing essential to making the Mohists' case or to reconstructing their reasoning and the theories and assumptions underlying their views.

Second, I have omitted some longer chunks of material not directly relevant to the aim of understanding Mohist philosophy. This material includes the first two brief books, which are chronologically late and doctrinally very different from the rest of the *Mòzǐ*; all of the Mohist military texts (books 52–71); a few paragraphs scattered across the first thirty-seven books; and between one-third and one-half of the anecdotes and sayings in books 39 and 46 to 49. The principle of selection has been to include material of the greatest philosophical interest and omit other material that is either philosophically less acute or of mainly historical interest.

Third, to present a well-rounded picture of Mohist philosophy, it is crucial to include representative passages from the later Mohist dialectical texts. However, some passages in the canons, explanations, and the 'Greater Selection' present textual and interpretive problems so difficult that, with the resources currently available, they cannot be solved with enough confidence to justify translation. Others can tentatively be solved, but the problems are so complex that the lengthy discussion needed to explain and justify a solution would contravene the aims of the book. In both of these sorts of cases, I have chosen instead to omit the passages in question. In a third type of case, I have omitted passages on the grounds that their content extends too far beyond the intended philosophical focus of the translation. For instance, the canons include a series of discussions of optics and mechanics, both of which I have chosen to omit, as the extensive exposition needed to offer a plausible interpretation is beyond the scope of this volume.

The section divisions and section numbers in the translated text are my own and do not correspond to divisions in the Chinese text. The only divisions in the transmitted text are those between the various *piān* 篇 (bundles, scrolls), which I will refer to as 'books'. The section divisions generally correspond to shifts in topic. Some of the divisions agree with those of other editors, and some do not. The paragraph breaks within sections are also my own.

At the end of each numbered section—with the exception of the canons—readers will find a parenthetical citation giving chapter and line numbers corresponding to the text of that section in the Harvard–Yenching concordance to *Mòzǐ*.[8] These indices allow readers to locate the Chinese text for each section using the online concordance search tool at the Chinese Text Project.[9]

[8] W. Hung (ed.), *A Concordance to Mo Tzu* 墨子引得, Harvard–Yenching Institute Sinological Index Series, Supplement no. 21 (Cambridge, MA: Harvard University Press, 1956).

[9] See https://ctext.org/mozi.

The Dialectics

The Mohist 'Dialectics' (*Mò Biàn* 墨辯) are six books of the *Mòzǐ* devoted to topics in metaphysics, ethics, semantics, logic, epistemology, geometry, optics, mechanics, and economics, among other subjects. Two of these books (books 40 and 41) present series of short 'canons' (*jīng* 經), or terse, often one-line pronouncements. Two other books (42 and 43) present 'explanations' (*shuō* 說), or slightly longer elaborations, explanations, or justifications, for each individual canon.

The division between the two books of canons—and the two of corresponding explanations—reflects only the break between the two bamboo-strip scrolls on which they were written, rather than any major division in their content. The translation presents the canons in the order in which they appear in the *Mòzǐ*, with canons from book 40 indicated by 'A' and those from book 41 indicated by 'B'. The numbering system agrees with that introduced in Graham's edition.[10] Except in a few instances where a canon has no explanation, in the traditional text the explanations are indexed to the individual canons by one- or two-character headings corresponding to the first graph or two in the relevant canon. Following standard practice, the translation extracts the explanations from books 42 and 43 and pairs them with the canons to which they belong. Hence in the translation, the number 'A1' refers to both canon A1 and explanation A1. The formatting clearly indicates which part is the canon and which the explanation. The heading of each explanation is indicated by parentheses. I will refer to the canons and explanations from books 40 and 42 as 'part A', those from 41 and 43 as 'part B'.

The text of the canons and explanations adopted here is a new, abridged recension based on collation and critical evaluation of emendations proposed by more than a dozen Qīng dynasty and modern editors.[11] The base text is the Míng dynasty *Dào Zàng* 道藏

---

[10] A. C. Graham, *Later Mohist Logic, Ethics, and Science* (Hong Kong: Chinese University Press, 1978, reprint edition 2003).

[11] This work is indebted to my colleague Hong-Ki Lam, with whom I conducted a collaborative research project in 2004–5 at the Chinese University of Hong Kong to develop a new edition of the canons and explanations.

edition, the earliest surviving edition of the text, printed in 1445.[12]
Emendations to the *Dào Zàng* text are explained in the notes to each
canon and explanation in the digital supplement to the translation
published at http://www.mohistcanons.net. The editions consulted
in preparing the text are included in the Select Bibliography.

The corrected text diverges from other recent editions, including
Graham's, in many details and is generally more conservative in
emending the base text. This recension aims especially to avoid conjectural emendation—corrections to the text based solely on conjectures about its meaning, without support from variant readings,
counterpart passages, contextual parallels or contrasts, or familiar,
systematic instances of graphic error or graphic variation. The textual problems and the editorial methodology are summarized in the
introductory material to the digital supplement.

Because the canons and explanations are terse and often admit of
multiple, related interpretations, the translation frequently gives two
or more alternatives for key terms, separated by slashes. The aim is to
give readers a fuller sense of the semantic range of the words. The
result is an untidy translation, but for these highly specialized texts
this approach seems justifiable. The translation also includes extensive notes clarifying the significance of some of the canons and
explanations.[13]

The final pair of dialectical texts are book 44, '*Dà Qǔ* 大取', or
'Greater Selection', and book 45, '*Xiǎo Qǔ* 小取', or 'Lesser Selection'.
The titles of these books are unrelated to their content and most
likely refer to their having been compiled by salvaging two selections,
one larger and one smaller, from a pile of damaged bamboo-strip
scrolls.[14] Both comprise multiple, independent sections. Several

---

[12] The editions and manuscripts available as evidence of the text are described in detail
in Graham, *Later Mohist Logic*, 73–6. Wú Yùjiāng provides a complete list of variant
readings in all available early versions of the text. See his 墨子校注 [*Collated Annotations
on* Mòzǐ] (Beijing: Zhōnghuá Shūjú, 1993).

[13] For a more detailed discussion of the thought of the Dialectics, see C. Fraser,
'Mohist Canons', *Stanford Encyclopedia of Philosophy*, E. Zalta (ed.), https://plato.stanford.
edu/entries/mohist-canons/ (rev. 2018).

[14] One passage in book 44 refers to selecting the greater of two benefits as '*qǔ dà* 取大'
(selecting the greater) and the lesser of two harms as '*qǔ xiǎo* 取小' (selecting the lesser).
The similarity between these phrases and the titles '*Dà Qǔ*' and '*Xiǎo Qǔ*' has led some
interpreters to read the titles as 'Selecting the Greater' and 'Selecting the Lesser'.
However, the words 'selecting the lesser' have no obvious relation to any part of the content of book 45, and this interpretation parses the syntax of the titles incorrectly.

passages in book 44 break off in mid-sentence, indicating that in places the bamboo strips on which the texts were written were broken or lost. Graham conjectured that the 'Greater Selection' and 'Lesser Selection' represented the remnants of two essays, one on language and logic, the other on ethics, and attempted to rearrange and reconstruct the texts accordingly. However, the content of the distinct sections in these books is neither continuous nor coherent enough to justify the conclusion that they originally constituted exactly two discrete texts. The sections could have come from more than two damaged texts or from a collection of short discussions. Hence the translation presented here sets aside Graham's reconstruction and follows the sequence of the text as it appears in the *Dào Zàng* edition. For convenience, I have divided the texts into numbered sections but have not rearranged the order of the text. I have inserted ellipses at locations in which sentences seem incomplete or words appear to be missing. Because of the many textual problems in the 'Greater Selection', I have omitted several obscure sections.

SELECT BIBLIOGRAPHY

General Background Studies of Chinese Thought

Graham, A. C., *Disputers of the Tao* (La Salle, IL: Open Court, 1989).

Hansen, C., *A Daoist Theory of Chinese Thought* (Oxford: Oxford University Press, 1992).

Perkins, F., *Heaven and Earth are Not Humane* (Bloomington: Indiana University Press, 2014).

Schwartz, B., *The World of Thought in Ancient China* (Cambridge, MA: Harvard University Press, 1985).

Van Norden, B., *Virtue Ethics and Consequentialism in Early Chinese Philosophy* (Cambridge, UK: Cambridge University Press, 2007).

Critical Studies of Mohism

Ahern, D., 'Is Mo Tzu a Utilitarian?', *Journal of Chinese Philosophy* 3.2 (1976), 185–93.

Chiu, W., '*Jian ai* and the Mohist attack of Early Confucianism', *Philosophy Compass*, 8.5 (2013), 425–37.

Defoort, C., and N. Standaert (eds), *The 'Mozi' as an Evolving Text: Different Voices in Early Chinese Thought* (Leiden: Brill, 2013).

Defoort, C., 'The Growing Scope of *Jian* 兼: Differences between Chapters 14, 15 and 16 of the *Mozi*', *Oriens Extremus* 45 (2005), 119–40.

Duda, K., 'Reconsidering Mo Tzu on the Foundations of Morality', *Asian Philosophy* 11(1) (2001), 23–31.

Fraser, C., *The Philosophy of the* Mòzǐ*: The First Consequentialists* (New York: Columbia University Press, 2016).

Fraser, C., 'The *Mozi* and Just War Theory in Pre-Han Thought', *Journal of Chinese Military History* 5(2) (2016), 135–75.

Fraser, C., 'The Mohist Conception of Reality', in C. Li and F. Perkins (eds), *Chinese Metaphysics and Its Problems*, 69–84 (Cambridge, UK: Cambridge University Press, 2014).

Fraser, C., 'Mohism and Self-Interest', *Journal of Chinese Philosophy* 35.3 (2008), 437–54.

Fraser, C., 'Mohism', in E. Zalta (ed.), *Stanford Encyclopedia of Philosophy*, https://plato.stanford.edu/entries/mohism/ (2002; rev. 2015).

Lai, W., 'The Public Good That Does the Public Good: A New Reading of Mohism', *Asian Philosophy* 3(2) (1993), 125–41.

Lowe, S., *Mo Tzu's Religious Blueprint for a Chinese Utopia* (Lewiston, NY, Mellen Press, 1992).

Loy, H., 'A Theological Voluntarist Conception of Morality in the *Mozi*', in J. Tiwald (ed.), *Oxford Handbook of Chinese Philosophy* (forthcoming).

Loy, H., 'Mohist Arguments on War', in P. Lo and S. Twiss (eds), *Chinese Just War Ethics: Origin, Development, and Dissent*, 226–48 (London: Routledge, 2015).

Loy, H., 'On the Argument for *Jian'ai*', *Dao: A Journal of Comparative Philosophy* 12(4) (2013), 487–504.

Loy, H., 'Justification and Debate: Thoughts on Mohist Moral Epistemology', *Journal of Chinese Philosophy* 35(3) (2008), 455–71.

Loy, H., 'On a *Gedankenexperiment* in the *Mozi* Core Chapters', *Oriens Extremus* 45 (2005), 141–58.

Perkins, F., 'The Mohist Criticism of the Confucian Use of Fate', *Journal of Chinese Philosophy* 35(3) (2008), 421–36.

Robins, D., 'Mohist Care', *Philosophy East and West* 62(1) (2012), 60–91.

Robins, D., 'The Mohists and the Gentlemen of the World', *Journal of Chinese Philosophy* 35(3) (2008), 385–402.

Taylor, R., 'Religion and Utilitarianism: Mo Tzu on Spirits and Funerals', *Philosophy East and West* 29(3) (1979), 337–46.

Vorenkamp, D., 'Another Look at Utilitarianism in Mo-Tzu's Thought', *Journal of Chinese Philosophy* 19(4) (1992), 423–43.

Wong, B., and H. Loy, 'War and Ghosts in Mozi's Political Philosophy', *Philosophy East and West* 54(3) (2004), 343–63.

Wong, D., 'Chinese Ethics', in E. Zalta (ed.), *Stanford Encyclopedia of Philosophy*, https://plato.stanford.edu/entries/ethics-chinese/ (2008; rev. 2018).

Wong, D., 'Universalism vs. Love with Distinctions: An Ancient Debate Revived', *Journal of Chinese Philosophy* 16(3) (1989): 251–72.

Studies of Mohist Dialectics

Chong, C., 'The Neo-Mohist Conception of *Biàn* (Disputation)', *Journal of Chinese Philosophy* 26(1) (1999), 1–19.

Fraser, C., 'Mohist Canons', in E. Zalta (ed.), *Stanford Encyclopedia of Philosophy*, https://plato.stanford.edu/entries/mohist-canons/ (2005; rev. 2018).

Fraser, C., 'Rationalism and Antirationalism in Later Mohism and the *Zhuangzi*', in C. Defoort and R. Ames (eds), *Having a Word with Angus Graham* (Albany: SUNY Press, 2018), 251–74.

Fraser, C., 'Distinctions, Judgment, and Reasoning in Classical Chinese Thought', *History and Philosophy of Logic* 34(1) (2013), 1–24.

Fraser, C., 'Truth in Moist Dialectics', *Journal of Chinese Philosophy* 39(3) (2012), 351–68.

Fraser, C., 'Knowledge and Error in Early Chinese Thought', *Dao: A Journal of Comparative Philosophy* 10 (2011), 127–48.

Fraser, C., 'Language and Ontology in Early Chinese Thought', *Philosophy East and West* 57(4) (2007), 420–56.

Geaney, J., 'A Critique of A. C. Graham's Reconstruction of the "Neo-Mohist Canons"', *Journal of the American Oriental Society* 119(1) (1999), 1–11.

Graham, A. C., *Later Mohist Logic, Ethics, and Science* (Hong Kong: Chinese University Press, 1978; reprinted 2003).

Hansen, C., *Language and Logic in Ancient China* (Ann Arbor: University of Michigan Press, 1983).

Liu, F., and J. Zhang, 'New Perspectives on Moist Logic', *Journal of Chinese Philosophy* 37(4) (2010), 605–21.

Robins, D., 'Names, Cranes, and the Later Mohists and Logic', *Journal of Chinese Philosophy* 39(3) (2012), 369–85.

Robins, D., 'The Later Mohists and Logic', *History and Philosophy of Logic* 31(3) (2010), 247–85.

Saunders, F., 'Semantics without Truth in Later Mohist Philosophy of Language', *Dao: A Journal of Comparative Philosophy* 13(2) (2014), 215–29.

Stephens, D., 'Realism and Conventionalism in Later Mohist Semantics', *Dao: A Journal of Comparative Philosophy* 16(4) (2017), 521–42.

Willman, M., 'Logical Analysis and Later Mohist Logic: Some Comparative Reflections', *Comparative Philosophy* 1(1) (2010), 53–77.

Editions Consulted for Part IV, 'The Dialectics'

Chén Mènglín 陳孟麟. 墨辯邏輯學新探 [*New Inquiries into the Logic of the Mohist Dialectics*] (Taipei: Wunan Book Publishing, 1996).

Gāo Hēng 高亨. 墨經校詮 [*Collation and Interpretation of the Mohist Canons*] (Beijing: Zhonghua Book Company, 1962).

Graham, A. C., *Later Mohist Logic, Ethics, and Science* (Hong Kong: Chinese University Press, 1978; reprinted 2003).

Jiāng Bǎochāng 姜寶昌. 墨經訓釋 [*Explication and Interpretation of the Mohist Canons*] (Jinan: Qí Lǔ Books, 1993).

Liáng Qǐchāo 梁啟超. 墨經校釋 [*Collation and Interpretation of the Mohist Canons*] (Shanghai: Commercial Press, 1923).

Liu Tsun-yan 柳存仁. 〈墨經箋疑〉 ['Commentary on Problems in the Mohist Canons']. 新亞學報 (*New Asia Academic Bulletin*) 6(1) (1964): 45–140; 7(1) (1965): 1–134.

Luán Diàofǔ 欒調甫. 墨子研究論文集 [*Essays on Mòzǐ Research*] (Beijing: People's Press, 1957).

Shěn Yǒudǐng 沈有鼎. 墨經的邏輯學 [*The Logic of the Mohist Canons*], in 沈有鼎文集 [*Works of Shěn Yǒu Dǐng*] (Beijing: People's Press, 1992).

Sūn Yíràng 孫詒讓. 墨子閒詁 [*Interspersed Commentaries on* Mòzǐ] (Beijing: Zhōnghuá Shūjú, 2001).

Tǎn Jièfǔ 譚戒甫. 墨辯發微 [*Detailed Explications of the Mohist Dialectics*] (Beijing: Zhonghua Book Company, 1964).

Wǔ Fēibǎi 伍非百. 墨辯解故 [*Explanations of the Mohist Dialectics*]. In 中國古名家言 [*Doctrines of China's Ancient School of Names*] (Beijing: Zhōngguó Shèhuì Kēxué Publishing, 1983).

Wú Yùjiāng 吳毓江. 墨子校注 [*Collated Annotations on* Mòzǐ] (Beijing: Zhōnghuá Shūjú, 1993).

Yáng Jùnguāng 楊俊光. 墨經研究 [*Research on the Mohist Canons*] (Nanjing: Nanjing University Press, 2002).

Zhāng Chúnyī 張純一. 墨子集解 [*Collected Explications of* Mòzǐ]. In 墨子大全 [*Complete Works on* Mòzǐ], vol. 31 (Beijing: Beijing Book Company, 2003).

Zhōu Yúnzhī 周雲之. 墨經校注、今譯、研究—墨經邏輯學 [*Collated Notes, Modern Translation, and Research on the Mohist Canons—The Logic of the Mohist Canons*] (Lanzhou: Gansu People's Press, 1993).

Previous Translations

Johnston, Ian (tr.), *The Mozi* (Hong Kong: Chinese University Press, 2010). (The only complete translation. A revised version has been published as *The Book of Master Mo* (London: Penguin Books, 2014).)

Knoblock, John, and Jeffrey Riegel (trs), *Mozi: A Study and Translation of the Ethical and Political Writings,* China Research Monograph 68 (Berkeley, CA: Institute of East Asian Studies, 2013).

Mei, Yi-Pao (tr.), *The Ethical and Political Works of Motse* (London: Probsthain, 1929).

Watson, Burton, *Mo Tzu: Basic Writings* (New York: Columbia University Press, 1963). (Selected ethical and political writings.)

Yates, Robin, 'The Mohists on Warfare: Technology, Technique, and Justification', *Journal of the American Academy of Religion* 47(3) (1980), 549–603. (Includes a translation of the military writings.)

Chinese Editions

Lǐ Shēnglóng 李生龍 and Lǐ Zhènxīng 李振興, 新譯墨子讀本 [*A Newly Translated* Mòzǐ *Reader*] (Taipei: Sanmin Book Company, 1996).

Lǐ Yúshú 李漁叔, 墨子今註今譯 [Mòzǐ: *Contemporary Notes and Translation*] (Taipei: Commercial Press, 1974).

Sūn Yíràng 孫詒讓, 墨子閒詁 [*Interspersed Commentaries on* Mòzǐ] (Beijing: Zhonghua Book Company, 2001).

Wáng Huànbiāo 王煥鑣, 墨子校釋 [*Collated and Explicated* Mòzǐ] (Hangzhou: Zhèjiāng Arts Publishing, 1984).

Wú Lónghuī 吳龍輝, 墨子白話今譯 [*A Vernacular Contemporary Translation of* Mòzǐ] (Beijing: Zhōngguó Shūdiàn, 1992).

Wú Yùjiāng 吳毓江, 墨子校注 [*Collated Annotations on* Mòzǐ] (Beijing: Zhonghua Book Company, 1993).

CHRONOLOGY

(All dates are BC)

c.481–221	Warring States period
479	Death of Confucius
c.470	Birth of Mòzǐ (?)
453–403	Major state of Jìn 晉 partitioned into three states, Zhào 趙, Wèi 魏, and Hán 韓
c.400	Mohist movement flourishes
c.390	Death of Mòzǐ (?)
386–343	Tián 田 clan usurp throne and build power in state of Qí 齊
371–340	After conflicts between Zhào, Wèi, and Hán, Qí in east and Qín 秦 in west emerge as especially powerful states
334	Chǔ 楚 conquers Yuè 越 to consolidate power in the south
334–249	Shifting alliances and conflicts among seven powerful states of Qín, Qí, Chǔ, Hán, Zhào, Wèi, and northern state of Yàn 燕
c.310	Confucian thinker Mencius attests to prominence of Mohism
c.275	Confucian thinker Xúnzǐ attacks Mohist economic doctrines
c.240	Legalist thinker Hán Fēi includes Mohism in discussion of 'eminent schools', mentions three branches of Mohists and their leaders
239	*Annals of Lǚ Bùwéi* indicates continuing influence of Mohism, mentions further Mohist leaders
230–221	Qín conquers six rival states to establish Qín dynasty
206	Qín 秦 dynasty falls, superseded by Hàn dynasty
200–150 (?)	Mohism gradually dies out

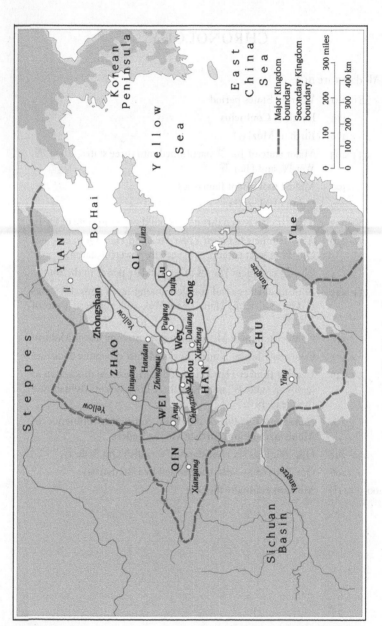

MAP 1 The Warring States, *c.*350 BC

Major Kingdom boundary
Secondary Kingdom boundary

0   100   200   300 miles
0   100   200   300   400 km

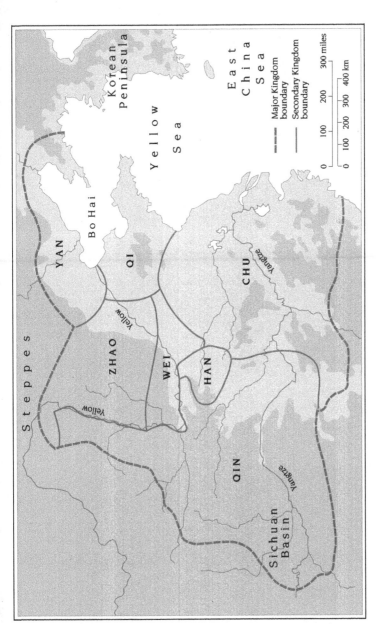

MAP 2 The Warring States, c.250 BC

The Essential *Mòzǐ*

PART I
MISCELLANEOUS ESSAYS

BOOK 4

MODELS AND STANDARDS

4.1 Our master Mòzǐ* said, 'Those in the world who undertake work cannot do without models and standards. There is no one who can accomplish their work without models and standards. Even officers* serving as generals or ministers, they all have models; even the hundred artisans undertaking their work, they too all have models. The hundred artisans make squares with the set square, circles with the compass,* straight lines with the string, vertical lines with the plumb line, and flat surfaces with the level.* Whether skilled artisans or unskilled artisans, all take these five as models.* The skilled are able to conform to them exactly. The unskilled, though unable to conform to them exactly, by following them in undertaking their work still do better than they do on their own. Thus the hundred artisans in undertaking their work all have models to measure by.

'Now for the greatest to order* the world and the next rank to order great states without models to measure by, this is to be less discriminating than the hundred artisans.' (4/1–5)

4.2 'That being so, then what can we take as a model for order? If all take their parents as a model, what would that be like? Those in the world who are parents are many, but the benevolent are few. If all take their parents as a model, this is taking the unbenevolent as a model. The model being unbenevolent, one can't take it as a model.

'If all take their teachers as a model, what would that be like? Those in the world who are teachers are many, but the benevolent are few. If all take their teachers as a model, this is taking the unbenevolent as a model. The model being unbenevolent, one can't take it as a model.

'If all take their ruler as a model, what would that be like? Those in the world who are rulers are many, but the benevolent are few. If all take their ruler as a model, this is taking the unbenevolent as a model. The model being unbenevolent, one can't take it as a model.

'So of the three, parents, teachers, and rulers, none can be a model for order.

'That being so, then what can we take as a model for order? So I say, nothing is better than taking Heaven* as a model. Heaven's conduct

is broad and impartial; its favours are rich and incur no debt; its brightness endures without fading. So the sage-kings took it as a model.'
(4/5–10)

4.3 'Having taken Heaven as a model, our actions and undertakings
must be measured against Heaven. What Heaven desires, do it; what
Heaven doesn't desire, stop.

'That being so, then what does Heaven desire and what does it detest?
Heaven surely desires people to care about each other and benefit each
other and doesn't desire people to detest each other and injure
each other. How do we know Heaven desires people to care about each
other and benefit each other and doesn't desire them to detest each other
and injure each other? By its inclusively caring about them and
inclusively benefiting them. How do we know Heaven inclusively
cares about them and inclusively benefits them? By its inclusively
possessing them and inclusively accepting offerings from them.

'Now across the world, whether great or small states, all are
Heaven's towns. Among people, whether younger or elder, noble or
lowly, all are Heaven's subjects. Hence none fail to fatten oxen and
sheep, feed hounds and pigs, and prepare pure offerings of wine and
grain to reverently serve Heaven. Is this not inclusively possessing
them and inclusively accepting offerings from them? If Heaven inclusively possesses them and accepts offerings from them, how could it
not desire people to care about each other and benefit each other? So
[it's] said, "Those who care about others and benefit others, Heaven
will surely bless them; those who detest others and injure others,
Heaven will surely afflict them with misfortune." [It's] said, "Those
who kill the innocent will get ill fortune from it." How is it that,
people killing each other, Heaven afflicts them with misfortune?
Hence we know Heaven desires people to care about each other and
benefit each other and doesn't desire people to detest each other and
injure each other.' (4/10–18)

4.4 'The sage-kings of the past, Yǔ, Tāng, Wén, and Wǔ,* inclusively cared about the common people of the world and led them to
honour Heaven and serve the ghosts. They benefited people much.
So Heaven blessed them, causing them to be established as Son of
Heaven,* and the various lords all respectfully served them. The
tyrants Jié, Zhòu, Yōu, and Lì* inclusively detested the common
people of the world and led them to insult Heaven and humiliate the

ghosts. They injured people much, so Heaven afflicted them with misfortune, causing them to lose their states, and to die and have their mutilated bodies displayed to all the world. Their sons and grandsons in later generations denounce them to this day. So those who did bad and were afflicted with misfortune—Jié, Zhòu, Yōu, and Lì are these. Those who cared about people and benefited people and were blessed—Yǔ, Tāng, Wén, and Wǔ are these. There have been those who cared about people and benefited people and were blessed, and there have also been those who detested people and injured people and were afflicted with misfortune.' (4/18–22)

BOOK 5

SEVEN TROUBLES

5.1 Our master Mòzǐ said, 'States have seven troubles. What are the seven troubles?

'The city walls and moats cannot be defended, yet they build palaces and houses—this is the first trouble.

'An enemy state arrives at the border, but no neighbouring states come to the rescue—this is the second trouble.

'The people's strength is exhausted in advance on useless projects and incapable people are rewarded. The people's strength exhausted in uselessness, wealth depleted in entertaining guests—this is the third trouble.

'Officials value only their salaries, travelling advisors care only about cultivating relationships, the ruler revises the models* to persecute his subjects, the subjects are fearful and dare not oppose him—this is the fourth trouble.

'The ruler takes himself to have sagely knowledge and so doesn't ask about affairs; he takes himself to be secure and strong and so makes no defence preparations; neighbouring states scheme against him but he doesn't know enough to be on guard—this is the fifth trouble.

'Those who are trusted are not loyal; those who are loyal are not trusted—this is the sixth trouble.

'Livestock and crops are inadequate for food; high ministers are inadequate for their tasks; rewards don't please; punishments don't intimidate—this is the seventh trouble.

'Residing in a state with these seven troubles, the altars to the spirits* of soil and grain will surely be lost. Defending a city with these seven troubles, enemies will arrive and the state will topple. Wherever these seven troubles apply, the state will surely face disaster.'* (5/1–7)

5.2 In all cases, the five grains* are what the people rely on and what the ruler is sustained by. So if the people have nothing to rely on, the ruler has no sustenance. If the people have no food, they cannot work. So as to food, one cannot fail to be diligent; as to land, one cannot fail to work it; and in using resources, one cannot fail to practise moderation . . . (5/7–8)

5.3 Now suppose there is a woman carrying her child while drawing water and she drops the child into the well. The mother will surely then rescue it. Now a bad harvest, the people starving, the roads filled with the hungry—this is even more serious than dropping one's child into a well. How can we not examine it?

So in years when the harvest is good, the people are benevolent and decent; in years when the harvest is bad, the people are stingy and mean. How could it be that the people are always this way?!* If those who work are few, while those who eat are many, the harvest is never plentiful. So [it's] said, 'If resources are insufficient, go back to the timing;* if food is insufficient, go back to use.'* So, since the people of former times produced resources with proper timing and used resources while maintaining strong fundamentals, resources were sufficient.

So even the sage-kings of past generations, how could they have made the five grains always yield a good harvest or droughts and floods not come?! Nevertheless, no people went cold or hungry. Why? They worked urgently at the proper times and were frugal in providing for themselves.

So the documents of Xià say, 'Yǔ had seven years of flooding.' The documents of Yīn say, 'Tāng had five years of drought.'* In these cases, they encountered extreme scarcity and famine. Nevertheless, the people were not cold or hungry. Why? They were meticulous in producing resources and moderate in using them. (5/13–19)

5.4 So the granaries not having prepared grain, it's not possible to cope with scarcity and famine. The armouries not having prepared weapons, even the righteous cannot conquer the unrighteous. The city walls not being fully prepared, it's not possible to defend oneself. The heart not having prepared plans, it's not possible to respond to contingencies . . . So preparation is most important for a state. Food is the state's treasure; weapons are its claws; and the city walls are its means of self-defence. These three are the basic provisions of the state. (5/19–23)

5.5 So [we] say, they* bestow the highest rewards on those of no achievement; empty the treasury to supply themselves with carriages and horses, clothing, and curios; and make their labourers suffer in order to build palaces to enjoy looking at. At their death, again, they are richly furnished with nested coffins and provided with much clothing. While alive, they build terraced pavilions; at death, again, they construct grave mounds and tombs. So, outside, the people suffer; inside, the treasury is depleted. Above, the rulers never tire of their pleasures; below, the people cannot bear their suffering. So if the state is attacked by bandits, it will be injured; if the people face scarcity and famine, they will perish—this is all the fault of inadequate preparation.

Moreover, food is what the sages treasure. So the documents of Zhōu* say, 'A state without three years of food—the state is not their state; a family without three years of food—the children are not their children.'* This refers to a state's preparation. (5/23–8)

BOOK 6

AVOIDING EXCESS

6.1 Our master Mòzǐ said, 'The people of antiquity, before they knew to build palaces and houses, resided by hills, dwelling in caves. The ground beneath was damp and injured people. So the sage-kings initiated the building of palaces* and houses. The model* for building palaces and houses said, "Houses, the height should be enough to avoid the damp, the sides thick enough to protect against the wind and cold, the top strong enough to withstand snow, frost, rain, and dew. The height of palace walls should be enough to maintain the propriety of separating men from women. Only this, then stop." Any expenditure of resources or exertion of labour that did not add benefit they did not undertake.

'If city walls are repaired using regular compulsory labour, the people will be weary but not injured. If rents and taxes are collected according to regular norms, the people incur expenses but are not distressed. What makes the people suffer is not this. They suffer from the heavy collection of taxes from the common people.*

'Thus the sage-kings initiated the building of palaces and houses for convenience in living, not to enjoy looking at. They initiated the making of clothes, robes, belts, and shoes for the convenience of the body, not for fashion. So they themselves practised moderation, and they taught this to the people. Hence the people of the world could be well ordered* and resources could be made sufficient.

'As to the rulers of today, on the other hand, they build palaces and houses differently from this. They inevitably collect heavy taxes from the common people, robbing the people of their resources for clothing and food, to build palaces and pavilions with zigzagging views and decorations of colourful paint and carvings. The ruler builds his palace like this, so those on his left and right all take him as a model. Hence their resources are insufficient to prepare against scarcity or famine or to relieve the orphaned and widowed. So the state is impoverished and the people are difficult to put in order.* If rulers really desire the world to be in order and detest its being in disorder, in building palaces and houses they cannot fail to practise moderation.' (6/1–9)

6.2 'The people of antiquity, before they knew to make clothing, wore fur coats and grass belts. In winter, these were not light and warm; in summer, they were not light and cool. The sage-kings took these to fail to conform to people's actual needs. So they initiated teaching women to handle silk and flax and to weave textiles to make clothing for the people. The model for making clothing* was, "In winter, clothing of heavy silk, sufficient to be light and warm; in summer, clothing of coarse linen, sufficient to be light and cool. Only this, then stop." So in making clothing, the sage-kings took fitting the body and feeling comfortable against the skin to be sufficient. It wasn't to impress the ears and eyes and show off to the commoners.

'In those times, they didn't know to value sturdy carts and fine horses; they didn't know to enjoy carvings and ornamentation. What is the reason? It was so because of the way they followed. So as to the people's resources for clothing and food, families had enough to cope with drought, flooding, scarcity, or famine. Why? They got what was actually needed to provide for themselves and were not confused by extraneous things. Hence their people were frugal and easy to put in order, and their ruler used resources in moderation and was easy to support. The treasury was full, sufficient to cope with difficulties. Weapons and armour were not in disrepair, officers and the people were not weary, and so their military was sufficient to conquer the disobedient. So the endeavour of the hegemon could be carried out in the world.*

'As to the rulers of today, on the other hand, they make clothing differently from this. Already provided both with clothes that in winter are light and warm and with those that in summer are light and cool, they inevitably collect heavy taxes from the common people, robbing the people of their resources for clothing and food, to make finely embroidered and ornamented garments with belt hooks of gold and pendants of pearls and jade. Female artisans make the ornamented finery and male artisans make the carved accessories for them to wear. These are not what in fact increases warmth. They deplete resources and expend labour, in the end amounting to no use. Looking at things this way, they make clothing not for the body but all to look good. Hence their people are dissolute and difficult to put in order, their rulers wasteful and difficult to advise. Now with a wasteful ruler leading a dissolute people, desiring the state to avoid disorder, they cannot succeed. If rulers really desire the world to be in order and detest its being in disorder, in making clothing they cannot fail to practise moderation.' (6/9–21)

6.3 'The people of antiquity, before they knew to make food and drink, ate only plain foods and dwelled apart from each other.* So the sage-kings initiated teaching men to plough and sow, and plant and cultivate, to produce food for the people. In producing food, they took it to be enough to replenish breath, satisfy hunger, strengthen the body, and fill the belly, and that's all. So they used resources in moderation and provided for themselves frugally. The people were wealthy and the state was in order.

'Nowadays, on the other hand, it is not so. They collect heavy taxes from the common people to prepare various gourmet meats, along with steamed and broiled fish and turtles. In a great state, the dishes total a hundred, in a small state ten. On a table with ten-foot sides, the eye cannot see all the dishes, the hand cannot reach them all, the mouth cannot taste them all. In winter, the uneaten food freezes; in summer it spoils. The ruler eats and drinks like this, so those on his left and right emulate him. Hence the wealthy and noble are wasteful, while the orphaned and widowed are cold and hungry. Even if they desire to avoid disorder, they cannot succeed. If rulers really desire the world to be in order and detest its being in disorder, in eating and drinking they cannot fail to practise moderation.' (6/21–6)

6.4 'The people of antiquity, before they knew to build boats and carts, did not move heavy loads or travel a long way. So the sage-kings initiated the building of boats and carts* to facilitate people's affairs. They built boats and carts that were sturdy and handy, able to hold a heavy load and travel far. They used few resources but produced much benefit, and hence the people were delighted to benefit from them. Legal decrees were carried out without urging; the people were not weary yet their superiors had enough resources to use, and so the people turned to them.

'As to the rulers of today, they build boats and carts differently from this. Their boats and carts are already both sturdy and handy, yet they inevitably collect heavy taxes from the common people to decorate them. They decorate the carts with ornamentation and decorate the boats with carvings. Women abandon their spinning and weaving to make the ornamentation, so the people are cold; men leave their ploughing and sowing to do the carving, so the people are hungry. The ruler builds his boats and carts like this, so those on his left and right emulate him, and hence their people face both hunger and cold and so do wicked deeds. When wicked deeds are many, punishments will be severe; when punishments are severe, the state is disordered. If rulers really desire the world to be in order and detest its being in disorder, in building boats and carts they cannot fail to practise moderation.' (6/27–33)

6.5 '. . . Even the most perfect sages of previous generations inevitably kept a harem. They did not let this injure their conduct, so the people did not resent it. In the palace, there were no confined women, so throughout the world there were no single men. Inside, there were no confined women, outside, there were no single men, and so the population of the world was large.

'As to the harems of the rulers of today, in a great state the confined women total in the thousands, in a small state they total in the hundreds. Hence many of the men in the world are single and lack wives, many women are confined and lack husbands, men and women lose the opportunity to mate, and so the population is small. If rulers really desire the population to be large and detest its being small, in keeping a harem they cannot fail to practise moderation.' (6/36–9)

6.6 'Regarding all of these five,* the sage is frugal and moderate, the petty person dissolute and indulgent. Frugality and moderation lead to prosperity; dissolution and indulgence lead to destruction. As to these five, one cannot fail to practise moderation. When husband and wife practise moderation, heaven and earth are harmonious; when the wind and rain are moderate, the five grains ripen; when clothing is moderate, the skin is comfortable.' (6/39–40)

BOOK 7

THREE DISPUTATIONS

7.1 Chéng Fán* asked our master Mòzǐ, 'Sir, you say, "The sage-kings did not make music." In the past, when the various lords tired of attending to government, they rested to the music of bells and drums. When officers and ministers tired of attending to government, they rested to the music of pipes and strings. The farmers plowed in spring, weeded in summer, harvested in autumn, and stockpiled in winter, resting to the music of jars and pots.* Now, Sir, you say, "The sage-kings did not make music." This is analogous to yoking horses to a carriage and never unhitching them or drawing a bow and never releasing it. Isn't this something no living creature could achieve?!' (7/1–3)

7.2 Our master Mòzǐ said, 'In the past, Yáo and Shùn lived in thatched huts, yet they performed ceremonies and they performed music. Tāng exiled the tyrant Jié to the Great Sea, unified the world, and established himself as king. Having accomplished these feats and established these achievements, with no major troubles in sight, on the basis of the former kings' music, he himself created music, titled "Hù", and arranged the "Jiǔ Zhāo". King Wǔ defeated the Yīn dynasty and executed the tyrant Zhòu, unified the world, and established himself as king. Having accomplished these feats and established these achievements, with no major troubles in sight, on the basis of the former kings' music, he himself created music, titled "Xiàng". King Chéng of Zhōu, on the basis of the former kings' music, created music himself, titled "Zōu Yú".

'In ordering the world, King Chéng of Zhōu was not the equal of King Wǔ; in ordering the world, King Wǔ was not the equal of Tāng; in ordering the world, Tāng was not the equal of Yáo and Shùn. So the more elaborate their music, the less they achieved good order. Looking at things this way, music is not the means by which to order the world.' (7/3–9)

7.3 Chéng Fán said, 'You say, "The sage-kings had no music." These cases are surely examples of music. How do you assert that the sage-kings had no music?'

Our master Mòzǐ said, 'The mandate of the sage-kings was to reduce the excessive. Eating is beneficial, but if knowing to eat when hungry is deemed knowledge, really this is no knowledge at all. Now the sages had music but very little; this too counts as none at all.'*
(7/9–11)

PART II
THE TRIADS

PROMOTING THE WORTHY

BOOK 8

PROMOTING THE WORTHY (I)

8.1 Our master Mòzĭ stated,* 'Nowadays kings, dukes, and great men who govern in states all desire the state to be wealthy, the population to be large, and the punishments and government* to be in order. Yet they get not wealth but poverty, not a large population but a small one, not order but disorder. So this is fundamentally missing what they desire and getting what they detest.'*

What is the reason for this?*

Our master Mòzĭ stated, 'This lies in kings, dukes, and great men who govern in states being unable to govern by promoting the worthy and employing the capable.* Thus if a state has many worthy and excellent officers,* order in the state is robust; if worthy and excellent officers are few, order in the state is weak. So the duty of great men will lie simply in making the worthy numerous.' (8/1–5)

8.2 [We] say,* 'That being so, then what will the method for making the worthy numerous be like?'

Our master Mòzĭ stated, 'Analogous to desiring to make the good archers and charioteers in the state numerous, one must enrich them, ennoble them, revere them, and praise them; then the good archers and charioteers in the state can be made numerous. How much more should this be done when there are worthy and excellent officers who are rich in virtuous conduct, discriminating in statements and discussion, and broadly learned in methods of the way! These are indeed treasures of the state and stewards of the altars of soil and grain. One must also enrich them, ennoble them, revere them, and praise them; then the excellent officers in the state can also be made numerous.' (8/5–8)

8.3 Thus the ancient sage-kings in governing stated, 'If not righteous, then not wealthy; if not righteous, then not ennobled; if not righteous, then not treated as kin; if not righteous, then not close.'

Hence when the wealthy and noble people of the state heard this, they all withdrew and planned, saying, 'At first, what I relied on was wealth and nobility. Now the superior elevates the righteous and doesn't shun the poor or lowly. That being so, then I cannot fail to be righteous.' When those who were kin to the ruler heard it, they too withdrew and planned, saying, 'At first, what I relied on was kinship. Now the superior elevates the righteous and doesn't shun distant relations. That being so, then I cannot fail to be righteous.' When those close to the ruler heard it, they too withdrew and planned, saying, 'At first, what I relied on was closeness. Now the superior elevates the righteous and doesn't shun those far from him. That being so, then I cannot fail to be righteous.' When those far from the ruler heard it, they too withdrew and planned, saying, 'At first, I took it that, being far from the ruler, I had nothing to rely on. Now the superior elevates the righteous and doesn't shun those far from him. That being so, then I cannot fail to be righteous.' Eventually officials in distant cities and outlying regions, sons of court officials, the masses in the capital, and farmers along the four borders heard it, and they all competed to be righteous.

What is the reason for this?

[We] say, 'Superiors employed subordinates by means of just one thing; subordinates served superiors by means of just one method.* To give an analogy, a wealthy man has a high wall and a deep palace, and once the wall is erected, he pierces it with only one gate. If a robber enters, they shut the gate from which he entered and search for him, and the robber has no way out. What is the reason for this? It's that the superior holds the key point.' (8/8–16)

8.4 So the ancient sage-kings in governing ranked people's virtue and promoted the worthy. Even among farmers, artisans, and merchants, if there were capable people, [the sage-kings] elevated them, gave them high rank, granted them a generous salary, assigned them tasks, and authorized them to issue decrees. [They] said, 'If their rank is not high, the people will not revere them. If their salary is not rich, the people will not trust them. If their decrees are not authoritative, the people will not fear them.'* As to these three being given to the worthy, it wasn't to reward them for being worthy, it was from a desire for them to accomplish their tasks.

So, at that time, ranks were assigned on the basis of virtue, tasks allotted on the basis of the office held, and rewards given on the basis of the labour expended; achievements were measured and salaries apportioned accordingly. So no official was permanently ennobled, while none of the people were forever lowly. The capable were elevated; the incapable were demoted. This is what the statement 'Elevate public righteousness, prevent personal resentment'* refers to. (8/16–21)

8.5 So in antiquity Yáo elevated Shùn from the south side of Fú Marsh, authorized him to govern, and the world was at peace; Yú elevated Yì from amid Yīn Fāng, authorized him to govern, and the nine realms* were complete; Tāng elevated Yī Yǐn from within the kitchen, authorized him to govern, and his plan succeeded; King Wén elevated Hóng Yāo and Tài Diān from amid their hunting and fishing nets, authorized them to govern, and the western land submitted.*

So, at that time, even among ministers with rich salaries and honoured positions, none failed to discharge their duties with reverence and awe, while even among farmers, artisans, or merchants, none failed to encourage each other in promoting virtue.

So, worthy officers are those to serve as aides and deputies. So if one retains such officers, his plans will not encounter difficulties and his body will not be weary; his name will be established and his projects successful; beauty will be manifest and ugliness will not arise—all from retaining such officers. (8/21–5)

8.6 Thus our master Mòzǐ stated, 'When things go as one intends, one cannot fail to elevate worthy officers; when things don't go as one intends, one cannot fail to elevate worthy officers. Above, desiring to transmit the way of Yáo, Shùn, Yú, and Tāng, one cannot fail to promote the worthy. Promoting the worthy is the foundation of government.' (8/25–6)

BOOK 9

PROMOTING THE WORTHY (II)

9.1 Our master Mòzǐ stated, 'Now kings, dukes, and great men in ruling the people, heading the altars of soil and grain, and bringing order to the state desire to preserve them and not lose them. Why not examine how promoting the worthy is the foundation of government?'

How do we know promoting the worthy is the foundation of government?

[He] said, 'The noble and wise governing over the foolish and lowly, there is order; the foolish and lowly governing over the noble and wise, there is disorder.* Hence we know promoting the worthy is the foundation of government.' (9/1–3)

9.2 So the ancient sage-kings deeply honoured the worthy and appointed the capable, without partisanship toward fathers and sons, partiality toward the noble and wealthy, or favouritism for the handsome and fair. The worthy they elevated to superior rank, enriched and ennobled, and made heads of bureaus; the unworthy they demoted and dismissed, impoverished and lowered, and made servants. Hence the people all were encouraged by their rewards and feared their punishments, and they led each other to be worthy. In this way, the worthy were many and the unworthy few—this is called 'advancing the worthy'. After this, the sages listened to their statements, tracked their conduct, examined their abilities, and carefully assigned them offices—this is called 'employing the capable'. So those who could be employed to order* the state were employed to order the state; those who could be employed as heads of bureaus were employed as heads of bureaus; those who could be employed to order the towns were employed to order the towns. All those who were employed to order the state, government bureaus, and towns and villages, these all were the worthies of the state. (9/3–8)

9.3 When worthies order a state, they come to court early and retire late, to hear legal cases and order government affairs. Hence the state is in order and the punishments and models* are correct. When worthies head bureaus, they go to bed late and rise early, collecting taxes from the profits on passes, markets, forests, and fish weirs* to fill the treasury. Hence the treasury is full and resources are not squandered. When worthies order the towns, they go out early and come in late, ploughing and sowing, planting and cultivating, harvesting crops.* Hence crops are plentiful and the people have enough to eat.*

So the state being in order, the punishments and models are correct; the treasury being full, the myriad people are wealthy. Above, there are the means to make pure offerings of wine and grain to sacrifice to Heaven and the ghosts; abroad, there are the means to prepare furs and coins to befriend the various lords of neighbouring states; within the state, there are the means to feed the hungry and rest the weary, so as to provide for the myriad people; while abroad, there are the means to attract worthy persons from all the world. Thus, above, Heaven and the ghosts enrich them; abroad, the various lords join with them; within the state, the myriad people feel kinship with them, and worthy people turn to them. In this way, planning affairs, one is effective; undertaking affairs, one is successful; entering to defend, one is strong; emerging to punish, one is powerful.* So as to how the sage-kings of the three dynasties of the past, Yáo, Shùn, Yǔ, Tāng, Wén, and Wǔ, reigned over the world and rectified the various lords, this indeed was their model. (9/8–14)

9.4 Having spoken of this model, if we don't yet know the method for putting it into practice, then the task remains incomplete. Hence we must establish the Three Foundations.*

What are called the 'Three Foundations'?

[We] say, 'If their rank is not high, the people will not revere them. If their salary is not rich, the people will not trust them. If their decrees are not authoritative, the people will not fear them.'* So the ancient sage-kings gave them high rank, granted them a generous salary, assigned them tasks, and authorized them to issue decrees. How could this have been to reward their subjects?! It was from a desire for them to accomplish their tasks.

An ode says:*

> I instruct you to feel concern for others' worries.
> I teach you to confer ranks.
> Who can hold something hot
> Without first rinsing their hand in cold water?

So this expounds how in ancient times the rulers of states and the various lords could not fail to get hold of good people to serve as aides and deputies. It is analogous to rinsing when holding something hot so as to relieve one's hand.

The ancient sage-kings, if they found worthy people and employed them, conferred titles to ennoble them and apportioned land to enfeoff them, their whole life never spurning them. Worthy people, if they found an enlightened ruler to serve, exerted the strength of their four limbs to the utmost in discharging their responsibilities for the ruler's tasks, their whole life never tiring. If there was beauty and good, they credited it to their superior; hence beauty and good lay with the superior, while grievances and complaints lay with the subordinates. Peace and joy lay with the ruler; worries and grief lay with the ministers. So the ancient sage-kings governed like this. (9/14–22)

9.5a Nowadays kings, dukes, and great men also desire to emulate ancient people in governing by promoting the worthy and employing the capable.* They give them high rank but not a corresponding salary. As to officials who hold high rank without a corresponding salary, the people will not trust them. The officials say, 'This is not, within, really caring about me. It's just a pretence for using me.' As for people who have been the victims of pretence, how could they ever feel kinship with their superior?! So the former kings stated, 'Those who are greedy for government power cannot apportion tasks to others; those who put too much weight on goods cannot apportion salaries to others.' Tasks not being assigned, salary not being apportioned, we ask, how will the worthy people of the world come to the side of kings, dukes, and great men?

If the worthy don't come to the side of kings, dukes, and great men, then this is the unworthy being on their left and right. If the unworthy are on their left and right, then what they praise doesn't coincide with the worthy, while what they punish doesn't coincide with the vicious. If kings, dukes, and great men honour these people in governing the state, rewards too will surely not coincide with the worthy, while punishments too will surely not coincide with the vicious.* If rewards don't coincide with the worthy and punishments don't coincide with the vicious, then this is those who do what's worthy not being encouraged and those who do what's vicious not being discouraged. Hence, entering the home, people are not kind and filially devoted to their parents; going out, they are not respectful and fraternal to the townspeople. In their living habits, they lack moderation; in their comings and goings, they lack measure; in relations between men and women, they have no proper separation. If employed to order government bureaus, they steal; to defend a city, they betray it. If the ruler encounters difficulty, they don't die for him; if he is exiled, they don't follow him. If employed to judge legal cases, their adjudication is inaccurate; to apportion resources, they do it unfairly. Planning affairs with them, one is ineffective; undertaking affairs, one is unsuccessful; entering to defend, one is not strong; emerging to punish, one is not powerful. So as to how the tyrants of the three dynasties of the past, Jié, Zhòu, Yōu, and Lì, lost their states and caused their altars of soil and grain to be overturned, it was caused by this.* (9/22–32)

9.5b What is the reason? All this is brought about by understanding the little things but not understanding the big things.* Now kings, dukes, and great men, if they have a suit of clothes they cannot make, they surely employ a good tailor; if they have an ox or a sheep they cannot slaughter, they surely employ a good butcher. So in cases like these two, kings, dukes, and great men all know to adopt promoting the worthy and employing the capable as a government policy. When it comes to their state being in disorder and the altars of soil and grain being endangered, on the other hand, they don't know to employ the capable to put them in order. If people are their relatives, they employ them; if they happen to have wealth and noble rank, or if they have attractive looks, they employ them. As for people employed because they happen to have wealth and noble rank or they have attractive looks, how are they necessarily wise and intelligent?! If they are employed to order the state, then this is employing the unwise and unintelligent to order the state; that the state will be in disorder can thus be known.

Moreover, when kings, dukes, and great men have someone they employ because they care for his looks, without their hearts examining his knowledge they give him their care. Thus someone incapable of ordering* a hundred people is employed in an office in charge of a thousand; someone incapable of ordering a thousand people is employed in an office in charge of ten thousand. What is the reason for this? [I] say, the occupant of such an office has high rank and a rich salary, so, caring for his looks, they employ him in it.*

As for someone incapable of ordering a thousand people, if he is employed in an office in charge of ten thousand, this office exceeds his capability tenfold. Now the model for good order is that what arrives each day is to be put in order that day. The day cannot be extended tenfold. Knowledge* is the means of putting things in order. If his knowledge is not increased tenfold, yet he is given an office that exceeds his capability tenfold, then this is putting one matter in order and neglecting nine. Even if he works day and night continuously to put this office in order, the office will be just as if not put in order. What is the reason for this? It's because kings, dukes, and great men don't understand to govern by promoting the worthy and employing the capable.

So, governing by promoting the worthy and employing the capable and so achieving order, those statements above* refer to this. Governing by demoting the worthy and so bringing disorder, my statements here* refer to this. Now kings, dukes, and great men, if, within, they really desire to bring order to their state, if they desire to preserve it and not lose it, why not examine how promoting the worthy is the foundation of government? (9/32–43)

9.6a Moreover, as for taking promoting the worthy to be the foundation of government, how indeed could this be the statement of our master Mòzǐ alone?! This is the way of the sage-kings, the documents of the former kings, and the statement of distant years.* A tradition says, 'Seek a sagely ruler or wise person to assist you.' The 'Oath of Tāng' says, 'Hence seek a great sage with whom to join your efforts and unite your heart.' So these state how the sages didn't neglect to govern by promoting the worthy and employing the capable. So only because the ancient sage-kings were able to judiciously govern by promoting the worthy and employing the capable, with no extraneous matters mixed into things, all the world benefited from it. (9/43–6)

9.6b In antiquity, Shùn ploughed at Mount Lì, made pottery on the banks of the river, and fished at Thunder Marsh. Yáo found him on the south side of Fú Marsh, elevated him as the Son of Heaven, and handed over to him the government of the world, to order the people of the world. Yī Zhì was a personal servant of the Prince of Xīn's daughter when she married and was personally a cook. Tāng found him, elevated him to be his chief minister, and handed over to him the government of the world, to order the people of the world. Fù Yuè wore coarse clothing with a belt of rope and worked as a servant building the city walls of Fù Yán. Wǔ Dīng found him, elevated him to be one of the three dukes, and handed over to him the government of the world, to order the people of the world.*

Why did these men start off lowly and end up noble, start off impoverished and end up wealthy? It's because kings, dukes, and great men understood to govern by promoting the worthy and employing the capable. Hence none of the people were hungry without getting food, cold without getting clothing, weary without getting rest, or in disorder without being put in order. (9/46–51)

9.7 So the ancient sage-kings judiciously governed by promoting the worthy and employing the capable, taking Heaven as a model. Even Heaven too doesn't distinguish between the poor or wealthy, noble or lowly, far or near, closely or distantly related—the worthy, it elevates and promotes; the unworthy it demotes and dismisses.

That being so, then who were the wealthy and noble who by being worthy got its rewards? [We] say, these were such as the sage-kings of the three dynasties of the past, Yáo, Shùn, Yǔ, Tāng, Wén, and Wǔ. How did they get its rewards? [We] say, in governing the world, they inclusively cared about them and thus benefited them, and furthermore they led the myriad people of the world to honour Heaven above and serve the ghosts and to care about and benefit the myriad people. Thus Heaven and the ghosts rewarded them and established them as Son of Heaven, to serve as the parents of the people. The myriad people thus praised them, calling them sage-kings to this day. So these are the wealthy and noble who by being worthy got its rewards.

That being so, then who were the wealthy and noble who by being vicious got its punishments? [We] say, these were such as the tyrants of the three dynasties of the past, Jié, Zhòu, Yōu, and Lì. How do we know it is so? [We] say, in governing the world, they inclusively despised them and thus injured them, and furthermore they led the people of the world to insult Heaven and humiliate the ghosts and to slaughter the myriad people. Thus Heaven and the ghosts punished them, causing their bodies to die and be mutilated, their sons and grandsons to scatter, and their houses to perish, cut off without descendants. The myriad people thus condemned them, calling them tyrants to this day.* So these are the wealthy and noble who by being vicious got its punishments. . . .* (9/51–60)

9.8 Now kings, dukes, and great men desire to reign over the world and govern the various lords, but without virtue and righteousness, by what means will they do this? Their doctrine is surely by displaying might and power. Now why do kings, dukes, and great men select might and power? This leads the people to their death. As for the people, life is what they most desire, death what they most despise. They don't get what they desire, while what they despise comes again and again. From antiquity until today, there has never been someone who could reign over the world and govern the various lords in this way.

Now if great men desire to reign over the world and govern the various lords, if they desire to achieve their ambitions throughout the world and make a name for themselves in later generations, then why not examine how promoting the worthy is the foundation of government? This is something the sages practised deeply. (9/70–4)

BOOK 10

PROMOTING THE WORTHY (III)

10.1 Our master Mòzǐ stated, 'The kings, dukes, and great men of the world all desire their state to be wealthy, their population to be large, and their punishments and models* to be in order. Yet by not recognizing that they should govern their state and the common people by promoting the worthy, kings, dukes, and great men fundamentally neglect that promoting the worthy is the foundation of government.

'If kings, dukes, and great men fundamentally neglect that promoting the worthy is the foundation of government, can we not cite cases to show them? Now suppose there is a feudal lord here governing his state. He says, "All officers in my state who are capable at archery and chariot driving, I will reward and ennoble them. Officers incapable of archery and driving, I will punish and demote them." Ask of the officers of this state who is pleased and who is fearful. I take it that surely the officers capable of archery and driving are pleased, the officers incapable of archery and driving are fearful.

'Let's try on this basis to lead them further. Suppose the lord says, "All officers in my state who are loyal and trustworthy, I will reward and ennoble them. Officers who are not loyal and trustworthy, I will punish and demote them." Ask of the officers of this state who is pleased and who is fearful. I take it that surely the loyal and trustworthy officers are pleased and the officers who are not loyal and trustworthy are fearful.

'Now if they govern their state and the common people by promoting the worthy, this encourages those in the state who do good and discourages those in the state who are vicious. On a larger scale, adopted to govern the world,* it encourages those in the world who do good and discourages those who are vicious. That being so, then previously,* why I valued the way of Yáo, Shùn, Yǔ, Tāng, Wén, and Wǔ, what was the reason for it? That in overseeing the masses, issuing government policies, and so ordering the people, they brought it about that those in the world who do good could be encouraged and those in the world who are vicious could be discouraged. That being so, then as for this promoting the worthy, it is the same as the way of Yáo, Shùn, Yǔ, Tāng, Wén, and Wǔ.' (10/1–10)

10.2 'Moreover, now the officers and gentlemen of the world in their statements and sayings in daily life all promote the worthy, but when it comes to overseeing the masses, issuing government policies, and ordering the people, none know to promote the worthy and employ the capable. By this I know the officers and gentlemen of the world understand the little things but don't understand the big things.* How do we know it is so? Now kings, dukes, and great men, if they have as a resource an ox or a sheep they're unable to slaughter, they surely seek a good butcher. If they have the resources for a suit of clothes they're unable to make, they surely seek a good tailor. When kings, dukes, and great men are in these situations, even if there are those available who are their flesh and bone kin, who happen to have wealth and noble rank, or who have attractive looks, they really know that these people are incapable, so they don't employ them. What is the reason for this? They fear they will ruin the resource.* When kings, dukes, and great men are in these situations, they don't neglect to promote the worthy and employ the capable.

'Kings, dukes, and great men, if they have a sick horse they're unable to heal, they surely seek a good doctor. If they have a stiff bow they can't draw, they surely seek a good craftsman. When kings, dukes, and great men are in these situations, even if there are those available who are their flesh and bone kin, who happen to have wealth and noble rank, or who have attractive looks, they really know these people are incapable, so surely they don't employ them. What is the reason for this? They fear they will ruin the resource. When kings, dukes, and great men are in these situations, they don't neglect to promote the worthy and employ the capable.

'When it comes to their state, on the other hand, it's not so. If someone is the flesh and bone kin of kings, dukes, and great men, happens to have wealth and noble rank, or has attractive looks, they elevate the person. So, do kings, dukes, and great men hold their state to be less dear to them than the resources of a stiff bow, a sick horse, a suit of clothes, an ox, or a sheep? By this I know the officers and gentlemen of the world all understand the little things but don't understand the big things. This is analogous to someone being mute yet employed as a court liaison or deaf yet employed as a musician.' (10/10–20)

10.3 Thus as to how the ancient sage-kings put the world in order, those they enriched and those they ennobled were not necessarily those who were the flesh and bone kin of kings, dukes, and great men, those who happened to have wealth and noble rank, or those who had attractive looks. Thus, in the past, Shùn ploughed at Mount Lì, made pottery on the banks of the river, fished at Thunder Marsh, and traded at Cháng Yáng. Yáo found him on the south side of Fú Marsh and established him as the Son of Heaven, letting him take over the government of the world, to order the people of the world. In the past, Yī Yǐn was a personal servant of the Prince of Xīn's daughter when she married and was employed as a cook. Tāng found and elevated him, establishing him as one of the three dukes and letting him take over the government of the world, to order the people of the world. In the past, Fù Yuè lived in the North Sea district on the walls of a prison. His clothing was coarse, his belt was a rope. He worked as a servant building the city walls of Fù Yán. Wǔ Dīng found and elevated him, establishing him as one of the three dukes and letting him take over the government of the world, to order the people of the world.*

Thus, in the past, as to Yáo's elevating Shùn, Tāng's elevating Yī Yǐn, and Wǔ Dīng's elevating Fù Yuè, how could it have been because they deemed them flesh and bone kin, those who happened to have wealth and noble rank, or those with attractive looks?! It was only because, by taking their statements as a model, using their plans, and practising their way, above, one could benefit Heaven; in the middle, one could benefit the ghosts; and below, one could benefit people—thus they advanced them to superior positions. (10/20–8)

10.4 The ancient sage-kings, having inspected promoting the worthy, desired to adopt it as a basis for government. So they wrote it on bamboo and silk* and inscribed it on dishes and bowls to pass down to their sons and grandsons in later generations. In the documents of the sage-kings, the document of the 'Punishments of Lǚ' is so. The king says:

O! Come! You who possess states and lands, I will tell you about fair punishments. Now you seek to pacify the common people. What should you choose, if not the right people? What should you revere, if not punishment? What should you consider, if not how to achieve this?*

To be able to choose the right people and carry out punishment with reverence, this can be achieved through the way of Yáo, Shùn, Yǔ, Tāng, Wén, and Wǔ. Why is this? It is achieved by promoting the worthy. In the documents of the former kings, a statement established over the years is so.* It says, 'Hope for sagely, brave, and wise people to assist you.' This states that the former kings in ordering the world surely chose worthies as their attendants and aides. (10/28–32)

10.5a [They] say,* 'Nowadays the officers and gentlemen of the world all desire wealth and noble rank and detest poverty and low rank.'

[We] say, 'It's so. What do you do to get wealth and noble rank and avoid poverty and low rank? Nothing is better than being worthy.'

What will the way of being worthy be like?

[We] say, 'Those with strength urgently help others, those with resources exert themselves to share with others, those with ways are encouraged to teach others. Things being like this, the hungry get food, the cold get clothing, and the disordered are put in order. If the hungry get food, the cold get clothing, and the disordered are put in order—this is living life with security.' (10/32–5)

10.5b Nowadays kings, dukes, and great men, those they enrich, those they ennoble, are all those who are the flesh and bone kin of the kings, dukes, and great men, those who happen to have wealth and noble rank, or those with attractive looks. Now as to the flesh and bone kin of kings, dukes, and great men, those who happen to have wealth and noble rank, or those with attractive looks—why would they necessarily be knowledgeable?!* If they are not knowledgeable, yet they are employed to order their state, that their state will be in disorder can be known.

Now the officers and gentlemen of the world all desire wealth and noble rank and detest poverty and low rank. That being so, then what do you do to get wealth and noble rank and avoid poverty and low rank? [They] say, 'Nothing is better than being the flesh and bone kin of kings, dukes, and great men, those who happen to have wealth and noble rank, or those with attractive looks.' Being the flesh and bone kin of kings, dukes, and great men, happening to have wealth and noble rank, or having attractive looks, these are not what one can learn to be capable of. (10/35–40)

10.5c Supposing rulers don't know how to draw distinctions, being rich in virtuous conduct like Yǔ, Tāng, Wén, and Wǔ gains one nothing, while if one is the flesh and bone kin of kings, dukes, and great men, being lame, mute, deaf, or vicious like Jié and Zhòu costs one nothing. Thus rewards don't coincide with the worthy, and punishments don't coincide with the vicious; those they reward have no reason to be rewarded, those they punish likewise have committed no crime. Hence this makes the common people all anxious and shattered, discouraged from doing good. Laying down the strength of their limbs, they don't labour for each other; letting surplus resources rot, they don't share materials; concealing good ways, they don't instruct each other. Things being like this, the hungry don't get food, the cold don't get clothing, and the disordered are not put in order.... (10/40–4)

10.7 Moreover, now the kings, dukes, great men, officers, and gentlemen of the world, if, within, they really desire to be benevolent and righteous and seek to be superior* officers; above, they desire to conform to the way of the sage-kings; and below, they desire to conform to the benefit of the state and the common people, so, this is why they cannot fail to examine the doctrine of promoting the worthy. Promoting the worthy is to the benefit of Heaven, the ghosts, and the common people and is the foundation of government affairs. (10/46–8)

IDENTIFYING UPWARD

BOOK 11

IDENTIFYING UPWARD (I)

11.1 Our master Mòzǐ stated, 'In antiquity, when people first arose, before there were punishments and government, probably the saying was, "People have different norms of righteousness."* Hence for one person, one norm; for two people, two norms; for ten people, ten norms—the more people, the more too the things they called "righteous". Hence people deemed their norm right and by it deemed others' norms wrong, so in interacting they deemed each other wrong.* Thus, within the family, fathers and sons, elder and younger brothers became resentful and scattered, unable to remain together with each other peacefully. The common people of the world all injured each other with water, fire, or poison. It reached the point that, having surplus strength, they couldn't use it to labour for each other; letting surplus resources rot, they didn't share them with each other; and concealing good ways, they didn't teach them to each other. The disorder in the world was like that among the birds and beasts.' (11/1–5)

11.2 Now it being understood that what brought about the world's disorder arose from there being no government leaders, thus the most worthy and capable person in the world was chosen and established as the Son of Heaven.* Once the Son of Heaven was established,* deeming his strength insufficient, again the most worthy and capable people in the world were chosen and installed as the three dukes. Once the Son of Heaven and the three dukes were established, deeming the world so vast that the people of distant states and different lands, along with the distinctions between right and wrong and benefit and harm, could not clearly be known one by one, so, the divisions between the myriad states were drawn and the various lords and rulers of states were established. Once the various lords and rulers of states were established, deeming their strength insufficient, again the most worthy and capable people in their states were chosen and installed as government leaders. (11/5–8)

11.3 Once the government leaders were in place, the Son of Heaven issued a government policy to the common people of the world, stating, 'Hearing of good or bad, in all cases report it to your superiors. What superiors deem right, all must deem right; what superiors deem wrong, all must deem wrong.* If superiors commit errors, admonish them; if subordinates do good, recommend them. Identify upward and don't align together below. This is what superiors will reward and subordinates will praise.

'Or, if you hear of good or bad but don't report it to superiors; are unable to deem right what superiors deem right; are unable to deem wrong what superiors deem wrong; don't admonish superiors when they commit errors; don't recommend subordinates when they do good; align together below and don't identify upward, this is what superiors will punish and the common people will denounce.' Superiors rewarded and punished on this basis. They examined things extremely clearly so as to be judicious and trustworthy. (11/9–13)

11.4 Thus the village head was the most benevolent man in the village. The village head issued a government policy to the common people of the village, stating, 'Hearing of good or bad, you must report it to the district head. What the district head deems right, all must deem right; what the district head deems wrong, all must deem wrong. Eliminate your bad statements and learn the good statements of the district head; eliminate your bad conduct and learn the good conduct of the district head.' Then how could the district be in disorder?! Examine what put the district in order: it's just that the district head was able to unify the district's norms of righteousness, and hence the district was in order.

The district head was the most benevolent man in the district. The district head issued a government policy to the common people of the district, stating, 'Hearing of good or bad, you must report it to the lord of the state. What the lord of the state deems right, all must deem right; what the lord of the state deems wrong, all must deem wrong. Eliminate your bad statements and learn the good statements of the lord of the state; eliminate your bad conduct and learn the good conduct of the lord of the state.' Then how could the state be in disorder?! Examine what put the state in order: it's just that the lord of the state was able to unify the state's norms of righteousness, and hence the state was in order.

The lord of the state was the most benevolent man in the state. The lord of the state issued a government policy to the common people of the state, stating, 'Hearing of good or bad, you must report it to the Son of Heaven. What the Son of Heaven deems right, all deem right; what the Son of Heaven deems wrong, all deem wrong. Eliminate your bad statements and learn the good statements of the Son of Heaven; eliminate your bad conduct and learn the good conduct of the Son of Heaven.' Then how could the world be in disorder?! Examine what put the world in order: it's just that the Son of Heaven was able to unify the world's norms of righteousness, and hence the world was in order.* (11/13–22)

11.5 If the common people of the world all identify upward with the Son of Heaven but don't identify upward with Heaven, then disasters still will not go away. Now if in the heavens whirlwinds and bitter rain come again and again, this is how Heaven punishes the common people for not identifying upward with Heaven.* (11/22–4)

11.6 Thus our master Mòzĭ stated, 'The ancient sage-kings in fact made the five punishments* to order their people. Analogous to the tie around a skein of silk or the drawstring of a net, they are for gathering in the common people of the world who don't identify upward with their superiors.'* (11/24–5)

BOOK 12

IDENTIFYING UPWARD (II)

12.1 Our master Mòzǐ said, 'In the present time, returning back to the ancient era when people first arose, before there were government leaders, probably the saying was, "The people of the world have different norms of righteousness." Hence for one person there was one norm, for ten people, ten norms, for a hundred people, a hundred norms. The greater the number of people, the greater too the number of things they called "righteous". Hence people deemed their own norm right and deemed others' norms wrong, and so they deemed each other wrong. Within the family, fathers and sons, elder and younger brothers resented each other and all had the intention to break up, unable to stay together peacefully. It got to the point that people wasted their surplus strength and did not use it to labour for each other, concealed good ways and did not teach them to each other, and let surplus resources rot and did not share them with each other. The disorder in the world got like that among the birds and beasts. There were no norms of moderation for ruler and subject, superior and subordinate, elder and youth, nor norms of ceremonial propriety for father and son or elder and younger brother, and hence the world was in disorder.' (12/1–5)

12.2 It was understood that the people lacked government leaders to unify the world's norms of righteousness and so the world was in disorder. Thus the most worthy, sagely, and intelligent person in the world was chosen, established as the Son of Heaven, and commissioned to undertake to unify the world's norms of righteousness.* Once the Son of Heaven was established, he deemed that from just the facts his ears and eyes could hear and see, he could not unify the world's norms all alone, and thus he chose the next most worthy, sagely, intelligent people in the world and installed them as the three dukes, to undertake together to unify the world's norms. Once the Son of Heaven and the three dukes were established, they deemed the world so vast that they could not successfully unify the people of the mountains, forests, and distant lands. Thus they divided up the world, set up the myriad feudal lords and rulers of states, and commissioned them to undertake to unify the norms of their states. Once the rulers of states were established, they in turn deemed that from just the facts their ears and eyes could hear and see, they could not unify the norms of their state. Thus they chose the most worthy people from their state and installed them as aides, generals, and ministers, all the way down to the heads of districts and villages, to undertake together to unify the norms of their state. (12/5–11)

12.3 Once the Son of Heaven, various lords, and government leaders of the people were decided, the Son of Heaven issued a government policy and promulgated an instruction, saying, 'All those who hear or see something good must report it to their superior; all those who hear or see something bad must also report it to their superior. What the superior deems right, you must also deem right; what the superior deems wrong, you must also deem wrong. If you do something good, present it; if superiors commit errors, admonish them. Identify upward with your superiors and have no heart to align together below. When superiors get hold of people who do these things, they will reward them, and when the myriad people hear about them, they will praise them.

'Or, if you hear or see something good but don't report it to your superior; hear or see something bad but also don't report it to your superior; are unable to deem right what the superior deems right; are unable to deem wrong what the superior deems wrong; do something good but are unable to present it; when superiors commit errors, are unable to admonish them; align together below and deem your superiors wrong—when superiors get hold of people who do these things, they will punish them, and when the myriad people hear about them, they will denounce them.'

So the ancient sage-kings in administering punishments and government, along with rewards and praise, examined things extremely clearly so as to be judicious and trustworthy. Hence the people of the entire world all desired to get the superiors' rewards and praise and feared the superiors' denunciation and punishment. (12/12–18)

12.4 Thus the village heads followed the Son of Heaven's government policy and unified their villages' norms of righteousness. Once the village heads had unified their villages' norms, they led the myriad people of their villages in identifying upward to the district heads, saying, 'As to all the myriad people of the village, all will identify upward with the district head and dare not align together below. What the district head deems right, you must also deem right; what the district head deems wrong, you must also deem wrong. Eliminate your bad statements and learn the good statements of the district head; eliminate your bad conduct and learn the good conduct of the district head.'

The district head was certainly the most worthy person in the district. All the people of the district taking the district head as a model, how could the district not be in order? Examine how the district heads put the districts in order; what is the reason for it? [We] say, it's just that they were able to unify their districts' norms, and hence the districts were in order.

The district heads put their districts in order, and once the districts were in order, they in turn led the myriad people of their districts to identify upward with the rulers of states, saying, 'As to all the myriad people of the district, all will identify upward with the ruler of the state and dare not align together below. What the ruler of the state deems right, you must also deem right; what the ruler of the state deems wrong, you must also deem wrong. Eliminate your bad statements and learn the good statements of the ruler of the state; eliminate your bad conduct and learn the good conduct of the ruler of the state.'

The ruler of the state was certainly the most worthy person in the state. All the people of the state taking the ruler of the state as a model, how could the state not be in order? Examine how the rulers of states put the states in order, such that the states were in order; what is the reason for it? [We] say, it's just that they were able to unify their states' norms, and hence the states were in order.

The rulers of states put their states in order, and once the states were in order, they in turn led the myriad people of their states to identify upward with the Son of Heaven, saying, 'As to all the myriad people of the state, all will identify upward with the Son of Heaven and not dare align together below. What the Son of Heaven deems right, you must also deem right; what the Son of Heaven deems wrong, you must also deem wrong. Eliminate your bad statements and learn the good statements of the Son of Heaven; eliminate your bad conduct and learn the good conduct of the Son of Heaven.'

The Son of Heaven was certainly the most benevolent person in the world. All the myriad people of the world taking the Son of Heaven as a model, how could the world not be in order? Examine how the Son of Heaven put the world in order; what is the reason for it? [We] say, it's just that he was able to unify the world's norms, and hence the world was in order. (12/18–31)

12.5 Now having identified upward to the Son of Heaven, but not yet identifying upward to Heaven, natural disasters will still not cease. So, as when Heaven sends down unseasonable cold or heat, or untimely snow, frost, rain, or dew, or the five grains don't ripen and the six livestock* don't breed, or there is disease or pestilence, or when whirlwinds and bitter rain come again and again—these are punishments sent down by Heaven to punish the people below for not identifying upward to Heaven.* (12/31–3)

12.6 So the ancient sage-kings, understanding what Heaven and the ghosts desired and avoiding what Heaven and the ghosts despised, sought to promote the benefit of the world and eliminate harm to the world. Hence they led the myriad people of the world to purify and bathe themselves and prepare pure offerings of wine and grain to sacrifice to Heaven and the ghosts. In serving the ghosts and spirits, they dared not offer wine and grain that were not pure, dared not offer sacrificial animals that were not plump, and dared not offer jade tablets, jade discs, coins, and silk that did not conform to the proper measures. In the spring and autumn sacrifices, they dared not miss the proper timing. In hearing legal cases, they dared not be inaccurate; in apportioning resources, they dared not be unfair; and in their living habits they dared not be neglectful.

[We] say, they served as government leaders like this, and thus, above, Heaven and the ghosts richly supported their serving as government leaders, while, below, the myriad people facilitated their serving as government leaders. Since Heaven and the ghosts deeply supported them, they were able to strive hard in their tasks, so they could get the blessings of Heaven and the ghosts. Since the myriad people facilitated them, they were able to strive hard in their tasks, so they could get the kinship of the myriad people. They governed like this, hence in planning affairs, they were effective; in undertaking affairs, successful; in entering to defend, strong; in emerging to punish, victorious.* What is the reason for this? [We] say, it's just that they governed by identifying upward. So the ancient sage-kings governed like this. (12/33–41)

12.7a Now the people of the world say, 'At the present time, the government leaders of the world not having been removed from the world, what's the reason why the world is in disorder?'

Our master Mòzǐ said, 'As to being a government leader in the present time, it's fundamentally different from antiquity. To give an analogy, it's like the Miáo tribes'* use of the five punishments. In the past, the sage-kings instituted the five punishments and used them to order the world. When it came to the Miáo tribes' instituting the five punishments, they used them to disorder the world. Yet how did this entail the punishments were bad?! It's the use of the punishments that was bad.

'Hence in the documents of the former kings, the "Penal Code of Lǚ" teaches,* "The Miáo people did not follow commands in instituting punishments but only created punishments consisting of five forms of execution,* calling them 'models'."* So this states that those who use punishments well use them to order the people; those who don't use punishments well use them as five forms of execution. Yet how does this entail the punishments are bad?! It's the use of the punishments that was bad. So consequently they became five forms of execution. . . .

'So in antiquity when government leaders were installed, it was for them to order the people. To give an analogy, it was like the tie around a skein of silk and the drawstring of a net, to use in gathering in the dissolute and vicious in the world and unifying their norms of righteousness'. (12/41–8)

12.7b Hence in the documents of the former kings, the 'Xiāng Nián' teaches:*

Now constructing states and building cities, and then appointing kings and lords—this was not to make them proud. Appointing ministers, officials, teachers, and heads—this was not to give them ease. It was to distinguish various tasks and employ them to assist in ordering Heaven's calm.*

So this speaks of how, in antiquity, when the Lord on High* and the ghosts and spirits constructed states and cities and established government leaders, it was not to give them high rank and a rich salary, so that they could live in wealth, honour, and leisure. It was for them to promote benefit and eliminate harm to the myriad people, to enrich the poor, increase the few, secure the endangered, and bring order to the disordered. So the ancient sage-kings governed like this. (12/49–52)

12.7c Nowadays kings, dukes, and great men in administering punishments and government are the opposite of this. They govern for the sake of flatterers, clansmen, fathers, brothers, acquaintances, and friends, placing them on their left and right, and installing them as government leaders. The people know that the superiors' installing of government leaders is not really to order the people. Hence they all ally together, concealing things, and none are willing to identify upward with their superiors. Thus superiors and subordinates have different norms of righteousness. If superiors and subordinates have different norms of righteousness, rewards and praise are not enough to encourage good, while punishments and penalties are not enough to discourage viciousness.

How do we know it is so?

[I] say, 'Suppose a superior is established to govern in a state and serve as the people's government leader. He says, "People it's appropriate to reward, I will reward them." If superiors and subordinates have different norms of righteousness, those the superior rewards are those the masses condemn.* [It's] said, "People dwell together in masses."* If people are condemned among the masses, then in this case even supposing they are rewarded by the superior, this is not enough to encourage them.

'Suppose a superior is established to govern in a state and serve as the people's government leader. He says, "People it's appropriate to punish, I will punish them." If superiors and subordinates have different norms of righteousness, those the superior punishes are those the masses praise. [It's] said, "People dwell together in masses." If people are praised among the masses, then in this case even supposing they are punished by the superior, this is not enough to discourage them.*

'If one is established to govern a state and to act as the people's government leader, yet one's rewards and praise are not enough to encourage good, while one's punishments and penalties are not enough to discourage viciousness, then isn't this the same as what I previously stated originally about when people first arose, before there were government leaders? If there being government leaders is the same as the time when there were no government leaders, then this is not the way by which to order the people and unify the masses.' (12/52–61)

12.8 So only because the ancient sage-kings were able to apply identifying upward in acting as government leaders,* thus the facts about

superiors and subordinates were genuinely communicated.* If superiors had unnoticed deeds or overlooked benefits, subordinates found
out and benefited from them. If subordinates had standing grievances
or accumulated harms, superiors found out and eliminated them.
Hence if there was someone thousands or tens of thousands of *lǐ**
away who did good, before his household all knew and before the
townspeople all heard about it, the Son of Heaven found and rewarded
him. If there was someone thousands or tens of thousands of *lǐ* away
who did bad, before his household all knew and before the townspeople all heard about it, the Son of Heaven found and punished him.
Hence all the people of the entire world were fearful, astonished, and
intimidated and dared not be dissolute or vicious. They said, 'The
Son of Heaven's seeing and hearing are spirit-like.'* The former
kings stated, 'They're not spirit-like. It's just that they are able to
employ others' ears and eyes to assist them in seeing and hearing, employ
others' mouths to assist them in stating and discussing, employ others' hearts to assist them in thinking and considering, and employ
others' limbs to assist them in acting.' Since those who assist them in
seeing and hearing are many, what they hear and see is far-reaching.
Since those who assist them in stating and discussing are many, those
consoled by their virtuous voices are extensive. Since those who assist
them in thinking and considering are many, the plans they discuss are
swiftly drawn up. Since those who assist them in acting are many,
their undertakings are swiftly completed. So how the ancient sages
were successful in undertaking affairs and had their names handed
down to later generations was due to no other reason or different
thing than this. [I] say, it's just that they were able to govern by identifying upward.* (12/61–9)

. . .

12.10 Thus our master Mòzǐ said, 'Now the kings, dukes, great men,
officers, and gentlemen of the world, if they in fact desire to enrich
their states, increase their population, put their punishments and
government* in order, and secure their altars of soil and grain, then
they cannot fail to examine identifying upward, for it is the foundation of these.' (12/74–6)

13.1 Our master Mòzǐ stated, 'As to the task of the wise,* they must calculate what puts the state and the common people in order and do it, and they must calculate what puts the state and the common people in disorder and avoid it.

'So, if we are calculating what puts the state and the common people in order, what is it? If superiors in governing get the facts about subordinates, there is order; if they don't get the facts about subordinates, there is disorder.

'How do we know it is so? If superiors in governing get the facts about subordinates, then this is understanding what the people have done good or wrong.* If they understand what the people have done good or wrong, they get hold of good people and reward them and get hold of vicious people and punish them. If good people are rewarded and vicious people punished, the state will surely be in order.

'If superiors in governing don't get the facts about subordinates, this is not understanding what the people have done good or wrong. If they don't understand what the people have done good or wrong, this is not getting hold of good people and rewarding them and not getting hold of vicious people and punishing them. Good people not being rewarded and vicious people not being punished, if one governs like this, the state and the masses will surely be in disorder. So, in rewards and punishments, not getting the facts about subordinates is something one cannot fail to examine.' (13/1–7)

13.2 So, if we have calculated that we must get the facts about subordinates, how will it be possible to do so?

So our master Mòzǐ said, 'Only if you are capable of governing by identifying upward to a unified norm of righteousness, only then is it possible.' How do we know that identifying upward to a unified norm can be the basis for governing throughout the world? 'That being so, then why not investigate the explanation of the beginning of government in antiquity?'

'In antiquity, when Heaven first gave rise to people, before there were government leaders, the common people were persons.* If the common people were persons, this is one person, one norm of righteousness; ten people, ten norms; a hundred people, a hundred norms; a thousand people, a thousand norms, until it got to the point that the number of people was incalculable, and the things they called "righteous" were also incalculable. These people all deemed their norm of righteousness right and deemed others' norms wrong, and hence in serious cases there was fighting, in lighter cases there was contention.

'Thus, all the world desiring to unify the world's norms of righteousness, thus they chose a worthy and established him as the Son of Heaven.* The Son of Heaven deemed his knowledge and strength insufficient to order the world all alone, and hence he chose his deputies and established them as the three dukes. The three dukes in turn deemed their knowledge and strength insufficient to serve at the Son of Heaven's left and right all alone, and hence they divided the world into various states and set up the various lords. The various lords in turn deemed their knowledge and strength insufficient to order the territory within their four borders all alone, and hence they chose their deputies and established them as ministers and chancellors. The ministers and chancellors in turn deemed their knowledge and strength insufficient to serve at their lord's left and right all alone, and hence they chose deputies to establish as district heads and clan heads.

'Thus, in antiquity, when the Son of Heaven established the three dukes, various lords, ministers and chancellors, and district heads and clan heads, it was not simply to bestow wealth and nobility or leisure and ease that he chose them. It was to employ them to help bring order to punishments and government. So, in antiquity, in constructing states and building cities, then establishing kings and lords and supporting them with ministers, officers, teachers, and heads, this was not from a desire for them to enjoy pleasure; it was to distinguish various tasks and employ them to assist in ordering Heaven's brightness.'* (13/7–17)

13.3 Nowadays why are those who are others' superiors unable to put their subordinates in order, while those who are others' subordinates are unable to serve their superiors? It's because in these cases superiors and subordinates undermine each other. Why is this so? Because their norms of righteousness are different. If norms are different, there is factionalism. Superiors take some people to be good and reward them. Even though these people get the superiors' rewards, they must avoid the common people's denunciation. Hence those who do good surely cannot be encouraged by seeing there are rewards. Superiors take some people to be vicious and punish them. Even though these people get the superiors' punishments, they possess the praise of the common people. Hence those who are vicious surely cannot be discouraged by seeing there are punishments. So, calculating the superiors' rewards and praise, they are insufficient to encourage good; calculating their denunciation and punishment, they are insufficient to discourage viciousness. Why is this so? It's because the norms of righteousness are different.* (13/17–22)

13.4 That being so, then desiring to unify the world's norms of righteousness, how will it be possible?

So our master Mòzǐ stated, 'That being so, then why not try letting clan heads issue a statute and announce a decree to their clans, saying, "If you see someone caring about and benefiting the clan, you must report it. If you see someone detesting and injuring the clan, you must also report it. Those who report it if they see care for and benefit to the clan are [to be treated] like those who care about and benefit the clan: when superiors get hold of them, they will reward them, and when the masses hear about it, they will praise them. Those who don't report it if they see detesting and injuring the clan are [to be treated] like those who detest and injure the clan: when superiors get hold of them, they will punish them, and when the masses hear about it, they will deem them wrong.' Hence the entire people of the clan all desire to get their leaders and superiors' rewards and praise and avoid their denunciation and punishment. Hence, seeing good, they state it; seeing bad, they state it. The clan head gets hold of good people and rewards them and gets hold of vicious people and punishes them. Good people being rewarded and vicious people punished, the clan will surely be in order. So, calculating what puts the clan in order, what is it? It's just because of governing by identifying upward to a single norm of righteousness.

'Once the clan is in order, is the way of the state completely covered by this? Not yet. The clans of the state are extremely many in number. These all deem their clan right and deem others' clans wrong, and hence in serious cases there is disorder, in lighter cases there is contention. So again let the clan heads unite their clans' norms of righteousness to identify upward with the ruler of the state. The ruler of the state also issues a statute and announces a decree to the masses in the state, saying, 'If you see someone caring about and benefiting the state, you must report it. If you see someone detesting and injuring the state, you must also report it. Those who report it if they see care for and benefit to the state are [to be treated] like those who care about and benefit the state: when superiors get hold of them, they will reward them, and when the masses hear about it, they will praise them. Those who don't report it if they see detesting and injuring the state are [to be treated] like those who detest and injure the state: when superiors get hold of them, they will punish them, and when the masses hear about it, they will deem them wrong.' Hence the entire people of the state all desire to get their leaders and superiors' rewards and praise and avoid their denunciation and punishment. Hence, when the people see good, they state it; when they see bad, they state it. The ruler of the state gets hold of good people and rewards them and gets hold of vicious people and punishes them. Good people being rewarded and vicious people punished, the state will surely be in order. So, calculating what puts the state in order, what is it? It's just because of governing by identifying upward to a single norm of righteousness.

'Once the state is in order, is the way of all the world completely covered by this? Not yet. The states of the world are extremely many in number. These all deem their state right and deem others' states wrong, and hence in serious cases there are wars, in lighter cases there is contention. So again let the rulers of states unite their states' norms of righteousness to identify upward with the Son of Heaven. The Son of Heaven also issues a statute and announces a decree to the masses of the world, saying, 'If you see someone caring about and benefiting the world, you must report it. If you see someone detesting and injuring the world, you must also report it. Those who report it if they see care about and benefit to the world are [to be treated] like those who care about and benefit the world: when superiors get hold of them, they will reward them, and when the masses hear about it, they will praise them. Those who don't report it if they see detesting and injuring the world are [to be treated] like those who detest and injure the world: when superiors get hold of them, they will punish them, and when the masses hear about it, they will deem them wrong.' Hence the entire people of the world all desire to get their leaders and superiors' rewards and praise and avoid their denunciation and punishment. Hence, when they see good or bad, they report it. The Son of Heaven gets hold of good people and rewards them and gets hold of vicious people and punishes them. Good people being rewarded and vicious people punished, the world will surely be in order. So, calculating what puts the world in order, what is it? It's just because of governing by identifying upward to a single norm of righteousness.

'Once the world is in order, the Son of Heaven again unites the world's norms of righteousness to identify upward with Heaven.' (13/22–42)

13.5 So as to the doctrine of identifying upward, used above, by the Son of Heaven, it can put the world in order; used in the middle, by the various lords, it can put their states in order; used on a small scale, by the clan heads, it can put their clans in order. Thus, used on a large scale, it puts the world in order without being inadequate; used on a small scale, it puts a single state or a single clan in order without being excessive—it's this way to which this refers.* So [it's] said, ordering all the states of the world is like ordering a single clan; employing all the people of the world is like employing a single man. (13/42–5)

13.6 Might it be that our master Mòzĭ alone has this and the former kings had no such thing? Yet they too were so. The sage-kings all governed by identifying upward, and so the world was in order. How do we know this is so? In the documents of the former kings, the statement of the 'Great Oath' is so. It says, 'If commoners see vileness or deceit and don't state what they have observed, their crime is equal.' This states that those who see dissolution but don't report it, their crime is also like that of the dissolute. (13/45–8)

13.7 So, as to how the ancient sage-kings put the world in order, those they chose to be aides on their left and right were all excellent, while the people on the outside who assisted them in seeing and hearing were many. So, when planning affairs with others, they found solutions before others did; when undertaking affairs with others, they accomplished them before others did; their honourable reputation and good name spread before others' did. Just because they undertook affairs in a trustworthy manner, the benefits were like this.

In antiquity there was a saying, 'The vision of one eye is not equal to the vision of two eyes; the hearing of one ear is not equal to the hearing of two ears; the grip of one hand is not equal to the strength of two hands.' Now if only one is able to undertake affairs in a trustworthy manner, the benefits are like this. Thus as to how the ancient sage-kings put the world in order, if there were worthy people a thousand *li* away, before their townspeople had all heard or seen them, the sage-kings found and rewarded them. If there were vicious people a thousand *li* away, before their townspeople had all heard or seen them, the sage-kings found and punished them. So shall we deem the sage-kings to have acute ears and keen eyes? How could they take one look and see everything thousands of *li* away or listen once and hear everything thousands of *li* away?! The sage-kings didn't go over to look or come closer to hear. Yet they forced those who were bandits, robbers, and thieves to tramp about the entire world with no place to rest their feet. How? Their governing by identifying upward was effective. (13/48–56)

13.8 Thus our master Mòzǐ said, 'All those who lead the people to identify upward, if they don't care about the people urgently, the people cannot be led to do it. I say, one must urgently care about them in leading them, be completely trustworthy in protecting them, use wealth and noble rank to guide the way before them, and use clear punishments to urge them along from behind. If one governs like this, then even if he desired the people not to identify with him, he could not succeed.' (13/56–8)

13.9 Hence our master Mòzǐ said, 'Now the kings, dukes, great men, officers, and gentlemen of the world, if, within, they in fact desire to be benevolent and righteous and seek to be superior* officers; above, they desire to conform to the way of the sage-kings; and below, they desire to conform to the benefit of the state and the common people, then they cannot fail to examine the doctrine of identifying upward. Identifying upward is the foundation of government and the key to order.' (13/58–60)

INCLUSIVE CARE

BOOK 14

INCLUSIVE CARE (I)

14.1 The sage, who takes ordering the world as his task, must know what disorder arises from; only then can he put it in order. If he doesn't know what disorder arises from, he can't put it in order. To give an analogy, it's like a doctor treating someone's disease. He must know what the disease arises from; only then can he treat it. If he doesn't know what the disease arises from, he can't treat it. How could putting disorder in order alone not be so?* One must know what disorder arises from; only then can one put it in order. If one doesn't know what disorder arises from, one can't put it in order. (14/1–3)

14.2 The sage, who takes ordering the world as his task, cannot fail to examine what disorder arises from. So let us examine what disorder arises from. It arises from not caring about each other. Subjects and sons not being filially devoted to their rulers and fathers is what's called 'disorder'. Sons care about themselves and don't care about their father, so they injure their father to benefit themselves; younger brothers care about themselves and don't care about their elder brothers, so they injure their elder brothers to benefit themselves; subjects care about themselves and don't care about their ruler, so they injure their ruler to benefit themselves—this is what's called 'disorder'.

Even fathers not being paternally kind to sons, elder brothers being unkind to younger brothers, rulers being unkind to subjects— this too is what the world calls 'disorder'. Fathers care about themselves and don't care about their sons, so they injure their sons to benefit themselves; elder brothers care about themselves and don't care about their younger brothers, so they injure their younger brothers to benefit themselves; rulers care about themselves and don't care about their subjects, so they injure their subjects to benefit themselves. Why is this? It all arises from not caring about each other.

Even in the case of those in the world who are robbers and thieves, they too are so. Robbers care about their house and don't care about other houses, so they steal from other houses to benefit their house. Thieves care about themselves and don't care about others, so they injure others to benefit themselves. Why is this? It all arises from not caring about each other.

Even in the case of great men who disorder each other's clans and the various lords who attack each other's states, they too are so. The great men each care about their clan and don't care about other clans, so they disorder other clans to benefit their clan. The various lords each care about their state and don't care about other states, so they attack other states to benefit their state.

The disorderly things in the world are all just these and nothing more. If we examine from what they arise, they all arise from not caring about each other. (14/4–12)

14.3 Suppose all the world inclusively cared about each other, caring about others as they care about themselves. Would there still be those who are not filially devoted? Viewing their father, elder brother, and ruler as themselves, how could they practise unfiliality? Would there still be those who are not paternally kind? Viewing their younger brother, son, and subject as themselves, how could they practise unkindness? So there would be no unfiliality or unkindness.

Would there still be robbers and thieves? Viewing others' houses as their house, who would steal? Viewing others as themselves, who would injure them? So there would be no robbers or thieves. Would there still be great men disordering each other's clans and various lords attacking each other's states? Viewing others' clan as their clan, who would disorder them? Viewing others' states as their state, who would attack them? So there would be no great men disordering each other's clans or various lords attacking each other's states.

Suppose all the world inclusively cared about each other. State and state would not attack each other, clan and clan would not disorder each other; there would be no robbers and thieves; rulers and subjects, fathers and sons could all be filially devoted and paternally kind. If things were like this, the world would be in order. So how could the sage, who takes ordering the world as his task, not prohibit detesting others and encourage caring about others? So if all the world inclusively cares about each other, there is order; if in interaction they detest each other, there is disorder. So this is why our master Mòzǐ said, 'One cannot fail to encourage caring about others.' (14/12–19)

BOOK 15

INCLUSIVE CARE (II)

15.1a Our master Mòzǐ stated, 'As to the purpose of the benevolent person* in undertaking tasks, it is surely to promote the benefit of the world and eliminate harm to the world—on this basis he undertakes tasks.'*

That being so, then what is the benefit of the world? What is harm to the world?

Our master Mòzǐ stated, 'Now things like states in their relations to other states attacking each other, clans in their relations to other clans subverting each other, persons in their relations to other persons injuring each other, ruler and subject not being generous and loyal, fathers and sons not being paternally kind and filially devoted, elder and younger brothers not being peaceful and harmonious, these are harms to the world.' (15/1–3)

15.1b That being so, then let's examine again how these harms are produced. Are they produced by not caring about each other?

Our master Mòzǐ stated, 'They are produced by not caring about each other. Now the various lords know only to care about their state and don't care about others' states, and hence they don't hesitate to deploy their state to attack others' states. Now the heads of clans know only to care about their clan and don't care about others' clans, and hence they don't hesitate to deploy their clan to subvert others' clans. Now people know only to care about themselves and don't care about others' selves, and hence they don't hesitate to deploy themselves to injure others' selves.

'Thus the various lords not caring about each other, they inevitably go to war; heads of clans not caring about each other, they inevitably subvert each other; people not caring about each other, they inevitably injure each other; rulers and subjects not caring about each other, they are not generous and loyal; fathers and sons not caring about each other, they are not paternally kind and filially devoted; elder and younger brothers not caring about each other, they are not peaceful and harmonious. The people of the world all not caring about each other, the strong inevitably oppress the weak, the wealthy inevitably humiliate the poor, the noble are inevitably contemptuous of the lowly, and the cunning inevitably deceive the foolish.

'All of the calamities, subversion, resentment, and hatred in the world, as to what they arise from, they are produced by not caring about each other. Hence the benevolent deem it wrong.'* (15/4–10)

15.1c Having deemed it wrong, with what do we replace it?

Our master Mòzǐ stated, 'Replace it with the model of inclusively caring about each other and in interaction benefiting each other.'*

That being so, then the model of inclusively caring about each other and in interaction benefiting each other, what will it be like?

Our master Mòzǐ stated, 'View others' states as you view your state; view others' clans as you view your clan; view others' selves as you view yourself.

'Thus if the various lords care about each other, they will not go to war; if the heads of clans care about each other, they will not subvert others; if people care about each other, they will not injure each other. If rulers and subjects care about each other, they will be generous and loyal; if fathers and sons care about each other, they will be paternally kind and filially devoted; if elder and younger brothers care about each other, they will be peaceful and harmonious. The people of the world all caring about each other, the strong will not oppress the weak, the many will not intimidate the few, the wealthy will not humiliate the poor, the noble will not be contemptuous of the lowly, and the cunning will not deceive the foolish. All the world's calamities, subversion, resentment, and hatred, what can prevent them from arising is produced from caring about each other. Hence the benevolent praise it.'* (15/10–15)

15.2 Yet now the officers and gentlemen of the world say, 'It's so. As for inclusion, it's indeed good. Nevertheless, it's the most difficult thing in the world.'*

Our master Mòzǐ stated, 'The officers and gentlemen of the world just don't recognize its benefit and distinguish the reasons for it. Now as to things like besieging a city, battling in the fields, or sacrificing one's life for a good name, these are what the common people of the world all find difficult. If their ruler is pleased by them, the officers and masses can do them. How much more so in the case of inclusively caring about each other and in interaction benefiting each other, which is different from these! As for those who care about others, others will surely then care about them; those who benefit others, others will surely then benefit them. Those who detest others, others will surely then detest them; those who harm others, others will surely then harm them. What difficulty is there in this?! It's just because superiors don't adopt it as a basis for governing, while officers don't adopt it as a basis for conduct.

'In the past, Duke Wén of Jìn was fond of officers wearing rough clothing. So Duke Wén's subjects all wore sheepskin coats, leather swordbelts, and plain silk caps, whether entering for an audience with the ruler or exiting to stride through the court. What was the reason for this? The ruler was pleased by it, so the subjects did it.

'In the past, King Líng of Chǔ was fond of officers with slim waists. So King Líng's subjects all restricted themselves to one meal a day, sucked in their breath before tightening their belts, and could stand up only by supporting themselves against a wall. Within a year, the whole court had a dark, sickly appearance. What was the reason for this? The ruler was pleased by it, so the subjects were capable of it.

'In the past, King Gōu Jiàn of Yuè was fond of officers' courage. He trained his subjects and assembled them, set fire to a boat so it was in flames, and tested his officers, saying, "The national treasures of Yuè are all here!" The King of Yuè personally sounded the drum for his soldiers to advance. When the soldiers heard the sound of the drum, they broke ranks and rushed forward. Those who ran into the fire and died numbered more than a hundred before the King of Yuè struck a gong to signal retreat.'

Thus our master Mòzǐ stated, 'As for eating little, wearing rough clothes, or sacrificing oneself for a good name, these are what the common people of the world all find difficult. If the ruler is pleased by them, the masses can do them. How much more so in the case of inclusively caring for each other and in interaction benefiting each other, which is different from these! As for those who care about others, others too will then care about them; those who benefit others, others too will then benefit them. Those who detest others, others too will then detest them; those who harm others, others too will then harm them. What difficulty is there in this?! It's just because superiors don't adopt it as a basis for governing, while officers don't adopt it as a basis for conduct.' (15/15–29)

15.3 Yet now the officers and gentlemen of the world say, 'It's so. As for inclusion, it's indeed good. Nevertheless, it's something that's impossible to put into practice, analogous to picking up Mount Tài and leaping the Jì river.'*

Our master Mòzǐ said, 'This is not the proper analogy. Now picking up Mount Tài and leaping the Jì river can be said to demand the utmost strength. From antiquity until today, there's never been anyone who could put this into practice. How much easier is inclusively caring for each other and in interaction benefiting each other, which is different from this! The ancient sage-kings practised it.

'How do we know this is so? In antiquity, Yǔ brought order to the world. In the west, he dredged the west river and the Yúdú River to drain the waters of the Qú, Sūn, and Huáng rivers. In the north, he dammed the Yuán and Gū rivers to fill Hòuzhǐdǐ and the Hūchí River, used Mount Dǐzhù to form a bypass, and tunnelled through Mount Lóngmén. This was to benefit the people of Yān, Dài, Hú, Mò, and the west river. In the east, he drained the great plain and dammed the wetlands of Mèngzhū, so that the waters flowed into the nine canals, regulating the waters of the eastern lands to benefit the people of Jìzhōu. In the south, he dredged the Yangtze, Hàn, Huái, and Rǔ rivers so they flowed east and filled the Five Lakes, to benefit the people of Jīng, Chǔ, Hán, Yuè, and the southern barbarian tribes. This states Yǔ's deeds; I now practise inclusion.

'In the past, King Wén put the western lands in order. Like the sun, like the moon, he shone light on the four corners of the world and on the western lands. He did not allow great states to humiliate small states, did not allow the many to humiliate the few, and did not allow the violent and powerful to rob farmers of their grain, dogs, and hogs. Heaven endorsed King Wén's kindness. Hence the old and childless had the means to live out their lifespan, the solitary and brotherless had the means to mingle among living people, and the young who had lost their parents had the means of support to grow up. These being King Wén's deeds, I now practise inclusion. . . .' (15/29–38)

15.4 Thus our master Mòzǐ stated, 'Now the officers and gentlemen of the world, if, within, they really desire the world to be wealthy and detest its being poor, and they desire the world to be in order and detest its being in disorder, then as to inclusively caring about each other and in interaction benefiting each other, this is the model of the sage-kings and the way of order in the world. One cannot fail to diligently practise it.' (15/41–2)

BOOK 16

INCLUSIVE CARE (III)

16.1a Our master Mòzǐ stated, 'The task of the benevolent person is surely to diligently seek to promote the benefit of the world and eliminate harm to the world.'

So, nowadays, among harms to the world, which is greatest?

[He] said, 'Things like great states attacking small states, great clans disordering small clans, the strong oppressing the weak, the many tyrannizing the few, the cunning deceiving the foolish, the noble being contemptuous of the lowly, these are harms to the world. Moreover, those who are rulers being ungenerous, subjects disloyal, fathers unkind, sons unfilial, these too are harms to the world. Moreover, the vulgar people of today taking up their weapons, poison, water, or fire to damage and injure each other, this too is harm to the world.

'If we try to fundamentally investigate what these many harms are produced from, what are these produced from? Are these produced from caring about others and benefiting others? Then we must say, it's not so. We must say, they are produced from detesting others and injuring others. If we demarcate and name detesting others and injuring others in the world, is it "inclusion"? Or is it "exclusion"?* Then we must say it is "exclusion". That being so, then doesn't this interacting by exclusion turn out to produce great harm to the world? Thus exclusion is wrong.'* (16/1–7)

16.1b Our master Mòzǐ said, 'Those who deem others wrong must have something to replace their view. If one deems others wrong without having anything to replace their view, to give an analogy, it's like using a flood to rescue people from a flood. One's doctrine will surely be in no respect acceptable.'

Thus our master Mòzǐ said, 'Replace exclusion with inclusion.'

That being so, then what is the reason that inclusion can replace exclusion?

[He] said, 'Suppose people were for others' states as for their state. Then who alone would deploy his state to attack others' states? One would be for others as for oneself. Were people for others' cities as for their city, then who alone would deploy his city to assault others' cities? One would be for others as for oneself. Were people for others' clans as for their clan, then who alone would deploy his clan to disorder others' clans? One would be for others as for oneself. That being so, then states and cities not attacking and assaulting each other, people and clans not disordering and injuring each other, is this harm to the world? Or is it benefit to the world? Then we must say, it is benefit to the world.

'If we try to fundamentally investigate what these many benefits are produced from, what are these produced from? Are these produced from detesting others and injuring others? Then we must say, it's not so. We must say, they are produced from caring about others and benefiting others. If we demarcate and name caring about others and benefiting others in the world, is it "exclusion"? Or is it "inclusion"? Then we must say, it is "inclusion". That being so, then doesn't this interacting by inclusion turn out to produce great benefit to the world?'

Thus our master Mòzǐ said, 'Inclusion is right.'

Moreover, previously I originally stated, 'The task of benevolent people is surely to diligently seek to promote the benefit of the world and eliminate harm to the world.' Now I have fundamentally investigated what inclusion produces, and it is great benefit to the world. Now I have fundamentally investigated what exclusion produces, and it is great harm to the world.

Thus as to our master Mòzǐ's saying 'exclusion is wrong and inclusion is right', it issues from this method.* (16/7–18)

16.1c Now we sincerely seek to promote the benefit of the world and so select inclusion, adopting it as government policy.* Hence those with acute ears and keen eyes will see and hear for each other! Hence those with strong limbs will act for each other! And those having ways will diligently instruct each other. Hence the old without wives or children will have sustenance to live out their lifespan, while young, weak, orphaned children without parents will have the means of support to grow their bodies. Now if only inclusion were adopted as government policy, these would be its benefits. I wonder, what is the reason why the officers of the world all hear of inclusion and deem it wrong? (16/18–21)

16.2 Yet the statements of the officers of the world who deem inclusion wrong still don't stop. They say, 'So it's good. However, how can it possibly be used?'*

Our master Mòzĭ said, 'Were it used and found unacceptable, even
I too would deem it wrong.* Still, how can there be something that's
good but can't be used?

'Let's try developing the two alternatives. Suppose there are two
officers. Let one of the officers uphold exclusion, and let one of the
officers uphold inclusion. Thus the statement of the exclusive officer
says, "How can I be for my friend as I am for myself, for my friend's
parents as for my parents?" Thus he withdraws and observes his
friend. His friend being hungry, he doesn't feed him; cold, he doesn't
clothe him; ill, he doesn't attend to him; deceased, he doesn't bury
him. The exclusive officer's statement is like this and his conduct is
like this.*

'The inclusive officer's statement is not so, and his conduct is also
not so. He says, "I hear that the high officers* in the world surely are
for their friend as for themselves, for their friend's parents as for their
own. Only then can they be high officers in the world." Thus he withdraws and observes his friend. His friend being hungry, he feeds him;
cold, he clothes him; ill, he attends to him; deceased, he buries him.
The inclusive officer's statement is like this and his conduct is like
this. Two officers like these, don't their statements contradict each
other and isn't their conduct the opposite of each other?

'Let's suppose these two officers' statements are surely trustworthy
and their conduct surely brings results, such that the fit between their
statements and conduct is like the fit between two parts of a tally, there
being no statements that aren't carried out in conduct. That being so,
then let me ask: suppose there is a wide plain or vast wilderness here,
and a man is donning armour and helmet about to go to war, and the
balance of life or death can't be known. Again, suppose a lord or minister has dispatched him on a distant mission to Bā, Yuè, Qí, or Jīng,*
and whether he can get there and return or not can't be known. That
being so, then let me ask: I wonder, to which one he would entrust his
household, to look after his parents and support his wife and children?
I wonder, to the one who deems inclusion right? Or to the one who
deems exclusion right? I take it that when they are in this situation,
there are no foolish men or foolish women in the world. Even those
who deem inclusion wrong would surely entrust them to the one who
deems inclusion right. This is deeming inclusion wrong when making
statements, but selecting inclusion when making choices—so this is
statements and conduct contradicting each other. I wonder, what is

the reason why the officers of the world all hear of inclusion and deem it wrong?'* (16/18–34)

16.3 Yet the statements of the officers of the world who deem inclusion wrong still don't stop. They say, 'Might it be possible to choose officers by means of it but not to choose rulers?'

Let's try developing the two alternatives. Suppose there are two rulers. Let one of the rulers uphold inclusion, and let one of the rulers uphold exclusion. Thus the statement of the exclusive ruler says, 'How can I be for my myriad people as I am for myself? This runs too contrary to the facts of the world. People's life on earth is of hardly any duration—to give an analogy for it, it's like a team of horses galloping past a crack in the wall.' Thus he withdraws and observes his myriad people. His people being hungry, he doesn't feed them; cold, he doesn't clothe them; ill, he doesn't attend to them; deceased, he doesn't bury them. The exclusive ruler's statement is like this and his conduct is like this.

The inclusive ruler's statement is not so, and his conduct is also not so. He says, 'I hear that the enlightened rulers in the world surely put their myriad people first and put themselves last. Only then can they be enlightened rulers in the world.' Thus he withdraws and observes his myriad people. His people being hungry, he feeds them; cold, he clothes them; ill, he attends to them; deceased, he buries them. The inclusive ruler's statement is like this and his conduct is like this. That being so, then comparing two rulers like these, don't their statements contradict each other, and isn't their conduct the opposite of each other?

Let's suppose these two rulers' statements are surely trustworthy and their conduct surely brings results, such that the fit between their statements and conduct is like the fit between two parts of a tally, there being no statements that aren't carried out in conduct. That being so, then let me ask: suppose this year there is a plague, many of the myriad people face hardship, cold, and hunger, and already many have tumbled dead into ditches and gullies. I wonder, were people to choose between these two rulers, which would they follow? I take it that when they are in this situation, there are no foolish men or foolish women in the world. Even those who deem inclusion wrong would surely follow the ruler who deems inclusion right. They deem inclusion wrong when making statements, but select inclusion when making choices—this is statements and conduct contradicting each other. I wonder, what is the reason why the officers of the world all hear of inclusion and deem it wrong? (16/34–45)

16.4 Yet the statements of the officers of the world who deem inclusion wrong still don't stop. They say, 'So inclusion is indeed benevolent and righteous. However, how is it possible to do it?! We can give an analogy for the impossibility of undertaking inclusion: it's like picking up Mount Tài and stepping across a great river.* So as to inclusion, one can only wish for it. How is it something that could possibly be done?!'

Our master Mòzĭ said, 'As to picking up Mount Tài and stepping across a great river, from antiquity until today, ever since people arose, there has never been such a feat. Now as for inclusively caring about each other and in interaction benefiting each other, this the six former sage-kings personally practised.'

How do we know the six former sage-kings personally practised it?

Our master Mòzĭ said, 'It's not that I am their contemporary or from the same era as they and personally heard their voices and saw their faces. I know it by what they wrote on bamboo and silk, engraved in metal and stone, and inscribed on dishes and bowls to pass down to their sons and grandsons in later generations.'

The 'Great Oath' says, 'King Wén was like the sun and like the moon, shining light on the four corners of the world and on the western lands.' So this states the extensiveness of King Wén's inclusive care for the world, drawing an analogy between it and the impartiality with which the sun and moon inclusively shine on all the world. So this is King Wén's being inclusive. Even what our master Mòzĭ calls inclusion, the model for it is taken from King Wén.

Moreover, not only the 'Great Oath' is like this. Even the 'Oath of Yǔ' is also like this. Yǔ said:

Come together, you masses of people, and heed my statement. It is not that I, the little one, dare proceed to incite disorder. The Miáo have brought this about and Heaven's punishment applies to them. As such, I now lead you various lords on a punitive expedition against the Miáo.

Yǔ's punitive expedition against the Miáo was not to seek to multiply his wealth and rank, receive blessings and favours, or please his ears and eyes. It was to seek to promote the benefit of the world and eliminate harm to the world. So this is Yǔ's being inclusive. Even what our master Mòzĭ calls inclusion, it is taken from Yǔ.

Moreover, not only the 'Oath of Yǔ' is like this. Even the 'Doctrine of Tāng' is also like this. . . . (16/45–56)

If my own statements are not what's properly called expounding the way, then, in antiquity, when Kings Wén and Wǔ governed, they apportioned things fairly, rewarded the worthy, and punished the vicious, without partiality toward their relatives or brothers. So this is Wén's and Wǔ's being inclusive. Even what our master Mòzǐ calls inclusion, the model for it is taken from Wén and Wǔ. I wonder, what is the reason why the people of the world all hear of inclusion and deem it wrong? (16/61–3)

16.5 Yet the statements of those in the world who deem inclusion wrong still don't stop. They say, 'Might it fail to conform to the benefit of one's parents and so interfere with filial devotion?'*

Our master Mòzǐ said, 'If we try to fundamentally investigate a filially devoted son's planning on behalf of his parents, I wonder, in planning on behalf of his parents, does a filial son also desire others to care about and benefit his parents? Or does he desire others to detest and injure his parents? If we look at things on the basis of a persuasive explanation, then he desires others to care about and benefit his parents. That being so, then what do we undertake first to achieve this? If we first undertake to care about and benefit others' parents, will others then reciprocate by caring about and benefiting our parents? Or do we first undertake to detest and injure others' parents, and then others reciprocate by caring about and benefiting our parents? Then surely it's that we first undertake to care about and benefit others' parents, and then others reciprocate by caring about and benefiting our parents. That being so, then do these reciprocally filial sons turn out to have any alternative? Shouldn't they first undertake to care about and benefit others' parents? Or do you take the filial sons of the world to be so foolish they're incapable of doing what's correct?*

'If we try to fundamentally investigate it in the documents of the former kings, it's said in the "Great Odes":

> No statement is not requited.
> No generosity is not reciprocated.
> Offer me a peach
> I'll reciprocate with a plum.*

'So this states that those who care about others will surely be cared about, while those who detest others will surely be detested. I wonder, what is the reason why the officers of the world all hear of inclusion and deem it wrong?' (16/63–72)

16.6 Might it be they deem it so difficult that it can't be done?* There have been things more difficult than this that could be done. In the past, King Líng of Jīng was fond of small waists. During his time, the officers of Jīng ate no more than one meal a day, so they could stand up only by supporting themselves with a cane and walk only by leaning on a wall. So restricting one's diet is very difficult to do, yet they did it and King Líng was pleased by it. Within a generation, the people can be changed, as they seek to comply with their superiors.

In the past, King Gōu Jiàn of Yuè was fond of courage. He trained his soldiers and ministers for three years. Deeming his knowledge of them insufficient to know how courageous they really were, he set fire to a boat so it was in flames and sounded the drum for his soldiers to advance. Countless soldiers trampled those in the front ranks, leapt into the water or fire, and died. At this time, had he not drummed the signal to retreat, the soldiers of Yuè could be said to be finished. So, burning oneself alive is very difficult to do, yet they did it and the King of Yuè was pleased by it. Within a generation, the people can be changed, as they seek to comply with their superiors.

In the past, Duke Wén of Jìn was fond of rough clothing. During his time, the officers of Jìn wore clothes of coarse cloth, sheepskin coats, plain silk caps, and rough shoes, whether entering for an audience with Duke Wén or exiting to stride through the court. So wearing rough clothes is very difficult to do, yet they did it and Duke Wén was pleased by it. Within a generation, the people can be changed, as they seek to comply with their superiors.

Thus restricting one's diet, leaping into a burning boat, or wearing rough clothes—these are the most difficult things in the world to do, yet people did them and their superiors were pleased by them. Within a generation, the people can be changed. Why? It's that they seek to comply with their superiors. Now as to inclusively caring about each other and in interaction benefiting each other, this is incalculably beneficial and easy to do. I take it there are just no superiors who are pleased by it, that's all. If there were superiors pleased by it, who encouraged it with rewards and praise and enforced it with punishments, I take it that people's tendency to inclusively care about each other and in interaction benefit each other, to give an analogy, would be like fire tending upward and water tending downward. It would be unstoppable in the world. (16/72–83)

16.7 So inclusion is the way of the sage-kings, that by which kings, dukes, and great men achieve peace, and that by which the myriad people achieve sufficiency in clothing and food. So for gentlemen nothing is better than inspecting inclusion and diligently practising it. If one practises inclusion as someone's ruler, one will surely be generous; as someone's subject, one will surely be loyal; as someone's father, one will surely be paternally kind; as someone's son, one will surely be filially devoted; as someone's elder brother, one will surely be amicable; as someone's younger brother, one will surely be fraternal.* So, if gentlemen desire to be generous rulers, loyal subjects, kind fathers, filial sons, amicable elder brothers, and fraternal younger brothers, they cannot fail to practise inclusion. This is the way of the sage-kings and a great benefit to the myriad people. (16/83–6)

CONDEMNING AGGRESSION

BOOK 17

CONDEMNING AGGRESSION (I)

17.1 Now suppose a person enters someone's orchard and steals his peaches and plums. When the masses hear about it, they deem him wrong.* If superiors who govern get hold of him, they punish him. Why is this? Because he injures another to benefit himself.*

In the case of seizing someone's hounds, swine, chickens, and piglets, the unrighteousness is even greater than entering someone's orchard and stealing the peaches and plums. What is the reason for this? Because the more he injures another, the more he is unbenevolent and the heavier the crime.

In the case of entering someone's stable and taking the person's horses and oxen, the unbenevolence and unrighteousness are even greater than seizing someone's hounds, swine, chickens, and piglets. What is the reason for this? Because it injures another even more. If it injures another more, the more it is unbenevolent and the more serious the crime.

In the case of killing an innocent person, stripping him of his clothing, and taking his spear and sword, the unrighteousness is even greater than entering someone's stable and taking the person's horses and oxen. What is the reason for this? Because it injures another even more. If it injures another more, the more it is unbenevolent and the more serious the crime.

In these cases, the gentlemen of the world all know to deem these acts wrong and call them unrighteous. Now when it comes to the bigger case of attacking another state, they don't know to deem it wrong and thus they praise it, calling it righteous. Can this be called knowing the difference between righteous and unrighteous? (17/1–7)

17.2 Killing one person is called unrighteous and must count as one capital crime. If we proceed by this explanation, then killing ten people is ten times more unrighteous and must count as ten capital crimes. Killing one hundred people is a hundred times more unrighteous and must count as one hundred capital crimes.

In these cases, the gentlemen of the world all know to deem these crimes wrong and call them unrighteous. Now when it comes to the bigger case of unrighteously attacking another state, they don't know to deem it wrong and thus they praise it, calling it righteous. They really don't know it's unrighteous, so they write down their statements to pass down to later generations. If they knew it was unrighteous, how do we explain their writing down their unrighteousness to pass down to later generations?!

Now suppose there is a person here who on seeing a little black says 'black' but on seeing much black says 'white'.* Then surely we'd take this person to not know the distinction between white and black. Tasting a little of something bitter, he says 'bitter', but tasting much of something bitter he says 'sweet'. Then surely we'd take this person to not know the distinction between sweet and bitter. Now when someone commits a little wrong, they know to deem it wrong, but when someone commits the big wrong of attacking a state, they don't know to deem it wrong and thus they praise it, calling it righteous. Can this be called knowing the distinction between righteousness and unrighteousness?* Thus we know of the disorder of the gentlemen of the world in distinguishing righteousness from unrighteousness. (17/7–14)

BOOK 18

CONDEMNING AGGRESSION (II)

18.1 Our master Mòzǐ stated, 'In antiquity, kings, dukes, and great men who governed in states genuinely desired their praise to be judicious, their rewards and punishments to be fitting, and their punishments and government not to be faulty. . . .'*

Thus our master Mòzǐ said, 'In antiquity there was a saying, "If you plan and don't succeed, then know what is coming by what is past, know what is hidden by what is visible." If you plan like this, you can succeed in knowing.' (18/1–3)

18.2 Now when an army is to be mobilized for war, if they march in winter, one fears the cold; if they march in summer, one fears the heat. For these reasons, one cannot undertake it in winter or summer. If in spring, it forces the people to abandon their ploughing and sowing, planting and cultivating; if in autumn, it forces the people to abandon their harvesting and storing. Now if they abandon just one season, then those among the common people who go cold and hungry and die will be countless.

Now let's try to calculate the cost of the army setting out: countless arrows, banners, tents, armour, shields, and sword handles will go off with the troops and break or rot and not be brought back. And again, countless spears, halberds, lances, swords, chariots, and carts will go off and break or rot and not be brought back. And their oxen and horses will go off fat and return lean, while countless will die and not return at all. And countless common people will die because the road is distant and the supply of food is interrupted. And countless common people die from illness along the way because their living conditions are insecure, meals are irregular, and hunger and overeating are excessive. Countless troops are lost, countless entire armies are lost, and so also countless ghosts and spirits lose their chief descendants.* (18/3–9)

18.3 The state issues a government policy that robs the people of things they use and abandons the benefit of the people to this great extent—that being so, then for what purpose does it do this? [They] say, 'I covet the name won through conquest and the benefits of the assets gained, so I do it.'

Our master Mòzǐ stated, 'Calculate what they win for themselves, and there is nothing they can use. Calculate what they gain, and on the contrary it is not as much as what they lose. Now attacking a city of three *lǐ* with an outer wall of seven *lǐ*, to attack this without using weapons and capture it without killing, this is difficult. Only by killing people—whether many, surely numbering in the tens of thousands, or few, surely numbering in the thousands—can a city of three *lǐ* with an outer wall of seven *lǐ* be captured. Now states of ten thousand chariots have empty towns numbering in the thousands that can be entered without conquest and wilds numbering in the ten thousands that can be developed without conquest. That being so, then land is what's in surplus, while people are what's in shortage. Now to maximize the deaths of the people and aggravate the troubles of superiors and subordinates in order to fight for an empty city, this is to discard what's in shortage while multiplying what's in surplus.* Governing like this, it's not the [proper] duty of the state.'* (18/9–15)

18.4 The apologists for wars of aggression state, 'In the south, the kings of Jīng and Wǔ, in the north, the lords of Qí and Jìn, at the time they were first enfeoffed in the world, the area of their land reached less than several hundred *lǐ* and the size of their population reached less than several hundred thousand people. Because of wars of aggression, the breadth of their territory reached several thousand *lǐ* and the size of their population reached several million people. So as to wars of aggression, one cannot deem them wrong.'*

Our master Mòzǐ stated, 'Although four or five states benefited from it, we still call it not practising the way. It is analogous to a doctor medicating people who are sick. Suppose there is a doctor here who assembles for treatment all the sick people in the world and medicates them. A myriad people taking this medicine, if four or five people treated benefited from it, we still call it not practising medicine.* So filially devoted sons don't give it to their parents and loyal subjects don't give it to their ruler.

'Among those who in antiquity were enfeoffed in states in the world—the earlier ones we have heard about with our ears, the recent ones we have seen with our eyes—those who have perished in wars of aggression are countless. How do we know it is so? In the east, there was the state of Jǔ. It was a very small state situated between two big states. It did not revere and serve the bigger states, and the bigger states too thus did not care about and benefit it. Hence in the east the Yuè people surrounded and sliced off a piece of its territory, while in the west the Qí people annexed and took possession of the rest. Calculate how Jǔ perished between Qí and Yuè: it was by such wars of aggression.

'Even Chén and Cài in the south, how they perished between Wú and Yuè was also by wars of aggression. Even the Zhā tribe and Bùtúhé tribe in the north, how they perished between Yān, Dài, Hú, and Mò was also by wars of aggression.'

Thus our master Mòzǐ stated, 'If the kings, dukes, and great men of today in fact desire gain and detest loss, desire security and detest danger, then as to wars of aggression, one cannot fail to deem them wrong.' (18/15–26)

18.5 The apologists for wars of aggression state, 'Those others were unable to marshal and use their masses of people, and thus they perished. I am able to marshal and use my masses and by this wage wars of aggression across the world. Who dare not vow allegiance and submit?!'

Our master Mòzǐ stated, 'Although you may be able to marshal and use your masses, how could you be the equal of the ancient Hé Lǘ of Wú?! In antiquity, Hé Lǘ of Wú trained his soldiers for seven years. Wearing armour and carrying weapons, they could rush 300 *lǐ* before lodging there for the night. They garrisoned in Zhù Lín, emerged from the path at Dark Pass, and battled with Chǔ at Bǎi Jǔ. He occupied Chǔ and held court audiences for envoys from Sòng and Lǔ.* Then, in the reign of Fú Chā, he went north and attacked Qí, lodged by the Wèn river, battled at Àilíng, utterly defeated the Qí people, and forced them to retreat to Mount Tài. He went east to attack Yuè, crossed the three rivers and five lakes, and forced them to retreat to Kuài Jī. None of the states of the nine tribes failed to vow allegiance and submit. Returning home after this, he was unable to reward the surviving kin of soldiers who died in his campaigns or to distribute aid to the people. He relied on his strength, boasted of his achievements, praised his own knowledge, and neglected to instruct his people. Then he built the Gūsū Tower, which after seven years was still not complete. By this point, the people of Wú were demoralized and exhausted. King Gōu Jiàn of Yuè saw that the superiors and subordinates of Wú were in disharmony and marshalled his masses to take revenge. He entered the northern wall, towed away the royal barge, surrounded the king's palace, and thus the state of Wú perished.

'In the past, Jìn had six generals and none was stronger than Zhì Bó. Calculating the breadth of his land and the size of his population, he desired to use them to contend with the various lords so as to achieve a name for valour. Wars of aggression were the swiftest path, so he mustered his sharpest soldiers and assembled his boat and chariot forces to attack the house of Zhōngxíng and captured it. Taking his plans to have been sufficient, he then further attacked the house of Fàn and utterly defeated them. Combining the three clans into one, he did not stop there but again surrounded Zhào Xiāngzǐ at Jìnyáng.

'The situation reaching this point, the states of Hán and Wèi accordingly also planned together, saying, "In antiquity there was a saying, 'Once the lips perish, the teeth get cold.' The house of Zhào perishing in the morning, we follow it in the evening; the house of Zhào perishing in the evening, we follow it in the morning. An ode says, 'If the fish don't strive while in the water, once on land how will they manage?'" Hence the lords of the three houses united their hearts and joined their efforts, opened the gate and cleared the way, donned their armour and mobilized their soldiers, and with Hán and Wèi attacking from the outside and Zhào from the inside, they struck against Zhì Bó and utterly defeated him.' (18/26–39)

18.6 Thus our master Mòzǐ stated, 'In antiquity there was a saying, "The gentleman doesn't seek his reflection in water, he seeks it in others. Seeking our reflection in water, we see only the look of our face; seeking it in others, we know good and bad fortune." Now if you take wars of aggression to be beneficial, why not try reflecting this in the deeds of Zhìbó? That this is pursuing not good fortune but misfortune can thus be known.' (18/39–41)

BOOK 19

CONDEMNING AGGRESSION (III)

19.1a Our master Mòzǐ stated, 'Now what all the world praises as good, what is the explanation for it? Is it that, above, it conforms to the benefit of Heaven; in the middle, it conforms to the benefit of the ghosts; and below, it conforms to the benefit of people, so we praise it? Or is it that it does not, above, conform to the benefit of Heaven; in the middle, conform to the benefit of the ghosts; and below, conform to the benefit of people, so we praise it? Even supposing it's the lowest, most foolish of people, they will surely say, "It's that above, it conforms to the benefit of Heaven; in the middle, it conforms to the benefit of the ghosts; and below, it conforms to the benefit of people, so we praise it."' (19/1–4)

19.1b Now what all the world shares as the same norms of righteousness are the models of the sage-kings. Now many of the various lords of the world all still attack and annex each other; this is there being praise for righteousness in name without examining the reality* it refers to. This is analogous to the blind being able to name the names* 'white' and 'black' the same as others but being unable to divide the things referred to. How can one assert there is any difference?! (19/4–6)

19.2a Thus the wise people of antiquity in planning on behalf of the world surely carefully considered whether something was righteous and only then carried it out. Hence they could act without doubt, swiftly and competently achieving what they desired, while complying with the benefit of Heaven, the ghosts, and the common people. So this is the way of the wise.* (19/6–7)

19.2b* Thus the benevolent people of antiquity who possessed the world surely opposed the doctrine of great states,* united the harmony of the world, and brought together all within the four seas. Hence they led the common people of the world to diligently serve the Lord on High and the ghosts and spirits of the mountains and rivers. They benefited people much and their achievements were indeed great. Hence Heaven rewarded them, the ghosts enriched them, and the people praised them. They were made so noble as to be Son of Heaven and so wealthy as to possess all the world, their names forming a triad with Heaven and earth to this day. This, then, is the way of the wise, that by which the former kings possessed all the world. (19/7–10)

19.3 The kings, dukes, great men, and the various lords of the world today, on the other hand, are not so. They inevitably all muster their sharpest soldiers and all assemble their boat and chariot squads, and then, donning tough armour and carrying sharp weapons, set off to commit aggression against an innocent state. Entering the state's borders, they mow down its crops, fell its trees, raze its city walls, filling its moats with the rubble, slaughter its sacrificial animals,* burn its ancestral shrines, slaughter its myriad people, trample the old and weak, and carry off its treasures. The soldiers advancing, they are urged to fight, saying, 'Death in carrying out orders is the highest, killing many is next, getting injured is lowest. How much worse again is it to break ranks and run away! This is a capital crime without hope of pardon.' By this they instil fear in the troops.

Now to annex a state and overthrow its army, inflict cruelty on its people, and by this disorder the endeavours of the sages, might they deem this to benefit Heaven? Now to take Heaven's people and employ them to attack Heaven's towns, this is murdering Heaven's people, dispossessing spirits of their places in the shrines, overturning the altars of soil and grain, and slaughtering their sacrificial animals. So, above, this doesn't conform to the benefit of Heaven. Might they deem it to benefit the ghosts? Now killing these people wipes out the ghosts and spirits' chief descendants, dispenses with the former kings, inflicts cruelty on the myriad people, and causes the common people to scatter. So, in the middle, this doesn't conform to the benefit of the ghosts.* Might they take it to benefit people? Now the benefit to people of killing people is meagre. What's more, calculate the expense of this, and the extent to which it harms the basis for livelihood and exhausts the resources of the common people of the world is uncountable. So, below, this doesn't conform to the benefit of the people. (19/10–19)

19.4 . . . Now why not try observing states whose doctrines favour aggression. Suppose a state deploys its army. The gentlemen surely number several hundred, the commoners surely number several thousand, the foot soldiers* one hundred thousand—only then are there enough people to form an army and move out. Long campaigns take several years, quick ones several months. During this period, superiors will have no time to attend to government, officers no time to order their bureaus, farmers no time to plant or harvest, and women no time for spinning and weaving. In this case, then, the state loses proper leadership, and the common people abandon their duties.* Yet, even more, there's the damage and loss of carts and horses, and of tents and curtains, supplies for the three armies, and provisions of armour and weapons—if even one fifth is recovered, this still amounts to a substantial salvage. Yet, even more again, there are those who die on the road, as the road is distant, food supplies are interrupted, and meals are irregular. Incalculably many of those in service in this way succumb to hunger, cold, or disease and tumble dead into ditches and gullies.

This is not beneficial to people, and the harm to the world is serious indeed. Yet kings, dukes, and great men delightedly put it into practice. Then this is delighting in injuring and wiping out the myriad people of the world. How is this not perverse?!

Today the states in the world that favour war are Qí, Jìn, Chǔ, and Yuè. Suppose these four states could get whatever they intended in the world. They could all increase their state's population tenfold without being able to grow food on all their land. This is having a shortage of people but a surplus of land. Now, even worse, they instead injure each other to fight for land. That being so, then this is to lose what's in shortage while multiplying what's in surplus.* (19/22–30)

19.5 Now the rulers who favour aggression again defend their doctrine in order to deem our master Mòzǐ wrong,* saying, 'As for taking aggression to be unrighteous, is it not a beneficial thing? In the past, Yǔ subjugated the Miáo tribes, Tāng attacked Jié, and King Wǔ attacked Zhòu. These men were all established as sage-kings. What is the reason for this?'*

Our master Mòzǐ said, 'You have not examined the kinds referred to in my statements and have not understood the reasons for them.* Those cases are not what's called "aggression". They are what's called "punishment".* . . . (19/30–3)

'In the case of King Jié of the Xià, Heaven again issued its stern mandate.* The sun and moon did not appear on time; cold weather and hot came mixed together; the five grains withered and died; ghosts howled throughout the state; cranes cried for more than ten nights. Heaven then gave its mandate to Tāng in the Biāo Palace, bestowing on him the great mandate of Xià:

The virtue of Xià is in great disorder. I have ended its mandate in Heaven. Go and punish them. I will surely cause you to suppress them.

Only then did Tāng dare to follow orders and lead his masses, subsequently advancing to the Xià border. The Lord on High then made Yīn Bào* destroy the city of Xià. Shortly a spirit came to announce:

The virtue of Xià is in great disorder. Go to attack them. I will surely cause you to suppress them. I have received a mandate from Heaven. Heaven commands the fire-spirit Zhù Róng to send down fire on the northwest corner of the city of Xià.

Tāng absorbed Jié's troops into his own and led them to defeat Xià. He summoned the various lords to Bó and made clear Heaven's mandate, announced it to the four corners of the world, and none of the various lords of the world dared not submit to him. So this is how Tāng punished Jié.* . . . (19/37–42)

'If we look at things on the basis of these three sage-kings, their deeds are not what's called "aggression"; they're what's called "punishment".' (19/48)

19.6 Then the rulers who favour aggression again defend their doctrine in order to deem our master Mòzǐ wrong, saying, 'You take aggression to be unrighteous. Is it not a beneficial thing? In the past, Xióngli of Chǔ was first enfeoffed among the Suī mountains; King Yīkuī of Yuè emerged from Yǒu Jù and founded a country in Yuè; Tǎng Shú and Lǚ Shàng established countries in Qí and Jìn. These all had territories of several hundred *lǐ*. Today, because of annexation of other states, the four possess all the world divided among them. What is the reason for this?'

Our master Mòzǐ said, 'You have not examined the kinds referred to in my statements and have not understood the reasons for them. In antiquity, when the Son of Heaven first enfeoffed the various lords, there were more than ten thousand. Now, because of annexation of other states, more than ten thousand have all been destroyed and four states alone stand.* This is analogous to a doctor medicating more than ten thousand people, yet only four people are healed; then he cannot be called a good doctor.'* (19/48–53)

19.7 Then the rulers who favour aggression again defend their doctrine, saying, 'It's not that I deem my gold and jade, sons and daughters, and territory to be insufficient. I desire to establish a name throughout the world through righteousness and to attract the various lords through virtue.'

Our master Mòzǐ said, 'Now if there were someone able to establish a name throughout the world through righteousness and to attract the various lords through virtue, all the world would submit without delay. The world has been mired in aggression for a long time, analogous to children playing horse.* Now if there were someone able to be trustworthy in interacting with and take the lead in benefiting the various lords of the world—when great states are unrighteous, sharing the same concern; when great states attack small states, joining in the same rescue; when small states' city walls are damaged, ensuring they are repaired; when cloth and grain are depleted, supplying them; when money is insufficient, providing it—in this manner resisting the great states, the rulers of small states would be delighted.

'Others toiling while we are at ease, our armour and weapons are strong. If we are tolerant and generous, replacing urgency with calm, the people will surely be won over. Replace aggression toward others with putting our own state in order, and the achievements will surely be doubled. Measure the expense of deploying our army and use it instead to relieve the hardship of the various lords, and surely we can gain rich benefits from it. Inspect things on the basis of what's correct and make a name for righteousness, always striving to be tolerant of our masses, trustworthy toward our army, and in this way support others' armies, and then we will be matchless* in all the world. The benefits will be countless.

'This is to the benefit of the world, yet kings, dukes, and great men don't know to use it. So this can be called not knowing the greatest duty in benefiting the world.'* (19/53–62)

19.8 Thus our master Mòzǐ said, 'Now the kings, dukes, great men, officers, and gentlemen of the world, if, within, they in fact desire to seek to promote the benefit of the world and eliminate harm to the world, then as to incessant aggression, this is really an immense harm to the world. Now if they desire to be benevolent and righteous and seek to be superior officers; above, they desire to conform to the way of the sage-kings; and below, they desire to conform to the benefit of the state and the common people, then this is why one cannot fail to examine a doctrine like condemning aggression.' (19/62–4)

MODERATION IN USE

BOOK 20

MODERATION IN USE (I)

20.1 When a sage governs a single state, the state can double its resources; in the larger case in which he governs the world, the world can double its resources. His doubling them, it's not by taking land from outside. It's because his state eliminates its useless expenses, which are enough to double resources.

When sage-kings govern, in issuing decrees and undertaking affairs, employing the people and using resources, they do nothing that doesn't add usefulness. Thus they use resources without wasting anything, the people are not worn out, and they promote much benefit. (20/1–3)

20.2 Why did they* make clothing? They made it to protect against cold in winter and to protect against heat in summer. In all cases, the way of making clothing is, what adds warmth in winter and adds coolness in summer, select it. What doesn't add this, eliminate it.

Why did they make palaces and houses? They made them to protect against wind and cold in winter and to protect against heat and rain in summer. What adds security against robbers and thieves, select it. What doesn't add this, eliminate it.

Why did they make armour, shields, and the five weapons?* They made them to protect against bandits, robbers, and thieves. If there are bandits, robbers, and thieves, those who have armour, shields, and the five weapons are victorious; those who lack them are not victorious. Thus the sages initiated the making of armour, shields, and the five weapons. In all cases, in making armour, shields, and the five weapons, what adds lightness and sharpness, or makes them tougher and harder to break, select it. What doesn't add this, eliminate it.

Why did they make boats and carts? They made carts to travel on hills and plains and boats to travel through rivers and valleys to provide the benefit of transportation across the four corners of the world.

In all cases, the way of making boats and carts is, what adds lightness and convenience, select it. What doesn't add this, eliminate it.

In all cases of their making these things, they did nothing that did not add usefulness. Thus they used resources without wasting anything, the people were not worn out, and they promoted much benefit.* (20/3–9)

20.3 What's more, if we eliminate great men's fondness for collecting pearls and jade, birds and beasts, and hounds and horses and use the resources to increase the amount of clothing, palaces and houses, armour and shields, weapons, and boats and carts, would the amount be doubled? If this is done, doubling the amount wouldn't be difficult.

So what is difficult to double? Only the population is difficult to double. Yet as to population, there is a way one can double it. In the past, the sage-kings made a model, saying, 'Men of twenty years, none dare not settle down and start a family; women of fifteen years, none dare not marry.' This is the model of the sage-kings. Since the sage-kings passed away, the people do as they please. Of those who desire to start a family early, there are some who start a family at twenty years. Of those who desire to start a family late, there are some who start a family at forty years. Taking the average between the early and the late,* it is ten years later than the sage-kings' model. If families have a child every three years, two or three children could be born [in this ten-year period]. Doesn't this show that only by making people start families early can the population be doubled? Yet [things are] not like this.* (20/9–14)

20.4 Nowadays those who govern in the world have many ways by which they reduce the population. They wear the people out and they collect heavy taxes from them. The people's resources being insufficient, those who die from cold or starvation are countless. Moreover, when great men deploy the army to attack a neighbouring state, long campaigns last through the year, quick ones several months, and men and women don't see each other for a long time.* This is a way by which to reduce the population. And those who die from insecure living conditions, irregular meals, and disease, along with those who die from ambushes, fire attacks, sieges, and battles in the field, are countless.

Do these things not arise from the many methods in the way of reducing the population employed by those who govern today? When sages govern, there are simply no such things. Does this not arise from there also being many methods in the way of increasing the population employed by the sages in governing?

So our master Mòzǐ said, 'Eliminating useless expenses is the way of the sage-kings and a great benefit to the world.' (20/14–20)

BOOK 21

MODERATION IN USE (II)

21.1 Our master Mòzǐ stated, 'As to how the ancient enlightened kings and sages reigned over all the world and governed the various lords, they cared about the people extremely loyally and benefited the people extremely richly. They combined loyalty with trustworthiness and also presented the people with benefits, and hence to the end of their lives, people were not tired of them, and until the day they died, people were not weary of them. How the ancient enlightened kings and sages reigned over all the world and governed the various lords was this.' (21/1–3)

21.2 Thus the ancient sage-kings instituted a model for moderation in use, saying, 'All the various artisans of the world—wheelwrights, cartwrights, tanners, potters, smiths, and carpenters—let each undertake what he's capable of.' They said, 'In all cases, produce what is sufficient to provide for the people's use, then stop.' Anything that added expense without adding to the people's benefit, the sage-kings did not do it. (21/3–4)

21.3 The ancient sage-kings instituted a model for food and drink, saying, 'Enough to satisfy hunger, replenish breath, strengthen the limbs, and keep the ears acute and eyes keen, then stop. Don't go to extremes in blending the five flavours or harmonizing aromas. Don't pursue precious and rare delicacies from distant lands.'* How do we know it is so? In antiquity, when Yáo put the world in order, in the south he pacified Jiāozhǐ, in the north he won the surrender of Yōudū, in the east and west he reached where the sun comes out and goes in, and none did not submit to him. As to his favourite foods, he had only one grain dish and one meat dish per meal, ate from earthenware vessels, and drank wine with a wooden ladle. As to ceremonies with imposing rituals of bowing and standing, swirling and twirling, the sage-kings did not perform them. (21/4–8)

21.4 The ancient sage-kings instituted a model for clothing, saying, 'In winter, wear dark greyish-blue* silk clothing that is light and warm; in summer, wear linen clothing that is light and cool, then stop.'* Anything that added expense without adding to the people's benefit, the sage-kings did not do it. (21/8–9)

21.5 Because fierce, ferocious animals violently harmed people, the ancient sages taught people to travel with weapons. By day, they carried swords. When stabbing, they penetrate; when striking, they sever; when struck on the side, they don't break—these are the benefits of good swords. Armour that when worn is light and comfortable, when moving is flexible and doesn't hinder movement—these are the benefits of good armour. Carts are for carrying heavy loads and travelling long distances. When ridden, they are safe; when pulled, they are convenient. Safe so as not to injure people, convenient so as to reach the destination quickly—these are the benefits of carts. Because great rivers and broad valleys could not be crossed, the ancient sage-kings made boats and oars. They made them sufficient to cross, and then stopped. Even when superiors such as the three dukes and the various lords came, the boats and oars were not changed, and the ferrymen did not dress up. This is the benefit of boats.* (21/9–13)

21.6 The ancient sage-kings instituted a model for moderation in burials, saying, 'Three layers of shrouds are sufficient for the flesh to decay. A three-inch coffin is sufficient for the bones to decay. Dig the grave not so deep as to connect through to water, but deep enough that vapour doesn't leak out, then stop. Once the dead are buried, the living should not prolong mourning and grieving.'* (21/14–15)

21.7 In antiquity, when people first arose, before there were palaces and houses, they dug caves in hillsides and dwelled in them. The sage-kings were concerned about this and said of the caves, 'In the winter, they can give shelter from the wind and cold, but when summer comes, they are damp below and clammy above. We fear they will injure people's health.' Hence they initiated the building of palaces* and houses to benefit people.

That being so, then the model for building palaces and houses, what will it be like? Our master Mòzǐ stated, 'Build them such that the sides can protect against wind and cold and the top can protect against snow, frost, rain, and dew. Their interior must be clean so it can be used to offer sacrifices, and the palace walls sufficient to separate the men from women, then stop.'* Anything that added expense without adding to the people's benefit, the sage-kings did not do it. (21/15–19)

MODERATION IN BURIAL

BOOK 25

MODERATION IN BURIAL (III)

25.1 Our master Mòzǐ stated, 'The benevolent person's planning on behalf of the world, to give an analogy, is no different from a filially devoted son's planning on behalf of his parents. Now a filial son's planning on behalf of his parents, what will it be like? [I] say, if his parents are poor, he undertakes to enrich them; if their people are few, he undertakes to increase them; if their masses are in disorder, he undertakes to put them in order.* When he is in these situations, there are indeed cases when his strength is insufficient, his resources exhausted, or his knowledge lacking, and only then does he stop. In no case would he dare spare any effort, conceal any scheme, or withhold any benefit without pursuing them on behalf of his parents. These three duties—a filial son's planning on behalf of his parents is indeed like this.

'Even the benevolent person planning on behalf of the world is also like this. [I] say, if the world is poor, he undertakes to enrich it; if the people are few, he undertakes to increase them; if the masses are in disorder, he undertakes to put them in order. When he is in these situations, there are indeed cases when his strength is insufficient, his resources exhausted, or his knowledge lacking, and only then does he stop. In no case would he dare spare any effort, conceal any scheme, or withhold any benefit without pursuing them on behalf of the world. These three duties—the benevolent person's planning on behalf of the world is indeed like this.' (25/1–7)

25.2a 'Now that the sage-kings of the three dynasties of the past have passed away, the world has lost righteousness. The gentlemen of later generations, some deem rich burials and prolonged mourning benevolent, righteous, and the task of a filially devoted son; some deem rich burials and prolonged mourning unbenevolent, unrighteous, and not the task of a filially devoted son. [I] say, these two sides, their statements contradict each other and their conduct is the opposite of each other. They both say, "Above, we transmit the way of Yáo, Shùn, Yǔ, Tāng, Wén, and Wǔ", yet their statements contradict each other and their conduct is the opposite of each other. Thus gentlemen of later generations are all confused about these two sides' statements.

'If we are confused about these two sides' statements, that being so, then why not try promulgating them as government policy to the state and myriad people and observing them? Calculate how well rich burials and prolonged mourning accord with these three benefits.*

'Might it be that, supposing we take their statements as a model, use their plans, and have rich burials with prolonged mourning, this really can enrich the poor, increase the few, secure the endangered, and bring order to the disordered? Then this is benevolent, righteous, and the task of a filial son. In planning for others, one cannot fail to encourage it. The benevolent will promote it throughout the world, establish it and make the people praise it, and never abandon it.

'On the other hand, might it be that, supposing we take their statements as a model, use their plans, and have rich burials with prolonged mourning, this really cannot enrich the poor, increase the few, secure the endangered, and bring order to the disordered? Then this is not benevolent, not righteous, and not the task of a filially devoted son. In planning for others, one cannot fail to discourage it. The benevolent will seek to eliminate it from the world, abandon it and make people deem it wrong,* and never do it.' (25/7–16)

25.2b Moreover, from antiquity until today, there has never been a case in which a state and the common people have been led to disorder by promoting the benefit of the world and eliminating harm to the world. How do we know it is so?* (25/16–17)

25.3a Now many of the officers and gentlemen of the world are still all confused about whether rich burials and prolonged mourning conform to right or wrong, benefit or harm. So our master Mòzǐ stated, 'That being so, then let's try inspecting it. Now suppose we take the statements of those who uphold rich burials and prolonged mourning as a model and use them as a basis for carrying out affairs in the state.

'According to this, if there is a death among the kings, dukes, and great men, the inner and outer coffins must be nested in many layers, the burial must be deep, the grave clothes must be many, the embroidery must be elaborate, and the grave mound must be massive. If someone among the ordinary people and commoners dies, the expense exhausts the household's resources. If someone among the various lords dies, they empty the treasury to cover the body in gold, jade, and pearls and wrap it in silk and ribbons. Horses and carriages are placed in the tomb, and also they must prepare many curtains, cauldrons, drums, tables, mats, pots, vessels, spears, swords, feathered banners, ivory, and hides to inter in the burial chamber. The tomb is packed so full it is like moving house. [It's] said, the attendants buried alive to accompany the Son of Heaven to the grave range from as many as several hundred to as few as several dozen; those for generals or ministers from as many as several dozen to as few as several people.*

'What is the model for handling mourning like? [It's] said, the mourners must wail and cry intermittently until they are hoarse, wear coarse hemp mourning robes and caps while tears run down their faces, dwell in a mourning hut, and sleep on a grass mat with an earthen pillow. Also, they urge each other not to eat so as to be hungry, to wear thin clothes so as to be cold, and to make their eyes sunken and hollow, their complexion grim and dark, their ears and eyes dull and weak, and their limbs frail and feeble, so they cannot use them. Also, [it's] said, when superior officers are conducting mourning, they must be unable to stand up without support and unable to walk without a cane.* One is to apply all this for a total of three years.

'If we take such statements as a model and practise such ways, and make kings, dukes, and great men practise this, then surely they cannot go to court in the morning and retire late, hearing legal cases and ordering government affairs. If we make officers and great men practise this, then surely they cannot order the various government bureaus, develop crops and forests, and fill the granaries. If we make farmers practise this, surely they cannot go out in the morning and come in at night, ploughing and sowing, planting and cultivating. If we make the hundred artisans practise this, then surely they cannot build boats and carts and make tools and vessels. If we make women practise this, then surely they cannot rise at dawn and sleep late at night, doing their spinning and weaving.* [If we] calculate in detail the effects of rich burials, they bury many resources; [if we] calculate the effects of prolonged mourning, it prohibits work for a prolonged duration. Resources already produced are thrown away and buried; the people left alive are prohibited from undertaking work for a prolonged time. Seeking wealth by this means, this is analogous to seeking a harvest while prohibiting ploughing. No doctrine for producing wealth can be found in this.' (25/17–29)

25.3b 'Thus, since seeking to enrich the clan by this means is indeed impossible, desiring to increase the population by it, might that be possible? Their doctrine is again incapable.

'Now if rich burials and prolonged mourning are adopted as government policy, when the ruler dies, he is mourned for three years; when one's father or mother dies, they are mourned for three years; when a wife or eldest son dies, they are mourned for three years—all five are mourned for three years. Then for paternal uncles, elder and younger brothers, and other sons, it's one year. For other close relatives, it's five months. Paternal aunts, sisters, nephews, and maternal uncles, it's several months.

'As to emaciation, there must be regulations. Mourners are to make their eyes sunken and hollow, their complexion grim and dark, their ears and eyes dull and weak, and their limbs frail and feeble, so they cannot use them. Also, [it's] said, when superior officers are conducting mourning, they must be unable to stand up without support, unable to walk without a cane. One is to apply all this for a total of three years.

'If we take such statements as a model and practise such ways, if mourners indeed restrict their diet to starve themselves like this, thus in winter the common people will be unable to withstand the cold and in summer unable to withstand the heat, and incalculably many will fall ill and die. This greatly undermines relations between men and women. Seeking to increase the population by this means is analogous to seeking people's longevity while making them fall on their swords. No doctrine for increasing population can be found in this.' (25/30–6)

25.3c 'Thus, since seeking to increase the population by this means is indeed impossible, desiring to order punishments and government by it, might that be possible? Their doctrine is again incapable.

'Now if rich burials and prolonged mourning are adopted as government policy, the state will surely be poor, the population will surely be few, and punishments and government will surely be in disorder. If we take such statements as a model and practise such ways, making those who are superiors practise this, they cannot attend to government; making those who are subordinates practise this, they cannot undertake work. Superiors not attending to government, punishments and government will surely be in disorder; subordinates not undertaking work, resources for clothing and food will surely be insufficient. If resources are insufficient, those who are someone's younger brother will seek help from their elder brothers and not get it, and unfraternal younger brothers will surely resent their elder brothers.* Those who are someone's son will seek help from their parents and not get it, and unfilial sons will surely resent their parents. Those who are someone's subject will seek help from their ruler and not get it, and disloyal subjects will surely disorder their superiors. Hence dissolute and corrupt people, lacking clothing when going out and lacking food when entering the home, continually feel humiliated within and all engage in dissolution and violence, which cannot be prevented. Thus robbers and thieves are many, while the orderly are few. As for having many robbers and thieves but few of the orderly, seeking order by this means is analogous to making someone turn around three times without showing his back to you. No doctrine for achieving order can be found in this.' (25/36–43)

25.3d 'Thus, since seeking to order punishments and government by this means is indeed impossible, desiring to prevent great states from attacking small states by it, might that be possible? Their doctrine is again incapable.

'Thus the sage-kings of the past having passed away, the world has lost righteousness, and the various lords overcome others by force. In the south, there are the kings of Chǔ and Yuè, while in the north, there are the lords of Qí and Jìn. These all drill their armies and take attacking and annexing as their government policy in the world.* Thus, in all cases, the reason great states don't attack small states is that their provisions are many, their city walls are in good repair, and their superiors and subordinates are harmonious, and thus great states don't try to attack them. If they lack provisions, their city walls are in disrepair, or their superiors and subordinates are not harmonious, thus great states try to attack them. Now if rich burials and prolonged mourning are adopted as government policy, the state will surely be poor, the population will surely be small, and punishments and government will surely be in disorder. If the state is poor, this is to have no means of storing up provisions; if the population is small, this means the city walls and moats being deficient; if punishments and government are in disorder, this means failing to conquer when emerging to fight and failing to be strong when entering to defend.' (25/43–9)

25.3e 'Since seeking to prevent great states from attacking small states by this means is indeed impossible, desiring to get the blessings of the Lord on High and the ghosts and spirits by it, might that be possible? Their doctrine is again incapable.

'Now if rich burials and prolonged mourning are adopted as government policy, the state will surely be poor, the population will surely be small, and punishments and government will surely be in disorder. If the state is poor, this means its offerings of wine and grain will be impure; if the population is small, this means those who serve the Lord on High and the ghosts and spirits will be few; if punishments and government are in disorder, this means sacrificial rituals will be untimely. Now, moreover, they prohibit service to the Lord on High and the ghosts and spirits. If they govern like this, the Lord on High and the ghosts and spirits begin from on high to commiserate about it, saying, "Our having these people or not having these people, which is better?" They say, "Our having these people or not having these people, it makes no difference." Then even if the Lord on High and the ghosts and spirits punish their crimes by sending calamity and misfortune down upon them and abandoning them, how is this not fitting?!' (25/49–55)

25.4 Thus the ancient sage-kings instituted a model for burials, saying, 'A coffin three inches thick is sufficient for the body to decay. Three layers of shrouds are sufficient to cover the ugliness. As to the burial, below it should not reach water, above it should not let odour through; make the grave mound equal a plot three crop rows wide, then stop. Once the dead have been buried, the living must have no prolonged crying but hasten to undertake work, people doing what they're able so as to benefit each other in their interactions.'* This is the model of the sage-kings. (25/55–7)

25.5 Now the statement of those who uphold rich burials and prolonged mourning says, 'Even supposing rich burials and prolonged mourning cannot enrich the poor, increase the few, secure the endangered, and bring order to the disordered, still, this is the way of the sage-kings.'

Our master Mòzǐ said, 'It's not so. In the past, Yáo went north to instruct the eight Dí tribes, died on the way, and was buried on the northern slopes of Mount Qióng. He had three layers of shrouds and a coffin made of plain wood, bound with hemp. Only once the coffin was interred did they wail. The grave was filled and no mound was built. The burial finished, oxen and horses rode over it.

'Shùn went west to instruct the seven Róng tribes, died on the way, and was buried in Nánjǐ Market. He had three layers of shrouds and a coffin made of plain wood, bound with hemp. The burial finished, people in the market walked over it.

'Yǔ went east to instruct the nine Yí tribes, died on the way, and was buried at Mount Kuài Jǐ. He had three layers of shrouds and a coffin made of paulownia wood three inches thick, bound with hemp, with a poorly fitting cover. No tomb passage was formed. As to the depth of the pit, below it did not reach water, above it did not let odour through. Once he was buried, they gathered the remaining soil above it to form a mound equal to a plot three crop rows wide, then stopped.

'If we look at things on the basis of these three sage-kings, rich burials and prolonged mourning turn out not to be the way of the sage-kings. So, the three kings were all so noble as to be Son of Heaven and so wealthy as to possess all the world; how could they have worried about resources being insufficient?! They took it that this was the model for burials.*

'Nowadays, on the other hand, how kings, dukes, and great men undertake burials is different from this. They must have a great coffin and a middle coffin, with three layers of embroidered hides and jade discs and stones provided. Spears and swords, cauldrons and drums, pots and vessels, embroidery and silk, thousands of garments, carriages and horses, and women musicians are all provided. [It's] said, there must be passages connecting down to the tomb and the mound should be as big as a mountain. This interferes with the people's work and wastes the people's resources to an incalculable extent. They undertake useless activity to this extent.' (25/57–67)

25.6 Thus our master Mòzǐ said, 'Previously,* I originally stated, "Might it be that, supposing we take their statements as a model and use their plans, we calculate that rich burials with prolonged mourning in fact can enrich the poor, increase the few, secure the endangered, and bring order to the disordered? Then this is benevolent, righteous, and the task of a filial son. In planning for others, one cannot fail to encourage it. On the other hand, might it be that, supposing we take their statements as a model and use their plans, if people have rich burials with prolonged mourning, really this cannot enrich the poor, increase the few, secure the endangered, and bring order to the disordered? Then this is unbenevolent, unrighteous, and not the task of a filial son. In planning for others, one cannot fail to discourage it."

'Thus seeking to enrich the state by this means, one gets great poverty; desiring to increase the population by it, one greatly reduces it; desiring to order punishments and government by it, one gets great disorder. Seeking to prevent great states from attacking small states by it is indeed impossible; desiring to get the blessings of the Lord on High and the ghosts and spirits by it, one instead gets misfortune. Above, checking it against the way of Yáo, Shùn, Yǔ, Tāng, Wén, and Wǔ, it is directly contrary to it; below, checking it against the deeds of Jié, Zhòu, Yōu, and Lì, it's like fitting the two pieces of a tally together.* If we look at things on this basis, rich burials and prolonged mourning are not the way of the sage-kings.' (25/67–73)

25.7 Now those who uphold rich burials and prolonged mourning state, 'If rich burials and prolonged mourning turn out not to be the way of the sage-kings, then how do we explain why the gentlemen of the central states perform them without ceasing and maintain them without choosing something else?!'

Our master Mòzǐ said, 'This is what's called deeming their habits convenient and their customs righteous.* In the past, east of Yuè there was the country of Gài Shù. When their eldest son was born, they chopped him up and ate him, calling this "advantageous to the younger brothers". When their grandfather died, they carried off their grandmother and abandoned her, saying, "One cannot live with the wife of a ghost." These practices superiors took as government policy and subordinates took as custom, performing them without ceasing and maintaining them without choosing something else. Yet how could these really be the way of benevolence and righteousness?!* This is what's called deeming their habits convenient and their customs righteous.

'South of Chǔ there is the country of the Yán people. When their parents die, they let the flesh rot and throw it away, and only then bury the bones—thus they qualify as filial sons. West of Qín there is the country of Yí Qú. When their parents die, they collect firewood and burn them, and when the smoke rises, they call it "ascending"—only then do they qualify as filial sons. These practices superiors took as government policy and subordinates took as custom, performing them without ceasing and maintaining them without choosing something else. Yet how could these really be the way of benevolence and righteousness?! This is what's called deeming their habits convenient and their customs righteous.

'If we look at things on the basis of these three countries, their funerals are indeed too meagre; if we look at things on the basis of the gentlemen of the central states, their funerals are indeed too rich. That way is too rich, this way is too meagre—that being so, then burials are indeed subject to moderation. So clothing and food are to people's benefit when alive, yet still they are subject to moderation; burial is to people's benefit when dead, how could this alone not be subject to moderation?!' (25/74–83)

25.8 Our master Mòzĭ instituted a model for burials, saying, 'A coffin three inches thick is sufficient for the bones to decay. Three layers of shrouds are sufficient for the flesh to decay. Dig the grave to a depth such that no moisture leaks in below, no vapour leaks out above. Make the grave mound big enough to mark the spot and then stop. Cry on the way to and from the burial; on returning, undertake work to produce resources for clothing and food. Offer sacrifices regularly to fulfil one's filial duties to parents.'* So as to our saying that our master Mòzĭ's model neglects the benefit of neither the dead nor the living, it's for this reason. (25/83–6)

25.9 So our master Mòzĭ stated, 'Now the officers and gentlemen of the world, if, within, they in fact desire to be benevolent and righteous and seek to be superior officers; above, they desire to conform to the way of the sage-kings; and below, they desire to conform to the benefit of the state and the common people, then this is why they cannot fail to examine moderation in mourning as a government policy.' (25/86–8)

HEAVEN'S INTENT

BOOK 26

HEAVEN'S INTENT (I)

26.1 Our master Mòzǐ stated, 'The officers and gentlemen of the world know the little things but don't know the big things. How do we know this? We know it by how they live in their clans. If, living in a clan, you offend the clan head, there are still neighbouring clans to escape to. Yet parents, brothers, and acquaintances warn each other, all saying, "You mustn't fail to be cautious! You mustn't fail to be heedful! How can you live in a clan and offend the clan head?"

'It's not only living in a clan that's so; even living in a state is also so. If, living in a state, you offend the lord of the state, there are still neighbouring states to escape to. Yet parents, brothers, and acquaintances warn each other, all saying, "You mustn't fail to be cautious! You mustn't fail to be heedful! For who indeed can live in a state and offend the lord of the state?"

'In these cases there is somewhere to escape to, yet they warn each other as strongly as this. How much more so when there is no place to escape to—how could it be acceptable not to warn each other even more strongly? Moreover, there is a saying, "Committing an offence in broad daylight, where will you escape to?" [I] say, there is nowhere to escape to. As to Heaven, you cannot rely on forests, valleys, or dark secluded places where no one lives; its keen sight will surely see you. Yet in relation to Heaven, the officers and gentlemen of the world heedlessly don't know enough to warn each other. This is how I know the officers and gentlemen of the world know the little things but don't know the big things.'* (26/1–9)

26.2 'That being so, then indeed what does Heaven desire and what does it detest? Heaven desires righteousness and detests unrighteousness. That being so, then by leading the common people of the world to undertake righteousness, I am doing what Heaven desires. If I do what Heaven desires, Heaven too does what I desire. That being so, then what do I desire, what do I detest? I desire blessings and detest misfortune. If I don't do what Heaven desires, but do what Heaven doesn't desire, that being so, then I lead the common people of the world to undertake misfortune.

'That being so, then how do we know that Heaven desires righteousness and detests unrighteousness? [It's] said, "When there is righteousness in the world, there is life; when there is no righteousness, there is death. When there is righteousness, there is wealth; when there is no righteousness, there is poverty. When there is righteousness, there is order; when there is no righteousness, there is disorder." That being so, then Heaven desires life for the world and detests death; desires wealth and detests poverty; and desires order and detests disorder. This is how I know Heaven desires righteousness and detests unrighteousness.' (26/9–14)

26.3 [I] say, 'Moreover, righteousness is [good] government.* There is no such thing as subordinates governing superiors; it must be that superiors govern subordinates. Thus the commoners do their utmost in undertaking work but don't get to govern as they please; there are officers to govern them. The officers do their utmost in undertaking work but don't get to govern as they please; there are generals and ministers to govern them. The generals and ministers do their utmost in undertaking work but don't get to govern as they please; there are the three dukes and various lords to govern them. The three dukes and various lords do their utmost in attending to government but don't get to govern as they please; there is the Son of Heaven to govern them. The Son of Heaven doesn't get to govern as he pleases; there is Heaven to govern him. That the Son of Heaven governs over the three dukes, various lords, officers, and commoners, the officers and gentlemen of the world certainly clearly know. That Heaven governs over the Son of Heaven, the common people of the world don't yet clearly know it.

'So the sage-kings of the three dynasties of the past, Yǔ, Tāng, Wén, and Wǔ, desired to clearly explain to the common people of the world that Heaven governs over the Son of Heaven. So none failed to fatten oxen and sheep, feed hounds and hogs, and prepare pure offerings of wine and grain to sacrifice to the Lord on High and the ghosts and spirits, praying for blessings from Heaven.* I have never heard of someone in the world praying to the Son of Heaven for blessings. This is how I know Heaven governs over the Son of Heaven.' (26/14–21)

26.4 'So, the Son of Heaven is the most noble in the world and the most wealthy in the world. So those with wealth and nobility cannot fail to follow Heaven's intention.* Those who follow Heaven's intention, inclusively caring about each other and in interaction benefiting each other, surely get rewarded. Those who oppose Heaven's intention, excluding and detesting each other and in interaction injuring each other, surely get punished.'

That being so, then who are those who followed Heaven's intention and got rewarded? Who are those who defied Heaven's intention and got punished?

Our master Mòzǐ stated, 'The sage-kings of the three dynasties of the past, Yǔ, Tāng, Wén, and Wǔ, these followed Heaven's intention and got rewarded. The tyrants of the three dynasties of the past, Jié, Zhòu, Yōu, and Lì, these defied Heaven's intention and got punished.'

That being so, then how did Yǔ, Tāng, Wén, and Wǔ get rewarded?

Our master Mòzǐ stated, 'As to their deeds, above, they honoured Heaven; in the middle, they served the ghosts and spirits; and below, they cared about the people. So Heaven's intention said, "Those I care about, these people inclusively care about them; those I benefit, these people inclusively benefit them. As to caring about others, they do so extensively; as to benefiting others, they do so richly." So Heaven made them so noble as to be Son of Heaven and so wealthy as to possess all the world. Myriad generations of their descendants have continued to praise their goodness throughout the world. Even today people praise them, calling them sage-kings.'

That being so, then how did Jié, Zhòu, Yōu, and Lì get punished?

Our master Mòzǐ said, 'As to their deeds, above, they insulted Heaven; in the middle, they insulted the ghosts; below, they injured people. So Heaven's intention said, "Those I care about, these people exclude and detest them; those I benefit, these people in interaction injure them. As to detesting others, they do so extensively; as to injuring others, they do so deeply." So Heaven made them unable to live out their lifespan or finish their lives. Even today people denounce them, calling them tyrants.' (26/21–30)

26.5 'That being so, then how do we know that Heaven cares about the common people of the world? By its inclusively shining light on them.* How do we know it inclusively shines light on them? By its inclusively possessing them. How do we know it inclusively possesses them? By its inclusively accepting offerings from them. How do we know it inclusively accepts offerings from them? Within the four seas, among people who eat grain,* none fail to fatten oxen and sheep, feed hounds and hogs, and prepare pure offerings of wine and grain to sacrifice to the Lord on High and the ghosts and spirits. Heaven possesses the townspeople;* how would it not care about them?

'Moreover, I state, "Those who kill an innocent person will surely have an instance of ill fortune." Who is it that kills the innocent? It's people. Who is it that bestows ill fortune on them? It's Heaven. If we take Heaven to not care about the common people of the world, for what reason would it bestow ill fortune on people who kill each other? This is how I know Heaven cares about the common people of the world.' (26/30–6)

26.6 Following Heaven's intention is governing by righteousness. Opposing Heaven's intention is governing by force.

That being so, then what is governing by righteousness like?

Our master Mòzǐ stated, 'Those living in great states don't attack small states, those living in great clans don't subvert small clans, the strong don't oppress the few, the noble aren't contemptuous of the lowly, and the cunning don't deceive the foolish. This surely benefits Heaven above, benefits the ghosts in the middle, and benefits people below. These three benefiting, none fail to benefit. So the most beautiful name in the world is applied to those who govern this way, and they are called sage-kings.

'Those who govern by force, on the other hand, are different from this. Their statements contradict this, and their conduct is the reverse of this, like running in the opposite direction. Those living in great states attack small states, those living in great clans subvert small clans, the strong oppress the few, the noble are contemptuous of the lowly, and the cunning deceive the foolish. This doesn't benefit Heaven above, doesn't benefit the ghosts in the middle, and doesn't benefit people below. These three failing to benefit, none do benefit. So the ugliest name in the world is applied to those who govern this way, and they are called tyrants.' (26/36–41)

26.7 Our master Mòzǐ stated, 'I have Heaven's intent, analogous to the wheelwright's having a compass or the carpenter's having a set square.* The wheelwright and carpenter grasp their compass and set square and use them to measure square and round in the world, saying, "What conforms is right, what doesn't conform is wrong." Now the documents of the officers and gentlemen of the world are so many they cannot be completely recorded, and their statements and sayings are so many they cannot be fully calculated. Above, they persuade the various lords; below, they persuade the ranks of officers. Yet they are far indeed from benevolence and righteousness. How do we know this? [I] say, I've got the clearest model in the world to measure them.' (26/41–4)

BOOK 27

HEAVEN'S INTENT (II)

27.1a Our master Mòzǐ stated, 'Now the gentlemen of the world who desire to be benevolent and righteous cannot fail to examine what righteousness issues from.'

Having said they cannot fail to examine what righteousness issues from, that being so, then what does righteousness issue from?

Our master Mòzǐ said, 'Righteousness doesn't issue from the foolish and lowly. It must issue from the noble and wise.'*

How do we know righteousness doesn't issue from the foolish and lowly, but must issue from the noble and wise?

[He] said, 'Righteousness is good government.'*

How do we know righteousness is good government?

[He] said, 'When there is righteousness in the world, there is order; when there is no righteousness, there is disorder. This is how we know righteousness is good government. As for the foolish and lowly, they don't get to govern over the noble and wise. People must be noble and wise and only then do they get to govern over the foolish and lowly.* This is how I know righteousness doesn't issue from the foolish and lowly, but must issue from the noble and wise.'

That being so, then who is noblest? Who is wisest?

[He] said, 'Heaven is noblest and Heaven is wisest, and that's that. That being so, then righteousness turns out to issue from Heaven.' (27/1–6)

27.1b Now the people of the world say, 'As to things like the Son of Heaven being more noble than the various lords and the various lords being more noble than the ministers, we certainly clearly know this. Yet we've never known of Heaven's being more noble and wise than the Son of Heaven.'

Our master Mòzǐ said, 'There are grounds by which I know Heaven is more noble and wise than the Son of Heaven. [I] say, when the Son of Heaven does good, Heaven can reward him. When the Son of Heaven is vicious, Heaven can punish him. When the Son of Heaven has an illness or misfortune, he must fast and bathe, and prepare pure offerings of wine and grain to sacrifice to Heaven and the ghosts, for

Heaven can dispel it. Yet I've never known Heaven to pray for blessings to the Son of Heaven. This is how I know Heaven is more noble and wise than the Son of Heaven.

'It doesn't stop with only this. We also know it from the documents of the former kings that instruct us about aspects of Heaven's way that we don't understand, saying, "Bright and wise is Heaven, overseeing and ruling the land below." So this speaks of how Heaven is more noble and wise than the Son of Heaven.'

[You may] wonder, is there also one more noble and wise than Heaven?

'[I] say, Heaven is noblest, Heaven is wisest, and that's that. That being so, then righteousness turns out to issue from Heaven.'

Thus our master Mòzǐ said, 'Now the gentlemen of the world, if, within, they really desire to follow the way and benefit the people and to fundamentally examine the foundation of benevolence and righteousness, they cannot fail to heed Heaven's intention.' (27/6–14)

27.1c Since one cannot fail to heed Heaven's intention, that being so, then what does Heaven's intention desire and what does it despise?

Our master Mòzǐ said, 'Heaven's intention doesn't desire great states to attack small states, great clans to subvert small clans, the strong to tyrannize the few, the cunning to scheme against the foolish, and the noble to be contemptuous of the lowly. This is what Heaven doesn't desire. It doesn't stop with only this. Heaven desires people who have strength to work for each other, those who have ways to teach each other, and those who have resources to share them with each other. Also, it desires superiors to strive hard in attending to government and subordinates to strive hard in undertaking work.

'If superiors strive hard in attending to government, the state will be in order. If subordinates strive hard in undertaking work, resources will be sufficient. If the state is in order and resources sufficient, then within, there will be means to prepare pure offerings of wine and grain to sacrifice to Heaven and the ghosts, while abroad, there will be means to prepare bracelets and discs of pearl and jade to send envoys to befriend neighbouring states. The rancour of the various lords being calmed and fighting on the borders ceasing, within the state there will be means to feed the hungry, rest the weary, and support the myriad people. Then rulers and subjects, superiors and subordinates will be generous and loyal, and fathers and sons, elder and younger brothers paternally kind and filially devoted.

'So if people understand about following Heaven's intention, and promote and practise it throughout the world, then punishments and government will be in order, the myriad people will be harmonious, states
will be wealthy, resources will be sufficient, and the common people will
all get warm clothing and filling food and be calm and free of worries.'

Thus our master Mòzǐ said, 'Now the gentlemen of the world, if,
within, they really desire to follow the way and benefit the people and
to fundamentally examine the foundation of benevolence and righteousness, they cannot fail to heed Heaven's intention.' (27/14–22)

27.1d 'Moreover, the Son of Heaven possesses the world, to give an
analogy, no differently from how the rulers of states and the various
lords possess the territory within their four borders. Now as to the
rulers of states and the various lords possessing the territory within
their four borders, how could they desire their subjects, the myriad
people of their state, to do what doesn't benefit each other?! Now if
those living in great states attack small states and those living in great
clans subvert small clans, desiring by this to seek rewards and praise, in
the end they cannot get them, while punishment will surely come. As
for Heaven's possessing the world, it's no different from this. Now if
those living in great states attack small states, those living in great cities
assault small cities, desiring by this to seek blessings from Heaven, in
the end they will not get blessings, while misfortune will surely come.

'So, if there are people who don't do what Heaven desires, but do
what Heaven doesn't desire, then Heaven too will not do what people
desire, but will do what people don't desire. What is it that people don't
desire? [I] say, illness and misfortune. If we don't do what Heaven
desires, but do what Heaven doesn't desire, this is leading the myriad
people of the world to pursue misfortune. So, the ancient sage-kings
clearly knew what Heaven and the ghosts blessed and avoided what
Heaven and the ghosts despised, and by this sought to promote the
benefit of the world and eliminate harm to the world. Hence Heaven
made the cold and heat moderate, the four seasons regular, the *yīn*
and *yáng*, rain and dew timely, the five grains ripe, the six livestock
thrive, and diseases, disasters, epidemics, and famine not come.'

Thus our master Mòzǐ said, 'Now the gentlemen of the world, if,
within, they really desire to follow the way and benefit the people and
to fundamentally examine the foundation of benevolence and righteousness, they cannot fail to heed Heaven's intention.' (27/22–32)

27.2a 'Moreover, in the world there may well be those who are unbenevolent and inauspicious—[I] say, cases such as sons not serving their fathers, younger brothers not serving their elder brothers, or subjects not serving their rulers. So the gentlemen of the world all call them inauspicious. Now Heaven inclusively cares about all the world and provides the myriad things to benefit them. Not so much as the tip of a hair is not Heaven's doing, and the benefits the people get from these things can be said to be great indeed. Yet for them alone not to return the favour to Heaven, without knowing they are being unbenevolent and inauspicious, this is what I call the gentlemen understanding the little things but not understanding the big things.'* (27/32–5)

27.2b 'Moreover, there are grounds by which I know Heaven cares about the people deeply. [I] say, it arrayed the sun, moon, and stars to light the way for them; it regulates the four seasons, spring, autumn, winter, and summer, to direct and guide them; it sends down snow, frost, rain, and dew to grow the five grains, hemp, and silk, letting the people benefit from these resources. It arranged the mountains, rivers, streams, and valleys, and assigned the hundred offices to monitor the people's good and bad conduct. It set up the kings, dukes, and lords, making them reward the worthy and punish the vicious, collect metal and wood, birds and beasts, and undertake production of the five grains, hemp, and silk, to serve as the people's resources for clothing and food. From antiquity until today, these things have never not been available.

'Now suppose there is a person here who is fond of and cares about his son and does his utmost in striving to benefit him. The son grows up and doesn't repay his father, so the gentlemen of the world all call him unbenevolent and inauspicious. Now Heaven inclusively cares about all the world and provides the myriad things to benefit them. Not so much as the tip of a hair is not Heaven's doing, and the benefits the people get from these things can be said to be great indeed. Yet for them alone not to repay Heaven, without knowing they are being unbenevolent and inauspicious, this is what I call the gentlemen understanding the little things but not understanding the big things.' (27/35–42)

27.2c 'Moreover, as to how I know Heaven cares about the people deeply, it doesn't stop with only this as enough. [It's] said, "Those who kill the innocent, Heaven bestows ill fortune on them." Who are the innocent? [I] say, people. Who bestows ill fortune? [I] say, Heaven. If Heaven did not care about people deeply, how do we explain that

when people kill the innocent, Heaven bestows ill fortune on them?!
This is how I know Heaven cares about the people deeply.' (27/42–4)

27.2d 'Moreover, as to how I know Heaven cares about the people
deeply, it doesn't stop with only this. [I] say, there have been those
who cared about others and benefited others, followed Heaven's
intention, and got rewarded by Heaven. There have also been those
who despised others and injured others, defied Heaven's intention,
and got punished by Heaven.

'As for those who cared about others and benefited others, followed
Heaven's intention, and got rewarded by Heaven, who were they?
[I] say, these were people such as the sage-kings of the three dynasties
of the past, Yáo, Shùn, Yǔ, Tāng, Wén, and Wǔ. Yáo, Shùn, Yǔ, Tāng,
Wén, and Wǔ, what did they undertake? [I] say, they undertook inclusion; they did not undertake exclusion. As to inclusion, living in
a great state, they did not attack small states; living in a great clan,
they did not disorder small clans; the strong did not oppress the
weak; the many did not tyrannize the few; the cunning did not scheme
against the foolish; and the noble were not contemptuous of the lowly.
Observe their deeds: above, they benefited Heaven; in the middle,
they benefited the ghosts; below, they benefited people. These three
benefiting and none failing to benefit—this is called Heaven's virtue.* All the beautiful names in the world were collected and applied
to them, saying, these people were benevolent, righteous, and those
who cared about others and benefited others, followed Heaven's
intention, and got rewarded by Heaven.

'It doesn't stop with only this. It was written on bamboo and
silk, engraved in metal and stone, and inscribed on dishes and
bowls to pass down to sons and grandsons in later generations. [I] say,
what is the purpose of these? We use them to recognize those who
cared about others and benefited others, followed Heaven's intention,
and got rewarded by Heaven. The ode "Huáng Yǐ" speaks of it,
saying:

> The Lord on High said to King Wén,
> I cherish your bright virtue,
> It is not displayed with great fanfare.
> It did not change when you became head of the Xià.
> Without considering, without knowing,
> You follow the Lord's norms.

The Lord on High approved of his following the models and norms, so he offered the Yīn empire to reward him, making him so noble as to be Son of Heaven and so wealthy as to possess all the world. His name is praised to this day. So those who cared about others and benefited others, followed Heaven's intention, and got rewarded by Heaven can thus be remembered, that's all.

'As for those who despised others and injured others, defied Heaven's intention, and got punished by Heaven, who were they? [I] say, these are people such as the tyrants of the three dynasties of the past, Jié, Zhòu, Yōu, and Lì. Jié, Zhòu, Yōu, and Lì, what did they undertake? [I] say, they undertook exclusion; they did not undertake inclusion. As to exclusion, living in a great state, they attacked small states; living in a great clan, they disordered small clans; the strong oppressed the weak; the many tyrannized the few; the cunning schemed against the foolish; and the noble were contemptuous of the lowly. Observe their deeds: above, they did not benefit Heaven; in the middle, they did not benefit the ghosts; below, they did not benefit people. These three failing to benefit and none benefiting— this is called being a criminal to Heaven.* All the ugly names in the world were collected and applied to them, saying, these people were unbenevolent, unrighteous, and those who despised others and injured others, opposed Heaven's intention, and got punished by Heaven.

'It doesn't stop with only this. Even more, their deeds were written on bamboo and silk, engraved in metal and stone, and inscribed on dishes and bowls to pass down to sons and grandsons in later generations. [I] say, what is the purpose of these? We use them to recognize those who despised others and injured others, defied Heaven's intention, and got punished by Heaven. The "Great Oath" teaches it, saying:

Zhòu was insolent and arrogant, unwilling to serve the Lord on High. He abandoned his ancestors' spirits and did not sacrifice to them, saying, "I have the mandate." He neglected his duties to the world. Heaven indeed abandoned him and did not protect him.*

If we examine why Heaven abandoned Zhòu and did not protect him, it was that he defied Heaven's intention. So those who despised others and injured others, defied Heaven's intention, and got punished by Heaven can thus be known.'* (27/44–63)

27.3a Thus our master Mòzǐ's having Heaven's intent, to give an analogy, is no different from the wheelwright's having a compass or the carpenter's having a set square.* Now the wheelwright grasps his compass and uses it to measure the round and not round in the world, saying, 'What conforms to my compass, call it "round"; what doesn't conform to my compass, call it "not round".' Hence round and not round can both be known. What is the reason for this? It's that the model for round is clear. The carpenter too grasps his set square and uses it to measure the square and not square in the world, saying, 'What conforms to my set square, call it "square"; what doesn't conform to my set square, call it "not square".' Hence square and not square can both be known. What is the reason for this? It's that the model for square is clear.

Thus as for our master Mòzǐ's having Heaven's intention, above, he uses it to measure how the kings, dukes, and great men of the world administer punishments and government; below, he uses it to gauge how the myriad people of the world engage in writings and studies and present statements and discussions. Observe their conduct: if it follows Heaven's intention, call it good intentions and conduct; if it opposes Heaven's intention, call it bad intentions and conduct. Observe their statements and discussions: if they follow Heaven's intention, call them good statements and discussions; if they oppose Heaven's intention, call them bad statements and discussions. Observe their punishments and government: if they follow Heaven's intention, call them good punishments and government; if they oppose Heaven's intention, call them bad punishments and government. So he sets this up as a model, establishes this as a standard, and uses it to measure the benevolence or unbenevolence of kings, dukes, great men, secretaries, and ministers in the world, and, to give an analogy, it is like dividing black from white.* (27/63–72)

27.3b Thus our master Mòzǐ said, 'Now the kings, dukes, great men, officers, and gentlemen of the world, if, within, they really desire to follow the way, benefit the people, and fundamentally examine the foundation of benevolence and righteousness, then they cannot fail to follow Heaven's intention. Following Heaven's intention is a model of righteousness.' (27/72–3)

BOOK 28

HEAVEN'S INTENT (III)

28.1a Our master Mòzǐ stated, 'What is the explanation for why the world is in disorder? It's that the officers and gentlemen of the world all understand the little things but don't understand the big things.*

'How do we know they understand the little things but don't understand the big things? By their not understanding Heaven's intention.

'How do we know they don't understand Heaven's intention? We know it by how they live in someone's clan. Now if people live in a clan and commit an offence, there are still different clans to escape to. Yet fathers warn sons and elder brothers warn younger brothers, saying, "Be cautious! Be heedful! You may live in someone's clan without being cautious and heedful of them, but can you live in someone's state that way?"

'Now if people live in some state and commit an offence, there are still different states to escape to. Yet fathers warn sons and elder brothers warn younger brothers, saying, "Be cautious! Be heedful! Living in someone's state, you cannot fail to be cautious and heedful."

'Now people all live in the world under Heaven and serve Heaven. If you commit an offence against Heaven, there is nowhere to escape to. Yet no one knows to warn each other. By this I know that, as to the big things, they don't know them.'

Thus our master Mòzǐ stated, 'Be cautious! Be heedful! You must do what Heaven desires and eliminate what Heaven detests.' (28/1–8)

28.1b [I] say, 'What does Heaven desire? What does it detest? Heaven desires righteousness and detests unrighteousness.'

How do we know it is so?*

[I] say, 'Righteousness is [good] government.* How do we know righteousness is [good] government? When there is righteousness in the world, there is order; when there is no righteousness, there is disorder. By this we know righteousness is [good] government.

'Yet as to government, there's no such thing as subordinates governing superiors;* it must be that superiors govern subordinates. Thus commoners don't get to govern as they please. There are officers to govern them.* Officers don't get to govern as they please. There are ministers to govern them. The ministers don't get to govern as they please. There are the various lords to govern them. The various lords don't get to govern as they please. There are the three dukes to govern them. The three dukes don't get to govern as they please. There is the Son of Heaven to govern them. The Son of Heaven doesn't get to govern as he pleases. There is Heaven to govern him. Now the officers and gentlemen of the world all understand that the Son of Heaven governs the world, but they don't understand that Heaven governs the Son of Heaven.

'Thus the ancient sages clearly explained this to people, saying, "The Son of Heaven doing good, Heaven can reward him; the Son of Heaven committing errors, Heaven can punish him." If the Son of Heaven's rewards and punishments are not fitting and his hearing of legal cases is not accurate, the world will be afflicted by disease and misfortune and the frost and dew will be unseasonable. The Son of Heaven must then fatten and feed oxen, sheep, hounds, and hogs and prepare pure offerings of wine and grain to sacrifice to and pray for blessings from Heaven. I've never heard of Heaven praying for blessings from the Son of Heaven. By this I know that Heaven is more important and noble than the Son of Heaven.

'Thus righteousness doesn't issue from the foolish and lowly. It must issue from the noble and wise. [I] say, who is wisest? Heaven is wisest. That being so, then righteousness turns out to issue from Heaven.*

'Now as to the officers and gentlemen of the world who desire to be righteous, they cannot fail to follow Heaven's intention.' (28/8–18)

28.2a [You] say, 'What is following Heaven's intention like?'

[I] say, 'Inclusively care about the people of the world. How do we know [Heaven] inclusively cares about the people of the world? By its inclusively accepting offerings from them. How do we know it inclusively accepts offerings from them? From antiquity until today, there has never been any distant or isolated state but that fattens and feeds their oxen, sheep, hounds, and hogs and prepares pure offerings of wine and grain to reverently sacrifice to the Lord on High and the ghosts and spirits of the mountains and rivers. By this we know it inclusively accepts offerings from them. If it inclusively accepts offerings from them, it must inclusively care about them. To give an analogy, it's like the rulers of Chǔ and Yuè. Now the King of Chǔ accepts offerings from the territory within the four borders of Chǔ, so he cares about the people of Chǔ. The King of Yuè accepts offerings from Yuè, so he cares about the people of Yuè. Now Heaven inclusively accepts offerings from all the world. By this I know it inclusively cares about the people of the world.'* (28/18–23)

28.2b 'Moreover, Heaven's caring for the common people doesn't stop only with this. Now in all the states of the world, among people who eat grain,* those who kill an innocent person will surely have an instance of ill fortune. [I] say, "Who kills the innocent?" [I] say, "people". Who bestows ill fortune on them? [I] say, "Heaven". If Heaven, within, really did not care about these people, why is it that when people kill the innocent, Heaven bestows ill fortune on them?' (28/23–5)

28.2c 'Moreover, that Heaven cares about the common people deeply and Heaven cares about the common people comprehensively can be known. How do we know Heaven loves the common people? I know by how the worthy surely reward the good and punish the vicious.* How do we know the worthy surely reward the good and punish the vicious? I know it by the sage-kings of the three dynasties of the past. So, in the past, the sage-kings of the three dynasties, Yáo, Shùn, Yǔ, Tāng, Wén, and Wǔ, inclusively cared about the world and thus benefited it. They shifted the common people's intentions to this, leading them to revere the Lord on High and the ghosts and spirits of the mountains and rivers. Heaven deemed them to follow it in caring about those it cared about and benefiting those it benefited, and thus applied its rewards to them, causing them to occupy a superior position, establishing them as Son of Heaven to serve as models,* and naming them "sages". By this we know the evidence that the good are rewarded.

'Thus, in the past, the tyrants of the three dynasties, Jié, Zhòu, Yōu, and Lì, inclusively detested the world and thus harmed it. They shifted the common people's intentions to this, leading them to insult and humiliate the Lord on High and the ghosts and spirits of the mountains and rivers. Heaven deemed them not to follow it, by detesting those it cared about and injuring those it benefited, and thus applied its punishment to them, causing their fathers and sons to scatter, their states to perish, their altars of soil and grain to be lost, and troubles to come to them. Hence the commoners of the world one after another denounced them, and their descendants for myriad generations denounced them without cease, naming them "tyrants". By this we know the evidence that Heaven punishes the vicious.

'Now as to the officers and gentlemen of the world who desire to be righteous, they cannot fail to follow Heaven's intention.' (28/25–34)

28.3 [I] say, 'Following Heaven's intention is inclusion; opposing Heaven's intention is exclusion. To follow inclusion as a way is to govern by righteousness. To follow exclusion as a way is to govern by force.'*

[You] say, 'What is governing by righteousness like?'

[I] say, 'The great don't attack the small, the strong don't humiliate the weak, the many don't injure the few, the cunning don't deceive the foolish, the noble are not contemptuous of the lowly, the wealthy are not arrogant toward the poor, the hale don't rob from the old. Hence none of the numerous states of the world harm each other with water, fire, poison, or weapons. These things benefit Heaven above, benefit the ghosts in the middle, and benefit people below. These three benefiting and none failing to benefit—this is called Heaven's virtue. So anyone who undertakes this has sagely wisdom, is benevolent and righteous, is loyal and generous, and is kind and filial. Thus we collect all the finest names in the world and apply them to them. What is the reason for this? It's that they follow Heaven's intention.'

[You] say, 'What is governing by force like?'

[I] say, 'The great attack the small, the strong abuse the weak, the many injure the few, the cunning deceive the foolish, the noble are contemptuous of the lowly, the wealthy are arrogant toward the poor, the hale rob from the old. Hence the numerous states of the world then injure each other with water, fire, poison, or weapons. These things don't benefit Heaven above, don't benefit the ghosts in the middle, and don't benefit people below. These three failing to benefit and none benefiting—this is called being a criminal to Heaven. So anyone who undertakes this is a bandit, a robber, and a thief, is unbenevolent and unrighteous, is disloyal and ungenerous, and is unkind and unfilial. Thus we collect all the worst names in the world and apply them to them. What is the reason for this? It's that they oppose Heaven's intention.'* (28/34–43)

28.4 So our master Mòzǐ establishes Heaven's intent as a standard and model, as the wheelwright has the compass and the carpenter has the set square. Now the wheelwright uses the compass, the carpenter uses the set square, using these they know the difference between square and round.* (28/44–5)

28.5a Thus our master Mòzǐ establishes Heaven's intent as a standard and model; by this I know that the officers and gentlemen of the world have gone far from righteousness.

How do we know the officers and gentlemen of the world have gone far from righteousness? Now the rulers of the great states say, without scruples, 'Dwelling in a great state without attacking small states, how am I great?' Hence they muster their sharpest soldiers and assemble their boat and chariot forces to attack an innocent state. Entering the state's borders, they mow down its crops, fell its trees, raze its city walls, filling its moats with the rubble, burn its ancestral shrines, and slaughter its sacrificial animals.* People who resist are beheaded; those who don't resist are brought back in chains, the men to labour in stables and on chain gangs, the women to thresh grain.

So the rulers who favour aggression, they don't know this is unbenevolent and unrighteous. They announce it to the various lords of neighbouring states, saying, 'I attacked a state, defeated an army, and killed such-and-such many generals.' The rulers of the neighbouring states don't know this is unbenevolent and unrighteous, either. Some prepare furs and coins, opening their treasuries, and send envoys to offer gifts and congratulations. As to the rulers who favour aggression, there are those who are doubly ignorant of this being unbenevolent and unrighteous. They write their deeds on bamboo and silk and store them in their archives. Their descendants will surely desire to follow the practices of their former rulers and say, 'Why don't we open our archives to see the model and standard set by our former rulers?' Surely the records will not say, 'Kings Wén and Wǔ governed like this.' They will say, 'I attacked a state, defeated an army, and killed such-and-such many generals.' So, the rulers who favour aggression don't know this is unbenevolent and unrighteous, the rulers of neighbouring states don't know this is unbenevolent and unrighteous, and hence the aggression goes on for generation after generation without cease. This is what I call not knowing the big things.* (28/45–55)

28.5b What we call knowing the little things*—what's that like?

Now suppose there is a person here who enters someone's farm and takes the person's peaches, plums, gourds, and ginger. When superiors catch him, they will punish him; when the masses hear about it, they deem him wrong. Why is this? [I] say, he did not contribute his labour but received the fruits. The reason is that he took what was not his possession.*

How much worse is it for there to be a person who climbs over someone's wall and seizes the person's children?! Or who tunnels into someone's storehouse and steals the person's gold, jade, cloth, and silk? Or who climbs the fence into someone's paddock and steals the person's oxen and horses? And how much worse for there to be someone who kills an innocent person?

Now, as to how kings, dukes, and great men govern, from killing an innocent person to climbing someone's wall and seizing the person's children to tunnelling into someone's storehouse and stealing the person's gold, jade, cloth, and silk to climbing someone's paddock and stealing the person's oxen and horses to entering someone's farm and stealing the person's peaches, plums, gourds, and ginger—now, as to how kings, dukes, and great men apply punishment to these crimes, even Yáo, Shùn, Yǔ, Tāng, Wén, and Wǔ of antiquity in governing would indeed be no different from them.

Still, now the various lords of the world all invade, attack, and annex each other. This is many thousands and ten thousands of times worse than killing an innocent person. This is many thousands and ten thousands of times worse than climbing someone's wall and seizing the person's children or tunnelling into someone's storehouse and stealing the person's gold, jade, cloth, and silk. This is many thousands and ten thousands of times worse than climbing someone's paddock and stealing the person's oxen and horses or entering someone's farm and stealing the person's peaches, plums, gourds, and ginger. Yet they themselves say it is righteous. (28/55–64)

28.5c So our master Mòzǐ stated, 'As to how this confuses righteousness, how is there any difference between this and confusing the distinction between black and white or sweet and bitter?! Suppose there is a person here who when we show him a little black calls it "black", but when we show him much black calls it "white". Then he must say, "My eyes are disordered. I don't know the difference between black and white." Or suppose there is a person here who can taste a little of something sweet and say "sweet", but when he tastes much of it says "bitter". Then he must say, "My mouth is disordered. I don't know the flavours of sweet and bitter."*

'Now as to how kings, dukes, and great men govern, if someone kills a person, their state prohibits it. This . . .* But if someone is able to kill many of their neighbouring state's people, they respond by deeming it righteous. How is this different from confusing the difference between white and black or sweet and bitter?!' (28/64–9)

28.6a So our master Mòzǐ sets up Heaven's intent as a standard and model. It's not our master Mòzǐ alone who takes Heaven's intent as a model. In the documents of the former kings, the 'Great Xià' teaches so:

> The Lord on High said to King Wén,
> I cherish your bright virtue,
> It is not displayed with great fanfare.
> It did not change when you became head of the Xià.
> Without considering, without knowing,
> You follow the Lord's norms.

This expounds how King Wén took Heaven's intent as a model and followed the norms of the Lord on High. (28/69–71)

28.6b Moreover, now the officers and gentlemen of the world, if, within, they really desire to be benevolent and righteous and seek to be superior officers; above, they desire to conform to the way of the sage-kings; and below, they desire to conform to the benefit of the state and the common people, then they cannot fail to examine Heaven's intent. Heaven's intent is the canon of righteousness. (28/71–3)

UNDERSTANDING GHOSTS

BOOK 31

UNDERSTANDING GHOSTS (III)

31.1a Our master Mòzǐ stated, 'Once the sage-kings of the three dynasties of the past had passed away, the world lost righteousness and the various lords governed by force.* Hence, among those who were someone's ruler or subject, superior or subordinate, some were not generous and loyal; among fathers and sons, younger and elder brothers, some were not kind, filial, fraternal, respectful, honourable, and decent; among government leaders, some did not strive hard in attending to government, while among commoners some did not strive hard in undertaking work. People all over engaging in dissolution, viciousness, banditry, robbery, and thievery, using weapons, poison, water, or fire to stop innocent people on the roads and paths, seizing others' carts, horses, and clothing to benefit themselves—it all started from this. Hence the world was disordered.

'What is the reason this is so? It's all due to doubt and confusion about the difference between whether there are or aren't ghosts and spirits and to not understanding that ghosts and spirits are able to reward the worthy and punish the vicious. Now supposing the people of the world all trusted that ghosts and spirits are able to reward the worthy and punish the vicious, then how could the world be in disorder?!' (31/1–6)

31.1b Now those who hold there are no ghosts say, 'There definitely are no ghosts and spirits.' Morning and evening they instruct the world of this, spreading doubt among the masses of the world, causing the masses of the world to all be confused about the difference between whether there are or aren't ghosts and spirits. Hence the world is in disorder. Thus our master Mòzǐ said, 'Now the kings, dukes, great men, officers, and gentlemen of the world, if they really desire to seek to promote the benefit of the world and eliminate harm to the world, then they cannot fail to clearly examine the difference between whether there are or aren't ghosts and spirits.' (31/6–9)

31.2 Having deemed that one cannot fail to examine the difference between whether there are or aren't ghosts and spirits, that being so, then how can we clearly examine this doctrine?

Our master Mòzǐ said, 'This goes with the way by which all the world investigates to know whether there is or isn't anything. We must take the reality* that the masses' ears hear and eyes see as our standard to know whether there is something or not. If some have actually heard it or seen it, then we must deem that there is. If none have heard or seen it, we must deem that there isn't. If this is the case, why not try going into any one town or village and asking about it. From antiquity until today, from the time people first arose, if there have indeed been cases of seeing the things ghosts and spirits or hearing the sounds of ghosts and spirits, then how can we say there are no ghosts and spirits? If no one heard them and no one saw them, then how can we say there are ghosts and spirits?' (31/9–13)

31.3 Now those who hold there are no ghosts state, 'As for those in the world who engage in hearing and seeing the things ghosts and spirits, there are incalculably many of them. Just whom do you take to have heard or seen things indicating that there are or aren't ghosts and spirits?'

Our master Mòzǐ stated, 'If we go by what the masses have similarly seen and what they have similarly heard, then a case such as Dù Bó in the past is this. King Xuān of Zhōu killed his minister Dù Bó even though he was innocent. Dù Bó said, "My ruler kills me though I am innocent. If we take the dead to be unknowing, then it stops here. If I die yet am knowing,* within three years I will surely let my ruler know it."

'After a period of three years, King Xuān of Zhōu went hunting with the various lords at Pǔ Tián. The chariots numbered in the hundreds, while those following on foot numbered in the thousands, filling the fields. At midday, Dù Bó rode up in a plain chariot with white horses, wearing vermilion clothes and a vermilion cap, holding a vermilion bow, and clasping vermilion arrows. He pursued King Xuān of Zhōu and shot him in his chariot, striking his heart and snapping his spine. The king collapsed in his chariot, slumped over his bow case, and died. At this time, among the Zhōu people none of those following failed to see it and none of those far away failed to hear of it. They recorded it in the annals of the Zhōu court. Those who are rulers instruct their subjects by it, while those who are fathers warn their sons by it, saying, "Be cautious! Be heedful! Anyone who kills an innocent person will get ill fortune. The punishment of the ghosts and spirits is as swift as this." Looking at things on the basis of the explanation in this document,* how can one doubt there are ghosts and spirits?!'

'It's not only the explanation* in this document that's so . . .'.

Thus our master Mòzǐ stated, 'Even in deep valleys or vast forests, dark secluded places where no one lives, in conducting oneself one cannot fail to be heedful, for whatever you do there are ghosts and spirits watching it.' (31/13–21, 31/42)

31.4a Now those who hold there are no ghosts say, 'As for the facts the masses' ears hear and eyes see, how is that adequate to resolve doubt?! What's to be said about someone who desires to be a superior officer or gentleman in the world, yet turns to and trusts the facts the masses' ears hear and eyes see?!'*

Our master Mòzǐ said, 'If we take the facts the masses' ears hear and eyes see to be inadequate to trust and don't resolve doubt by them, then I wonder, those such as the sage-kings of the three dynasties of the past, Yáo, Shùn, Yǔ, Tāng, Wén, and Wǔ, are they adequate to take as models?'

So, to this, those of middle status and above all say, 'Those such as the sage-kings of the three dynasties of the past, they are adequate to take as models.'

If the sage-kings of the three dynasties of the past are adequate to take as models, that being so, then let's try, above, observing the deeds of the sage-kings.*

In the past, King Wǔ attacked Yīn and punished the tyrant Zhòu. He made the various lords divide up the sacrifices, saying, 'Let the more closely related take the inner sacrifices and the more distantly related take the outer sacrifices.' So King Wǔ surely took it that there are ghosts and spirits. Thus when he attacked Yīn and punished the tyrant Zhòu, he made the various lords divide up the sacrifices. If there are no ghosts and spirits, why did King Wǔ divide up the sacrifices?* (31/42–8)

31.4b It's not only King Wǔ's deeds that are so. When the ancient sage-kings rewarded someone, it had to be at the ancestral shrine; when they punished someone, it had to be at the altar of soil. Why reward at the ancestral shrine? To report to the ancestors that portions were fair.* Why punish at the altar of soil? To report that the hearing of the case was accurate. (31/48–50)

31.4c It's not only the explanation in this document* that's so. Moreover, in the past, the sage-kings of the three dynasties, Yú Xià, Shāng, and Zhōu,* on the day they began to establish their states and build their cities, surely chose the most correctly aligned altar in the state to set up their ancestral shrine. They surely chose the location where the trees were the healthiest and lushest to establish the altar of soil. They surely chose fathers and elder brothers who were the most kind, filial, honourable, and decent to serve as ancestral priests. They surely chose the plumpest and most purely coloured of the six domestic animals as sacrificial offerings. Jade tablets, discs, tubes, and pendants were prepared commensurate with the state's wealth. They surely chose the most fragrant and ripe of the five grains to make offerings of wine and grain, the quality varying with the harvest. So these are the respects in which the ancient sage-kings in ordering the world certainly surely put ghosts and spirits before people. So they said, when the government bureaus are being equipped, first a full set of sacrificial implements and sacrificial robes must be stored in the treasury, a full set of ancestral priests and officials installed at the court, and the sacrificial animals separated from their previous herds. So the ancient sage-kings governed like this.* (31/50–5)

31.4d The ancient sage-kings surely deemed that there are ghosts and spirits and their devotion to the ghosts and spirits was deep. Still, fearing their sons and grandsons in later generations would be unable to know these things, so they wrote them on bamboo and silk to pass down to their sons and grandsons in later generations. Some feared these documents might rot away and be destroyed, so their sons and grandsons in later generations would not get them and remember their content. So they inscribed them on dishes and bowls and engraved it in metal and stone, to repeat them. Again, they feared their sons and grandsons in later generations would be unable to venerate the ghosts and spirits enough to get good fortune, so, in the documents of the former kings and the statements of the sages, every foot of silk and every bundle of bamboo strips* speaks numerous times of there being ghosts and spirits, repeating it again and again. What is the reason for this? It's that the sage-kings were devoted to them.

Now those who hold there are no ghosts say, 'There definitely are no ghosts and spirits.' Then this opposes what the sage-kings were

devoted to. Opposing what the sage-kings were devoted to, this is not
the way by which to be a gentleman. (31/55–9)

31.5 Now the statement of those who hold there are no ghosts
says, '[You claim that] in the documents of the former kings,*
the statements of the sages, every foot of silk and every bundle of
bamboo strips speak numerous times of there being ghosts and
spirits, repeating it again and again. In just what documents is this
found?'

Our master Mòzĭ said, 'Among the documents of Zhōu, the "Great
Ode" has this. The "Great Ode" says:

> King Wén is above,
> Shining in the Heavens.
> Although Zhōu is an old country,
> Its mandate is new.
> Is Zhōu not illustrious!
> Was the Lord on High's mandate not timely!
> King Wén ascends and descends
> At the Lord on High's left and right.
> Conscientious was King Wén!
> His fame doesn't cease.

If there are no ghosts and spirits, then King Wén having died, how
could he be at the Lord on High's left and right? This is how I know
of ghosts in the documents of Zhōu.

'Now if the documents of Zhōu alone mentioned ghosts but the
documents of Shāng did not mention ghosts, this would be inadequate to take as a model. That being so, then let's try observing,
above, in the documents of Shāng. . . .*

'So first the documents of Xià and next the documents of Shāng
and Zhōu speak numerous times of there being ghosts and spirits,
repeating it again and again. What is the reason for this? It's that the
sage-kings were devoted to them. If we look at things on the basis of
the explanations in these documents, how can one doubt there are
ghosts and spirits?! . . .' (31/55–64, 31/73–5)

31.6a Thus our master Mòzĭ said, 'As to ghosts and spirits being able
to reward the worthy and punish the vicious, why not fundamentally
implement it in the state and implement it among the myriad people?*
It is really the way by which to order the state and benefit the myriad
people. . . .*

'Hence when there is dishonesty among officials managing government bureaus or failure to maintain proper separation between men and women, the ghosts and spirits will see it. When people engage in dissolution, viciousness, banditry, robbery, and thievery, using weapons, poisons, water, or fire to stop innocent people on the roads, seizing others' carts, horses, and clothing to benefit themselves, there will be ghosts and spirits to see it. Hence officials managing government bureaus dare not be dishonest; seeing good, they dare not fail to reward it; seeing viciousness, they dare not fail to punish it. People's engaging in dissolution, viciousness, banditry, robbery, and thievery, using weapons, poisons, water, or fire to stop innocent people on the roads, seizing carts, horses, and clothing to benefit themselves—it will all stop from this, . . .* and hence the world will be in order.

'So as to the keen sight of ghosts and spirits, one cannot rely on dark, secluded places or vast marshes, mountain forests or deep valleys—the keen sight of the ghosts and spirits* will surely know it. As to the punishments of the ghosts and spirits, one cannot rely on wealth or nobility, strength of numbers, bravery and strength or martial prowess, tough armour or sharp weapons—the punishments of the ghosts and spirits will surely overcome them.' (31/75–83)

31.6b 'If you deem it not so, in the past King Jié of the Xià dynasty was so noble as to be Son of Heaven and so wealthy as to possess the whole world. Above, he insulted Heaven and humiliated the ghosts; below, he cruelly slaughtered the myriad people of the world. He ruined the achievements of the Lord on High and rejected the conduct of the Lord on High.* So, consequently, Heaven commanded King Tāng of Shāng to carry out its enlightened punishment of him. Tāng arranged his nine chariots in the "bird formation" with the "goose march".* Tāng climbed Dàzàn, scattered the Xià troops, and entered Xià lands.* King Tāng captured Tuīchĭ Dàxì* with his own hands. So, in the past, King Jié of the Xià dynasty was so noble as to be Son of Heaven and so wealthy as to possess the whole world. He had Tuīchĭ Dàxì, a man of such bravery and strength he could tear apart a live rhinoceros or tiger and kill people with the touch of a finger. His people numbered so many millions that they filled the marshes and hills. Yet all this could not protect him from the punishment of the ghosts and spirits. This is what I was referring to by how, as to the punishment of the ghosts and spirits, one cannot rely on wealth or nobility, strength of numbers, bravery and strength or martial prowess, tough armour or sharp weapons—it's this.' . . .* (31/83–8)

31.7a Now those who hold there are no ghosts say, 'Might it fail to conform to the benefit of one's parents and so interfere with filial devotion?'*

Our master Mòzǐ stated, 'Whether in antiquity or today, those that are ghosts are none other than these: there are the ghosts of Heaven,* there are also ghosts and spirits of mountains and waters, and there are also people who die and become ghosts. Now, there are sons who die before their fathers and younger brothers who die before their elder brothers. Even supposing this is so, still, throughout the world it's a platitude that "Those born first, die first." If this is the case, then those who die first are, if not one's father, then one's mother, if not one's elder brother, then one's elder sister.

'Now we prepare pure offerings of wine and grain to reverently and attentively sacrifice to them. Supposing in fact* there are ghosts and spirits, this succeeds in providing food and drink for our parents and elder siblings. How is this not a rich benefit?! Supposing in fact there aren't ghosts and spirits, then this is just expending the resources used to make the offerings of wine and grain, that's all. Yet though we expend them, it's not that we just pour them in a sewage ditch and throw them away. Our relatives inside the clan and townspeople from outside the clan all get to drink and eat what's provided. Even supposing in fact there aren't ghosts and spirits, this can still make for an enjoyable gathering and build kinship among the townspeople.' (31/96–102)

31.7b Now those who hold there are no ghosts state, 'There definitely are in fact no ghosts and spirits. Hence we don't provide the resources for their offerings of wine and grain. Now surely it's not that we begrudge the cost of their offerings of wine and grain! But what's to be gained from it?!'

This is, above, contrary to the documents of the sage-kings, and, within the family, contrary to the conduct of people's filially devoted sons, yet these people undertake to be superior officers in the world. This is not the way by which to be superior officers.

Thus our master Mòzǐ said, 'Now when we perform sacrifices, it's not just pouring the offerings in a sewage ditch and throwing them away. Above, we use them to exchange blessings with the ghosts; below, we use them to hold an enjoyable gathering and build kinship among the townspeople. If there are spirits, then this succeeds in providing food for our parents and elder siblings. So how is this not a beneficial matter for the world?' (31/102–6)

31.8 Thus our master Mòzǐ said, 'Now the kings, dukes, great men, officers, and gentlemen of the world, if, within, they really desire to seek to promote the benefit of the world and eliminate harm to the world, then as to there being ghosts and spirits, they cannot fail to honour and understand them. This is the way of the sage-kings.' (31/107–8)

CONDEMNING MUSIC

BOOK 32

CONDEMNING MUSIC (I)

32.1 Our master Mòzǐ stated, 'The task of benevolence* is surely to diligently seek to promote the benefit of the world and eliminate harm to the world and to take this as a model throughout the world. Does it benefit people? Then do it. Does it not benefit people? Then stop.

'Moreover, the benevolent in planning for the world do not, for the sake of what is beautiful to the eye, enjoyable to the ear, delicious to the mouth, or comfortable to the body, rob the people of their resources for clothing and food. The benevolent do not do this.' (32/1–3)

32.2 Thus that by which our master Mòzǐ deems music wrong is not that he deems the sound of the great bells and sounding drums, zithers and lutes, and flutes and pipes unenjoyable. It's not that he deems the appearance of the carved decorations and ornaments unbeautiful. It's not that he deems the flavours of the roasted and broiled meats unsweet. It's not that he deems secluded dwelling in lofty pavilions on high terraces uncomfortable. Though the body knows their comfort, the mouth knows their sweetness, the eye knows their beauty, and the ear knows their enjoyment, still, examining them above, they don't conform to the deeds of the sage-kings, while measuring them below, they don't conform to the benefit of the myriad people. Thus our master Mòzǐ said, 'Making music is wrong.' (32/3–7)

32.3 Now kings, dukes, and great men, if they manufacture musical instruments, deeming this a service to the state, don't make them simply by scooping them up from the water or digging them up from the soil. They must collect heavy taxes from the myriad people to make the sounds of the great bells and sounding drums, zithers and lutes, and flutes and pipes. The ancient sage-kings too once collected heavy taxes from the myriad people, to make boats and carts. Once these were finished, people said, 'How will we use these?' [They] said,

'The boats are used on water, the carts are used on land. The gentlemen rest their feet with them, the commoners rest their shoulders and backs with them.' So the myriad people took out their resources and handed them over, not daring to resent it. Why? Because the boats and carts in return conformed to the benefit of the people. That being so, then if musical instruments in return also conformed to the benefit of the people like this, I wouldn't dare deem them wrong. That being so, then if the use of musical instruments was analogous to the sage-kings' making boats and carts, I wouldn't dare deem it wrong.* (32/7–12)

32.4 The people have three troubles: the hungry do not get food, the cold do not get clothing, and the weary do not get rest. These three are the major troubles of the people. That being so, then for their sake let's strike the giant bells, beat the sounding drums, strum the zithers and lutes, blow the flutes and pipes, and wave the shields and axes in the war dance. Can the resources for the people's clothing and food be got from this? I take it, not necessarily.

Or, setting this aside, now there are great states that attack small states, there are great clans that assault small clans, the strong oppress the weak, the majority tyrannize the few, the cunning deceive the foolish, the noble are contemptuous of the lowly, bandits, robbers, and thieves spring up everywhere, and all this cannot be stopped. That being so, then for the sake of these problems let's strike the giant bells, beat the sounding drums, strum the zithers and lutes, blow the flutes and pipes, and wave the shields and axes in the war dance. Can the disorder in the world be put in order by this? I take it, not necessarily.

Thus our master Mòzǐ said, 'If we try collecting heavy taxes from the myriad people to make the sounds of great bells, sounding drums, zithers and lutes, and flutes and pipes, to seek to promote the benefit of the world and eliminate harm to the world, it's of no help.' Thus our master Mòzǐ said, 'Making music is wrong.' (32/12–18)

32.5a Now kings, dukes, and great men, if they merely situate themselves in lofty pavilions on high terraces to view them, the bells just hang there like inverted cauldrons. Without their being struck, what enjoyment will be got from them? This explains why they must be struck. Since they are to be struck, the old and young mustn't be employed. The ears and eyes of the old and young are not acute and keen, their limbs are not strong, their voices are not harmonious, and their expressions are not varied. Those in the prime of life must be employed, for the acuity and keenness of their ears and eyes, the strength of their limbs, the harmony of their voices, and the variety of their expressions. Employing men to do it interferes with the men's seasons for ploughing and sowing, planting and cultivating. Employing women to do it interferes with the women's work in weaving and spinning.

Now kings, dukes, and great men, if they make music, rob the people's resources for clothing and food to this great extent to hold musical performances. Thus our master Mòzǐ said, 'Making music is wrong.' (32/18–23)

32.5b Now the sounds of the great bells, sounding drums, zithers and lutes, and flutes and pipes all being provided, if the great men quietly listen to the performance alone, what enjoyment will be got from it? This explains why, if not accompanied by gentlemen, they must be accompanied by commoners. Listening to it with gentlemen interferes with the gentlemen's attending to government. Listening to it with commoners interferes with the commoners' undertaking work.

Now kings, dukes, and great men, if they make music, rob the people's resources for clothing and food to this great extent to hold musical performances. Thus our master Mòzǐ said, 'Making music is wrong.' (32/23–6)

32.6 In the past, Duke Kāng of Qí delighted in music and the Wàn dance. The Wàn dancers cannot wear rough clothing and cannot eat coarse grains. [It's] said, if the food and drink are not fine, their faces and complexion are not worth looking at; if their clothing is not fine, their figures and movements are not worth viewing. Hence their food must be the finest grain and meat, their clothing must be finely embroidered. These were people who never undertook to produce resources for clothing and food but always lived on what others produced.

Thus our master Mòzǐ said, 'Now kings, dukes, and great men, if they make music, rob the people's resources for clothing and food to this great extent to hold musical performances.' Thus our master Mòzǐ said, 'Making music is wrong.' (32/26–30)

32.7a Now people are indeed different from birds, beasts, and other animals. Now birds, beasts, and other animals rely on their feathers and fur to serve as clothing, their hooves and claws to serve as trousers and shoes, and their water and grass to serve as food and drink. So even if we make their males not plough and sow or plant and cultivate and also their females not spin and weave, their resources for clothing and food are certainly already provided.

Now people are different from this. Those who rely on their efforts live, those who don't rely on their efforts don't live. If gentlemen do not strive hard in attending to government, punishments and government are in disorder. If commoners do not strive hard in undertaking work, resources are insufficient. (32/30–3)

32.7b Now the officers and gentlemen of the world take my statements to be not so.* That being so, then let's try enumerating the apportioned tasks in the world and observe the harms of music.

Kings, dukes, and great men go to court early and retire late, hearing legal cases and ordering government affairs. This is their apportioned task. Officers and gentlemen exhaust the strength of their limbs and wear out the knowledge of their wits, inside, ordering the bureaus, and outside, collecting taxes from profits on passes, markets, forests, and fish weirs, to fill the granaries and treasury. This is their apportioned task. Farmers go out in the morning and come in at dusk, ploughing and sowing, planting and cultivating, harvesting many crops. This is their apportioned task. Women rise at dawn and sleep late at night, spinning and weaving, making much linen, silk, hemp, and other textiles. This is their apportioned task.*

Now if kings, dukes, and great men are pleased by music and listen to it, then surely they cannot come to court early and retire late, hearing legal cases and ordering government affairs. Thus the state is in disorder and the altars of soil and grain endangered. Now if officers and gentlemen are pleased by music and listen to it, then surely they cannot exhaust the strength of their limbs and wear out the knowledge of their wits, inside, ordering the offices and bureaus, and outside, collecting taxes from profits on passes, markets, forests, and fish weirs, to fill the granaries and treasury. Thus the granaries and treasury are not full. Now if farmers are pleased by music and listen to it, then surely they cannot go out in the morning and come in at dusk, ploughing and sowing, planting and cultivating, harvesting many crops. Thus crops will be insufficient. Now if women are pleased by music and listen to it, then surely they cannot rise at dawn and sleep late at night, spinning and weaving, making much linen, silk, hemp, and other textiles. Thus textiles will not be produced.

[We] say, what is done that interferes with great men's government administration and commoners' undertaking work? [We] say, it's music. Thus our master Mòzǐ said, 'Making music is wrong.' (32/33–43)

32.8 How do we know it is so? [We] say, among the documents of the former kings, Tāng's official code of punishments has this:

Their constant dancing in the palace, this is called 'the Shaman's Air'. Their punishment is for a gentleman to pay two measures of silk, for commoners to pay double, two bolts of silk.*

The 'Yellow Path' then states:

Ah! Dancing everywhere, the sounds of music loud and clear. The Lord on High doesn't protect him.* The nine realms are lost.* The Lord on High doesn't comply and sends down a hundred misfortunes. Their house will surely perish.

Examine how the nine realms were lost: it's that he devoted himself to elaborate music. In the 'Wǔ Guān' it says:

King Qǐ indulged in music and dissolution, drinking and eating in the fields. Qiāng qiāng! the flutes and chimes resounded. He drowned himself in wine and gorged on food in the fields. The Wàn dance was magnificent and the sounds carried to Heaven, but Heaven did not approve.

So above, Heaven and the ghosts did not approve, while below, the myriad people did not benefit. (32/43–8)

32.9 Thus our master Mòzǐ said, 'Now the officers and gentlemen of the world, if they in fact desire to seek to promote the benefit of the world and eliminate harm to the world, then as to music this sort of thing, they cannot fail to prohibit and stop it.' (32/48–9)

CONDEMNING FATALISM

BOOK 35

CONDEMNING FATALISM (I)

35.1 Our master Mòzǐ stated, 'Ancient kings, dukes, and great men in governing the state all desired that the state be wealthy, the population large, and punishments and government in order. Yet they got not wealth but poverty, not a large population but a small one, not order but disorder. So this is fundamentally missing what they desired and getting what they detested.'*

What is the reason for this?

Our master Mòzǐ stated, 'Many fatalists were gathered among the people. The statements of the fatalists say, "If fated to be wealthy, then wealthy; if fated to be poor, then poor. If fated to be many, then many; if fated to be few, then few. If fated to be in order, then in order; if fated to be in disorder, then in disorder. If fated to be long-lived, then a long life; if fated to be short-lived, then a short life. Given fate, even if one devotes great effort, of what advantage is it?"* Above, they persuaded kings, dukes, and great men of this; below, they obstructed the common people from undertaking work. So the fatalists are unbenevolent. So as to the statements of the fatalists, one cannot fail to clearly distinguish them.'*

That being so, then how do we clearly distinguish this doctrine?*

Our master Mòzǐ stated, 'We must establish standards. Making statements without standards is analogous to establishing sunrise and sunset on a potter's wheel. The distinctions between right and wrong and benefit and harm can't be clearly known. So statements must have three markers.'*

What are called the 'three markers'?

Our master Mòzǐ stated, 'There is its foundation; there is its source; there is its use. In what is it founded? Above, found it in the deeds of the ancient sage-kings.* In what is it sourced? Below, source it by examining the reality the common people's ears hear and eyes see. In what is it used? Issue it as a basis for punishments and government and observe whether it conforms to the benefit of the state, the hundred clans, and the people.* This is what is referred to as statements having three markers.'* (35/1–10)

35.2 Yet now some of the officers and gentlemen of the world take it there is fate. Why not try, above, observing the deeds of the sage-kings? In antiquity, what Jié disordered, Tāng received and put in order; what Zhòu disordered, King Wú received and put in order. In these cases, the era hadn't changed and the people hadn't altered, but under Jié and Zhòu, the world was in disorder, while under Tāng and Wú, the world was in order. How can one assert there is fate?! (35/10–12)

36.2a* Now some of the officers and gentlemen of the world take it that there is fate and some take it that there isn't. As to how we know there is or there isn't fate, we know there is or there isn't by the facts the people of the masses' ears hear and eyes see. If some have heard it, some have seen it, we assert there is. If none have heard it, none have seen it, we assert there isn't. So, why not try confirming it against the facts of the common people? From antiquity until today, since people first arose, has there indeed been anyone who has seen this thing fate or heard the sound of fate? Then there never has been.

If we take the common people to be foolish and unworthy, the facts their ears hear and eyes see inadequate to be adopted as a model, that being so, then why not try confirming it against the statements and sayings passed along from the various lords? From antiquity until today, since people first arose, has there indeed been anyone who has heard the sound of fate or seen this item fate? Then there never has been. (36/5–7)

36.2b So, why not try confirming it against the deeds of the sage-kings? The ancient sage-kings elevated filially devoted sons and encouraged them to serve their parents, honoured the worthy and excellent and encouraged them to do good, issued statutes and announced decrees to instruct people, and clarified rewards and punishments to encourage people to do good and discourage them from doing bad. In this way, the disordered could be put in order and the endangered could be made secure. If anyone takes this not to be so, in the past, what Jié disordered, Tāng put in order; what Zhòu disordered, King Wú put in order. In these cases, the era didn't alter and the people weren't replaced; the superior switched government policies and the people changed their instructions. When they were under Tāng and Wǔ, they were in order; when under Jié and Zhòu, in disorder. Security or danger, order or disorder lie in the government policies that superiors issue. So how can one assert there is fate?!* So the claims of those who say there is fate are surely not so.* (36/7–13)

35.5 The fatalists state, 'Those whom superiors punish, fate fixes that they will be punished; it's not that they are vicious and so are punished. Those whom superiors reward, fate fixes that they will be rewarded; it's not that they are worthy and so are rewarded.'

If one acts as ruler on this basis, he will be unrighteous; as minister, disloyal; as father, unkind; as son, unfilial; as elder brother, not decent; as younger brother, not fraternal. And as to strongly holding this, this is simply the source of malicious statements* and the way of vicious people.

That being so, then how do we know fate is the way of vicious people? In the past, the poor people of previous eras were greedy for food and drink but lazy in undertaking work. Hence their resources for clothing and food were insufficient, and they were troubled by hunger and cold. They did not know to say, 'We are weak and unworthy and didn't work urgently enough.' Surely they said, 'My fate was fixed that I would be poor.'

In the past, the tyrants of previous eras did not resist the lusts of their ears and eyes or the proclivities of their heart and intention and did not obey their parents. Consequently, they lost their states and their altars of soil and grain were overturned. They did not know to say, 'I am weak and unworthy and governed badly.' Surely they said, 'My fate was fixed that I would lose them.'*

. . . In the 'Great Oath', it says:

Zhòu was insolent and would not serve the Lord on High or the ghosts and spirits. He abandoned his ancestors' spirits and did not sacrifice to them. He said, 'My people have fate' and neglected his work. Heaven indeed abandoned him and did not protect him.*

This states the grounds by which King Wǔ deemed wrong Zhòu's holding that there is fate.*

Now if we use the statements of the fatalists, superiors will not attend to government and subordinates will not undertake work. If superiors don't attend to government, punishments and government will be in disorder. If subordinates don't undertake work, resources will be insufficient. Above, they will lack the means to prepare pure offerings of wine and grain to sacrifice to the Lord on High and the ghosts and spirits. Below, they will lack the means to bring security to worthy and capable officers. Abroad, they will lack the means to entertain noble guests from among the various lords. Within the state, they will lack the means to feed the hungry, clothe the cold, and support the old and weak. So, above, fate is not beneficial to Heaven; in the middle, it is not beneficial to ghosts; below, it is not beneficial to people. And as to strongly holding this, this is simply the source of malicious statements and the way of vicious people. (35/33–46)

35.6 Thus our master Mòzǐ stated, 'Now the officers and gentlemen of the world, if, within, they really desire the world to be wealthy and detest its being poor, and they desire the world to be in order and detest its being in disorder, then, as to the statements of the fatalists, they cannot fail to deem them wrong.* These are a great harm to the world.' (35/46–7)

BOOK 36

CONDEMNING FATALISM (II)

36.1 Our master Mòzǐ stated, 'In all cases of pursuing a way of presenting statements and discussion or engaging in writing and studies, one cannot fail to first establish standards and models. Making statements without standards is analogous to establishing sunrise and sunset on a potter's wheel; even a skilled artisan surely can't get it right that way. That being so, now what in the world is factual or sham can't yet be recognized. So let there be three models for statements.

'What are the three models? There is its foundation; there is its source; there is its use. As to founding it, confirm it against the intent of Heaven and the ghosts and the deeds of the sage-kings. As to sourcing it, verify it in the documents of the former kings. How is it used? Issue it as a basis for punishments. These are the three models* for statements.' (36/1–5)

35.3* Yet now some of the officers and gentlemen of the world take it there is fate. Why not try, above, observing the documents of the sage-kings? Among the documents of the former kings, those issued throughout the states and distributed to the common people were the statutes. Did the statutes of the former kings ever say, 'Blessings cannot be sought, disasters cannot be avoided; reverence brings no advantage, viciousness no injury'?

The basis for hearing legal cases and regulating crime is the code of punishments. Did the code of punishments of the former kings ever say, 'Blessings cannot be sought, disasters cannot be avoided; reverence brings no advantage, viciousness no injury'?

The basis for organizing the army and commanding the troops to advance or retreat is the oaths. Did the oaths of the former kings ever say, 'Blessings cannot be sought, disasters cannot be avoided; reverence brings no advantage, viciousness no injury'?

Thus our master Mòzǐ stated, 'I haven't completely listed the excellent documents in the world, the number of which can't be exhaustively counted. Roughly sorted, they are of these three kinds. Now if we seek [in these documents] the statements of the fatalists, we don't surely find them. Is it not appropriate to give up looking?'

Now if we use the statements of the fatalists, this overturns the world's norms of righteousness. To overturn the world's norms of righteousness, this is to establish the doctrine of fate, the distress of the common people. Expounding a doctrine that brings distress to the common people,* this is destroying the people of the world. (35/12–19)

36.3 Now the fatalists state, 'It's not that we invented this in later eras. From the three dynasties in the past there have been similar statements that were passed down. Now why do you, Sir, oppose it?'*

[He] said, 'Now the fatalists, were they the sagely and good people of the three dynasties in the past? Or were they the vicious and unworthy people of the three dynasties in the past? How do we know? In the beginning, the ranked scholars and outstanding ministers were careful in their statements and wise in their conduct. By this, above there were the means to admonish their rulers; below, there were the means to instruct the common people. So, above, they won rewards from their ruler; below, they won praise from the common people. The reputation of the ranked scholars and outstanding ministers has never been cast aside, being passed down until today, and all the world says, "It was due to their effort." Surely they cannot say, "We see fate in this."' (36/13–18)

36.4* Thus, in the past, the tyrants of the three dynasties did not rectify the lusts of their ears and eyes and were not prudent about the proclivities of their heart and intention. Outside, they raced chariots and hunted; inside, they indulged in wine and music, disregarding the government of their state and the common people. They undertook scores of useless activities and were vicious and perverse to the common people, causing subordinates to be estranged from their superiors. Thus their states were ruined and their bodies were mutilated and executed. They were unwilling to say, 'I am weak and unworthy. I administered punishments and government badly.' Surely they said, 'My fate is fixed that I will perish.'

Even, in the past, the poor people of the three dynasties were also like this. Inside the family, they could not serve their parents well; outside in society, they could not serve their rulers well. They detested decorum and frugality and were fond of idleness and ease. They were greedy for food and drink but lazy in undertaking work. Their resources for clothing and food were insufficient, causing them to be troubled by hunger and cold. Surely they could not say, 'I am weak and unworthy. I didn't work urgently enough.' Surely they said, 'My fate was fixed that I would be poor.'*

Even, in the past, the charlatans of the three dynasties were also like this. They elaborately embellished the view that there is fate and taught it to the masses of foolish and simple people for a long time. The sage-kings were troubled by this, so they wrote about it on bamboo and silk and carved it into metal and stone. Among the documents of the former kings . . . the 'Great Oath' states so:

Zhòu was insolent and would not serve the Lord on High. He abandoned his ancestors' spirits and did not sacrifice to them. He said, 'My people have fate' and neglected his work. Heaven indeed abandoned him and did not protect him.*

This states that, as to Zhòu's holding there is fate, King Wǔ in the 'Great Oath' deemed it wrong . . . In the odes and documents of the Shāng and Xià, it says, 'As to fate, the tyrants invented it.' (36/18–30)

36.5 Moreover, now the officers and gentlemen of the world, if they desire to distinguish the reasons for right and wrong and benefit and harm, then as to holding that there is fate, they cannot fail to urgently deem this wrong. Holding that there is fate is a deep harm to the world. Thus our master Mòzǐ deems it wrong.* (36/30–1)

BOOK 37

CONDEMNING FATALISM (III)

37.1 Our master Mòzǐ stated, 'In all presenting of statements and discussion, one cannot fail to establish standards before making statements. If one doesn't establish standards before making statements, it is analogous to establishing sunrise and sunset on a potter's wheel. I take it that, although there is the distinction between sunrise and sunset, surely in the end they can never be determined. Thus statements have three models.'

What are called the 'three models'?

[He] said, 'There is its confirmation; there is its source; there is its use. How do we confirm it? Confirm it against the deeds of the former sages and great kings. How do we source it? Examine the facts the masses' ears hear and eyes see.* How do we use it? Issue it as government policy in the state, examine the myriad people and observe it.* These are called the "three models".'* (37/1–4)

37.2a So, in the past, the sage-kings of the three dynasties, Yǔ, Tāng, Wén, and Wǔ, when they first began to govern the world, said, 'We must diligently elevate filially devoted sons and encourage them to serve their parents; we must honour worthy and excellent people and instruct them to do good.' Thus they issued government policies and spread instructions, rewarded good and punished viciousness. Moreover, they took it that in this way the disorder in the world would become something that could be put in order and dangers to the altars of soil and grain would become something that could be settled.

If anyone takes this to not be so, in the past, what Jié disordered, Tāng put in order; what Zhòu disordered, King Wǔ put in order. At that time, the era didn't alter and the people didn't change; the superior switched government policies and the people reformed their customs. Living under Jié and Zhòu, the world was in disorder; living under Tāng and Wǔ the world was in order. The world's being in order was due to Tāng's and Wǔ's effort; the world's being in disorder was due to Jié's and Zhòu's crimes. If we look at things this way, security and danger, order and disorder lie in how superiors administer government; then how can one assert there is fate?!*

So, in the past, Yǔ, Tāng, Wén, and Wǔ, when they first began to govern the world, said, 'We must make the hungry get food, the cold get clothing, the weary get rest, and the disordered be put in order.' Consequently, they gained an honourable reputation and good name throughout the world. How can we take this to be due to their fate?! Certainly we take it to be due to their effort. Now worthy and excellent people honour the worthy and are accomplished in methods of the way, so, above, they get the rewards of their kings, dukes, and great men, while below, they get the praise of their myriad people, and consequently they gain an honourable reputation and good name throughout the world. In this case, too, how can we take this to be due to their fate?! Again, we take it to be due to effort.

That being so, now the fatalists, [I] wonder, were they the sagely and good people of the three dynasties in the past? Or were they the vicious and unworthy people of the three dynasties in the past? If we look at things on the basis of a persuasive explanation, surely they were not the sagely and good people of the three dynasties in the past. Surely they were the vicious and unworthy people. That being so, now those who hold there is fate, the tyrants of the three dynasties of the past, Jié, Zhòu, Yōu, and Lì, were so noble as to be Son of Heaven and so wealthy as to possess the world, and thus they could not correct the desires of their ears and eyes but instead followed the urges of their heart and intention. Outside, they raced chariots and hunted; inside, they indulged in wine and music, disregarding the government of their state and the common people. They undertook scores of useless activities and were vicious and perverse to the common people. Consequently, they lost their altars of soil and grain. In their statements, they did not say, 'I am weak and unworthy. In attending to government I didn't strive hard.' Surely they said, 'My fate was fixed that I would lose them.'

Even the weak and unworthy people of the three dynasties were also like this. They could not serve their parents and rulers well. They greatly detested decorum and frugality and were fond of idleness and ease. They were greedy for food and drink but lazy in undertaking work. Their resources for clothing and food were insufficient, and hence they were troubled by hunger and cold. In their statements, they did not say, 'I am weak and unworthy. In undertaking work I didn't strive hard.' Surely they said, 'My fate was fixed that I would be poor.'* The charlatans of the three dynasties in the past were also like this. (37/4–21)

35.4* That being so, then why desire righteousness to rule above? [We] say, 'When a righteous person rules above, the world is surely in order, the Lord on High and the ghosts and spirits of the mountains and rivers surely have a chief worshipper,* and the myriad people are greatly benefited.'

How do we know this?

Our master Mòzǐ said, 'In antiquity, Tāng was enfeoffed at Hào. Evening out the boundaries, his territory amounted to roughly a hundred square *lǐ*.* He and his common people inclusively cared about each other and in interaction benefited each other, and any surplus he shared. He led his common people to honour Heaven and serve the ghosts above, and hence Heaven and the ghosts enriched them, the various lords joined him, the common people regarded him as kin, and worthy officers turned to him. Before the end of his life, he reigned over the world and governed the various lords.

'In the past, King Wén was enfeoffed in Qízhōu. Evening out the boundaries, his territory amounted to roughly a hundred square *lǐ*. He and his common people inclusively cared about each other and in interaction benefited each other, and any surplus he shared. Hence the near were secure in his governance, while the distant turned to his virtue. Those who heard about King Wén all arose and hastened to him. The weak and unworthy and the disabled stayed where they were and wished for him, saying, "How can we make King Wén's territory extend to us, so we benefit? How could we not be King Wén's people too?" Hence Heaven and the ghosts enriched him, the various lords joined him, the common people regarded him as kin, and worthy officers turned to him. Before the end of his life, he reigned over the world and governed the various lords.

'Previously, [I] stated, "When a righteous person rules above, the world is surely in order, the Lord on High and the ghosts and spirits of the mountains and rivers surely have a chief worshipper, and the myriad people are greatly benefited." I use these cases to know it.'

Thus the ancient sage-kings issued statutes and presented decrees to set up rewards and punishments to encourage the worthy and discourage the vicious. Hence, entering the home, people were filially devoted and paternally kind to relatives, while going out, they were fraternal and respectful to the townspeople. In their daily habits, they were measured; in their comings and goings, they had moderation; in relations between men and women, they had proper distinctions.

Thus if employed to order government bureaus, they did not steal; to defend a city, they did not betray it. If the ruler encountered difficulty, they died for him; if he was exiled, they escorted him. This is what superiors rewarded and what the common people praised.

The statements of the fatalists say, 'Those whom superiors reward, fate fixes that they will be rewarded; it's not that they are worthy and so are rewarded. Those whom superiors punish, fate fixes that they will be punished; it's not that they are vicious and so are punished.' Thus, entering the home, people are not filially devoted and paternally kind to parents, while going out, they are not fraternal and respectful to the townspeople. In their daily habits, they are not measured; in their comings and goings, they lack moderation; in relations between men and women, they lack proper distinctions. Thus if employed to order government bureaus, they steal; to defend a city, they betray it. If the ruler encounters difficulty, they don't die for him; if he is exiled, they don't escort him. This is what superiors punish and what the common people denounce.* (35/19–33)

37.2b In the past, the tyrants initiated it and the poor people transmitted it, and this all sowed doubt among the masses and confounded the simple. As to the former sage-kings being troubled by this, it was indeed in a previous era. Hence they wrote it on bamboo and silk, engraved it on metal and stone, and inscribed it on dishes and bowls to pass down to their sons and grandsons in later generations.

[We] say, 'In what documents is it preserved?'

. . . In the statements of the 'Great Oath', the Crown Prince Fā* says:

Ah, my lords, Heaven has illustrious virtue; its conduct is brilliant. An example that reflects this is not far: it lies in the King of Yīn. He asserted people have fate, claimed that reverence could not be practised, asserted sacrifices were of no advantage, and asserted that viciousness brought no injury. The Lord on High did not aid him, and the nine realms were lost. The Lord on High did not approve and sent down his ruin. Only we, the Zhōu people, have received the empire from the great Lord on High.

In the past, King Zhòu of Yīn held there is fate and conducted himself accordingly. King Wǔ made the 'Great Oath' of the Crown Prince Fā to deem him wrong.

[We] say, 'Why don't you, above, confirm it against the records of the Shāng, Zhōu, and Yú Xià dynasties?* If among bundles of ten strips or more,* none have it,* what will you do?' (37/21–9)

37.3 Thus our master Mòzǐ said, 'Now as for the gentlemen of the world engaging in writing and studies and presenting statements and discussions, it's not to exercise their mouths or benefit their lips. It's that, within, they really desire to administer punishments and government for their state, town, and myriad people. Now why is it that kings, dukes, and great men go to court early and retire late, hearing legal cases and ordering government affairs, the whole day apportioning things fairly, not daring to be negligent?* [I] say, they take it that if they strive hard, there will surely be order, if they don't strive hard, there will surely be disorder; if they strive hard, there will surely be safety, if they don't strive hard, there will surely be danger; and so they dare not be negligent.

'Now why is it that secretaries and ministers exhaust the strength of their limbs and wear out the knowledge of their wits, inside, ordering the bureaus and, outside, collecting taxes from profits on passes, markets, forests, and fish weirs to fill the treasury, not daring to be negligent? [I] say, they take it that if they strive hard, they will surely be ennobled, if they don't strive hard, they will be commoners; if they strive hard, they will surely be honoured, if they don't strive hard, they will surely be humiliated; and so they dare not be negligent.

'Now why is it that farmers go out in the morning and come in at dusk, working hard at ploughing and sowing, planting and cultivating, harvesting many crops, not daring to be negligent? [I] say, they take it that if they strive hard, they will surely be wealthy, if they don't strive hard they will surely be poor; if they strive hard, they will surely be full, if they don't strive hard, they will surely be hungry; and so they dare not be negligent.

'Now why is it that women rise at dawn and sleep late at night, working hard at spinning and weaving, making much linen, silk, hemp, and other textiles, not daring to be negligent? [I] say, they take it that if they strive hard, they will surely be wealthy, if they don't strive hard, they will surely be poor; if they strive hard, they will surely be warm, if they don't strive hard, they will surely be cold; and so they dare not be negligent.

'Now if those among kings, dukes, and great men were to trust there is fate and thoroughly put this into practice, then surely they would be negligent in hearing legal cases and ordering government affairs; secretaries and ministers would surely be negligent in ordering the bureaus; farmers would surely be negligent in ploughing and sowing, planting and cultivating; women would surely be negligent in spinning and weaving. If kings, dukes, and great men are negligent in hearing legal cases and ordering government affairs, and secretaries and ministers are negligent in ordering the bureaus, then I take it the world will surely be in disorder. If farmers are negligent in ploughing and sowing, planting and cultivating, and women are negligent in spinning and weaving, then I take it the world's resources for clothing and food will surely be insufficient. If one adopts this as a policy for governing the world, above, serving Heaven and the ghosts with it, Heaven and the ghosts will not comply with our wishes; below, supporting the common people with it, the common people will not benefit and will surely scatter, such that a ruler cannot employ them. Hence entering to defend, one is not strong; emerging to punish, one is not victorious.* So even the tyrants of the three dynasties in the past, Jié, Zhòu, Yōu, and Lì, this was how their states were lost and their altars of soil and grain overturned.' (37/29–43)

37.4 Thus our master Mòzǐ stated, 'Now the officers and gentlemen of the world, if, within, they really desire to seek to promote the benefit of the world and eliminate harm to the world, as to statements such as those of the fatalists, they cannot fail to strongly deem them wrong.* [I] say, fate is the invention of the tyrants and the method of the impoverished. It's not the statement* of the benevolent. For those today who practise benevolence and righteousness, this is the reason they cannot fail to examine it and strongly deem it wrong.' (37/43–6)

PART III
CONDEMNING THE ERUDITES

39.1 The Erudites say, 'In treating kin as kin, there are methods; in honouring worthies, there are degrees.'* This states that there are differences between close and distant kin and between the honoured and the lowly. Their ceremonies say, 'At the loss of one's father or mother, three years of mourning; one's wife or eldest son, three years; for paternal uncles, elder and younger brothers, and other sons, one year; for other close relatives, five months.'

If the closeness or distance of the kinship determines the number of years and months, then close kin should have more and distant kin less. In these ceremonies, the wife and eldest son are the same as the father.* If honoured or low rank determines the number of years and months, then this is honouring their wife and son the same as their father and mother, and paternal uncles and brothers the same as younger sons. What could be more contrary than this?! (39/1–4)
. . .

39.4 Again, they strongly hold there is fate and expound contentions on this point, saying, 'Longevity or early death, poverty or wealth, security or danger, order or disorder are inherently fated by Heaven* and cannot be decreased or increased. Failure or success, reward or punishment, good fortune or bad have fixed limits. People's knowledge and effort cannot do anything about them.'*

If the various officials trust in this view, they will be neglectful in their apportioned duties. If the commoners trust in it, they will be neglectful in undertaking work. If officials don't order affairs, there will be disorder. If farm work is remiss, there will be poverty. Poverty and disorder are contrary to the foundation* of government, yet the Erudites take them to be the teachings of the way. These are men who injure the people of the world. (39/10–13)

39.5 Moreover, they elaborately embellish ceremonies and music to corrupt people; they practise prolonged mourning and fake grief to deceive parents. They establish the doctrine of fate, are remiss about poverty, and prize arrogance; they turn their backs on fundamentals, abandon work, and rest in idleness and complacency. They are greedy for food and drink but lazy in performing tasks. Falling victim to hunger and cold, endangered by freezing and starvation, they lack any means of avoiding them. They scrounge like beggars and hoard food like field rats, while staring like buck goats and jumping up like castrated pigs. When gentlemen laugh at them, they are furious, saying, 'Worthless people! How would you know a good Erudite?!'

In spring and summer, they beg for grain. Once the five grains are harvested, large funerals follow, and their sons and grandsons all come along to eat and drink their fill. Managing several funerals gives them enough to live on. They rely on others' families to become fat and depend on others' fields for their honour. When wealthy people have a funeral, they are overjoyed, delightedly saying, 'This is the source of clothing and food.'* (39/13–17)

39.6 The Erudites say, 'The gentleman must be ancient in his speech and attire,* only then can he be benevolent.'

Answer them by saying, 'What's called ancient speech and attire all were once new, and so when ancient people spoke it and wore it, they were not gentlemen. That being so, then must one wear the attire of non-gentlemen and speak the speech of non-gentlemen and only then be benevolent?' (39/17–19)

39.7 Again, they say, 'The gentleman follows and doesn't initiate.'*

Answer them by saying, 'In antiquity, Yì invented the bow, Shù invented armour, Xī Zhòng invented carts, and Artisan Chuí invented boats. That being so, then are today's tanners, armourers, cartwrights, and artisans all gentlemen, while Yì, Shù, Xī Zhòng, and Artisan Chuí are all petty people? Moreover, whatever they [the Erudites] follow, someone must have invented it. That being so, then what they follow is all the way of petty people.' (39/19–21)

39.8 Again, they say, 'The gentleman in victory doesn't pursue those fleeing, doesn't shoot arrows at those who have thrown off their armour, and, if they have fallen dead or wounded, helps put them into a cart.'*

Answer them by saying, 'If they are all benevolent people, then there is no good explanation for why they would join together in battle. Benevolent people inform each other of the patterns by which they select or reject, deem right or deem wrong. Those who lack a reason follow those who have a reason. Those who don't know something follow those who have knowledge. Lacking remarks to offer in their defence, they surely submit; seeing good, they surely reform. Why would they join together in battle?

'If two vicious parties fight with each other and the victors desire not to pursue the fleeing, not to shoot at those who have thrown off their armour, and, if they've fallen, to help them into a cart, even if they do so to the best of their ability, this still doesn't make them gentlemen. Or suppose one side is a violent, cruel state, and a sage is eliminating harm on behalf of the world by deploying his army to punish them. Winning a victory, he uses the Erudites' method and commands his soldiers, saying, "Don't pursue the fleeing, don't shoot at those who've thrown off their armour, and, if they've fallen, help them into a cart." Then vicious and disorderly people survive and the harm to the world is not eliminated. This is to inflict cruelty on the masses of fathers and mothers and is a deep injury to the world. No unrighteousness is greater than this.' (39/21–6)

39.9 Again, they say, 'The gentleman is like a bell. When struck, he chimes; when not struck, he doesn't chime.'

Answer them by saying, 'Benevolent people in serving their superiors are utterly loyal and in serving their parents strive to be filially devoted. When those they serve achieve good, they praise them; when they commit errors, they counsel them. This is the way by which to act as someone's subject.

'Now when struck, he chimes, when not struck, he doesn't chime—this is concealing knowledge and reserving strength, silently and indifferently waiting to be asked before replying. Even if there is great benefit to his ruler or parents, if they don't ask, he doesn't speak. Things like a large bandit attack about to occur and robbers and thieves about to spring up, like a crossbow bolt about to shoot—other people don't know, he alone knows it, but even though his ruler and parents are all present, if they don't ask, he doesn't speak—such a person is a criminal who causes great disorder. Acting as someone's subject in this way is disloyal; acting as a son this way is unfilial; serving elder brothers this way is unfraternal; interacting with acquaintances in this way is dishonourable and indecent.'. . . (39/26–31)

. . .

39.12 Confucius went to Qí and had an audience with Duke Jǐng. Duke Jǐng was pleased. He desired to enfeoff him in Ní Xī and reported this to Yànzǐ.*

Yànzǐ said, 'It's unacceptable. The Erudites are arrogant and follow only themselves, so they cannot instruct subordinates. They are fond of music and corrupt others, so they cannot be employed to personally order affairs. They establish the doctrine of fate and neglect work, so they cannot be made responsible for an office. They exalt funerals and prolong grief, so they cannot be employed to show kindness to the people. They wear strange attire and have a forced demeanour, so they cannot be employed to guide the masses.

'With his imposing demeanour and elaborate adornment, Confucius confuses the world; by singing to strings and dancing to drums, he gathers followers; with a profusion of rituals for ascending and descending stairs, he makes a display of ceremony; by devoting himself to the etiquette of scurrying and swirling he puts on a show for the masses.

'His broad studies cannot be employed to debate current events; his laboured thoughts cannot be used to assist the people. Several lifetimes would not be enough to complete all his studies; the prime of life would not be enough to perform all his rituals; no fortune would be enough to fund all his music.

'He elaborately embellishes dissolute methods to confuse the rulers of the age and extravagantly performs singing and music to corrupt foolish people. His way cannot be declared to the world; his studies cannot be used to guide the masses. Now my Lord enfeoffs him to benefit the customs of Qí; this is not how to guide the state and lead the masses.'

The Duke said, 'Good.' Hence he treated Confucius with rich ceremony but withheld his fief. He respectfully gave him audiences but did not ask about his way. . . . (39/44–51)

. . .

39.14 When Confucius was stranded between the states of Cài and Chén,* the soup of wild greens had no grain mixed in.* After ten days, his disciple Zǐlù boiled a suckling pig for him. Confucius ate it without asking where the meat came from. Zǐlù robbed someone's clothing to buy wine. Confucius drank it without asking where the wine came from.

When Duke Āi of Lǔ received Confucius, if his mat was not straight, he did not sit on it; if his meat was not cut properly, he did not eat it.*

Zǐlù came forward and asked, 'Why are you the opposite of the time at Chén and Cài?'

Confucius said, 'Come, I will tell you. Then, we were just trying to stay alive; now, we are just trying to be righteous.'

Now when starving and stranded, he did not refuse to take things unscrupulously to keep himself alive; when he could eat his fill, he conducted himself hypocritically to make himself look good. What vileness and deceit are greater than this? (39/55–9)

. . .

PART IV
THE DIALECTICS

A1

Canon: A reason/cause* is what must be obtained before something is completed/brought about.

Explanation: (Reason/cause.) Minor reason/cause—having it, something is not surely so; lacking it, something surely is not so. As to a unit/part, like having a tip. Major reason/cause—having it, something surely is so. Like coming into view [to an observer] completing seeing.*

A2

Canon: A unit/part is a division from a whole.

Explanation: (Unit/part.) Like one of two or the tip of a measured foot.*

A3

Canon: The knowing is the capacity.*

Explanation: (Knowing, capacity.) As to the knowing, it's that by which we know, such that we surely know. Like eyesight.*

A4

Canon: Considering is seeking.

Explanation: (Considering.) Considering* is, by means of the knowing, seeking something without necessarily getting it. Like peering.

A5

Canon. Knowing is connecting.

Explanation. (Knowing.) Knowing* is, by means of the knowing, passing something and being able to describe its features. Like seeing.

A6

Canon: Knowledge is understanding/clarity.

Explanation: (Knowledge.) Knowledge* is, by means of the knowing, discoursing on things such that one's knowing them is obvious. Like clear sight.

A7*

Canon: Benevolence is care for units/parts.

Explanation: (Benevolence.*) As to caring about oneself, it's not for the sake of using oneself. Not like caring about a horse.

A8

Canon: Righteousness is benefit.

Explanation: (Righteousness.) In intent, one takes all the world as one's portion, while in ability, one is able to benefit them. These are not necessarily used.*

A9

Canon: Ceremonial propriety is respect.

Explanation: (Ceremonial propriety.) The noble being called 'Sir', the common being called by their names, in both cases there are respect and rudeness. For various ranks to be treated differently is sorting/ranking.*

A10

Canon: Conduct is acting/doing.

Explanation: (Conduct.) What one does, without applying a fine name, is conduct. What one does, applying a fine name, is deviousness. Like being a robber.*

A11

Canon: Sincerity is honour/display.

Explanation: (Sincerity.) The display of one's intent and breath (*qi*) makes others know one. Not like metal tinkling or jade-embellished garments.*

A12

Canon: Loyalty is, taking something to be beneficial, strongly* . . .

Explanation: [Omitted.]

A13

Canon: Filial devotion is benefiting parents.

Explanation: (Filial devotion.) Taking one's parents as one's portion, in ability, one is able to benefit one's parents. One does not necessarily succeed.*

A14

Canon: Trustworthiness is statements matching with thought/ intention.

Explanation: [Omitted.]

A15–A18* [Omitted.]

A19

Canon: Bearing responsibility is an officer acting to his own loss but to the gain of those for whom he works.

Explanation: (Bearing responsibility.) He does what he himself detests in order to bring about what others urgently need.

A20

Canon: Courage is that by which the intent dares.

Explanation: (Courage.) On the basis of their daring to do this, one commands them; one does not, on the basis of their not daring to do that, harm them.

A21*

Canon: Strength is that by which the body/form exerts itself.

Explanation: (Strength.) It refers to weight. Lifting weight from below is exertion.

A22

Canon: Life is body/form located together with the knowing.*

Explanation: [Omitted.]*

A23

Canon: Sleep is the knowing having no knowing.*

Explanation: (None.)

A24

Canon: Dreaming is sleeping and taking things to be so.*

Explanation: (None.)

A25

Canon: Calm is the knowing not desiring or detesting anything.

Explanation: [Omitted.]

A26

Canon: Benefit is what one is pleased to get.

Explanation: (Benefit.) If one is pleased to get this, then this is benefit. The harm is not this.

A27

Canon: Harm is what one detests getting.

Explanation: (Harm.) If one detests getting this, then this is harm. The benefit is not this.

A28

Canon: Order/control/governance is getting what is sought.

Explanation: (Order.) Our affairs having been put in order, others also put in order north and south.*

A29

Canon: To praise is to clarify the beautiful/admirable.

Explanation: [Omitted.]

A30

Canon: To condemn is to clarify the ugly/detestable.

Explanation: [Omitted.]

A31

Canon: To mention/cite/bring up is to emulate objects.*

Explanation: (Mention/cite/bring up.) To inform is to use this name to mention that object.* So . . . for what is similar to stone [?] . . . use a similar name [?].

A32

Canon: To state is to utter mentions.*

Explanation: (To state.) Stating is the uttering of features of which all speakers are capable. Describing features is like drawing a tiger, but it is a statement. Saying statements—like 'stone'—is communicating.

A33

Canon: About to/will states what is about to be so.

Explanation: (About to/will.) From beforehand, we say 'about to'. From afterwards, we say 'already'. Just as it is so is also 'about to'.

A34*

Canon: The ruler is the connecting pact between ministers and the people.

Explanation: (None.)

A35

Canon: Achievement/merit is benefiting the people.

Explanation: (Achievement/merit.) It does not depend on the timing. Like clothing.*

A36

Canon: Reward is superiors repaying subordinates' achievement/merit.

Explanation: (Reward.) Superiors repaying subordinates' achievement/merit.*

A37

Canon: Crime is violating prohibitions.

Explanation: (Crime.) If not included in a prohibition, even if it is harmful, there is no crime.

A38

Canon: Punishment is superiors repaying subordinates' crimes.

Explanation: (Punishment.) Superiors repaying subordinates' crimes.*

A39*

Canon: The same is being different yet both being one in relation to something.

Explanation: (Same.) They are two people yet both see this pillar. Like serving a ruler.*

A40

Canon: Duration is pervading different times.

Explanation: (Duration.) Present and past contain morning and evening.

A41

Canon: Space is pervading different places.

Explanation: (Space.) East and west cover south and north.

A42

Canon: A limit is there being somewhere where, going forward, there is no room for a measured foot.*

Explanation: (Limit.) If somewhere there is no room for a measured foot, there is a limit. If everywhere there is room for a measured foot, there is no limit.

A43

Canon: All/completely/covering is none are not so.

Explanation: (All/completely/covering.) All stop moving.

A44

Canon: Starting is coinciding with the time.

Explanation: (Starting.) As to time, some has duration, some is durationless. Starting coincides with the durationless.*

A45

Canon: Transformation is the characteristics being exchanged.

Explanation: (Transformation.) Like a frog becoming a quail.

A46

Canon: Loss/decrease is part being removed.

Explanation: (Loss/decrease.) Part is a unit/part of a whole. Some of its units/parts being removed and some remaining, we say the remaining ones have suffered a loss/decrease.

A47*

Canon: To circle around . . .*

Explanation: (To circle.) Its features form a curve.

A48

Canon: To rotate is to change [direction?].

Explanation: (To rotate.) A demarcated hollow . . . the features are constant [?].*

A49

Canon: Movement is some part moving.

Explanation: [Omitted.]

A50

Canon: Staying/stopping/settling is with duration.

Explanation: (Staying/stopping/settling.) Durationless non-staying, something fits 'ox' and 'non-horse'.* Like a man passing a pillar. Non-staying with duration, something fits 'horse' and 'non-horse'.* Like a man passing over a bridge.

A51

Canon: Surely/definitely/must is unending.

Explanation: (Surely/definitely/must.) . . . Like younger brother and elder brother, one being so and one being not so—these are what is surely the case and what is not surely the case. This or not is surely the case.*

A52*

Canon: Level/flat is the same height.

Explanation: (None.)

A53

Canon: The same length is, when aligned straight, covering each other.

Explanation: (Same.) The same lengths of the door-bar and door-frame are straight.

A54

Canon: Centre is the same length.*

Explanation: (Centre.) Setting out from this, [the distance] is equal.

A55

Canon: Thickness/dimension is having size.

Explanation: (Thickness/dimension.) Only the dimensionless* has no size.

A 56

Canon: The sun at the centre (noon) is directly south.

Explanation: (None.)

A 57

Canon: Straight is in alignment.

Explanation: (None.)

A 58

Canon: Circular is from one centre, the same lengths.

Explanation: (Circular.) The compass draws . . .*

A 59

Canon: Square is four sides and angles balancing [?].*

Explanation: (Square.) The set square shows . . .*

A 60

Canon: Doubling is making two.

Explanation: (Doubling.) Two is measured foot and measured foot both departing from one.*

A 61

Canon: A tip is what, of a unit/part, is without thickness/dimension and is furthest front.

Explanation: (Tip.) This is not the same as anything.*

A 62

Canon: Having an interval/gap is not reaching the centre.

Explanation: (Having an interval/gap.) It refers to it being flanked.

A 63

Canon: An interval is not reaching the sides.

Explanation: (Interval.) It refers to the flanked . . .*

A 64

Canon: A lintel [?] is the interval being empty.*

Explanation: (Lintel.) [?] As to empty, of the interval between two pieces of wood, it refers to where there is no wood.

A65

Canon: To fill/filled is nowhere not present.

Explanation: (To fill/filled.) What does not fill is dimensionless. Along a measured foot, there is nowhere you can go and not find two.*

A66

Canon: Hard-white* is not excluding each other.

Explanation: (Hard.) Different locations do not fill each other. Not each other, this is excluding each other.*

A67

Canon: Touching/coinciding is obtaining each other.

Explanation: (Touching/coinciding.) Of a measured foot and a measured foot, neither fully covers the other. Of a tip and a tip, both fully cover each other. Of a measured foot and a tip, one is fully covered and one is not fully covered. Hard and white in coinciding fully cover each other. Units/parts in coinciding do not fully cover each other.*

A68

Canon: Side by side/measured against each other is having part that coincides with each other and part that does not coincide with each other.

Explanation: (Side by side.) It is possible only if the two have [the same?] tip.*

A69

Canon: Next/adjacent is having no interval but not coinciding.

Explanation: (Next/adjacent.) It is possible only if it is dimensionless.*

A70

Canon: A model is what, things being like it, they are so.*

Explanation: (Model.) Thought/intention, compass, and circle are three.* All can be used as models.

A71

Canon: The match/duplicate is wherein it's so.*

Explanation: (Match/duplicate.) Being so is the features being like the model.

A72

Canon: Explanations* are that by which one clarifies/understands.

Explanation: (None.)

A73

Canon: As to that/other, it's impermissible for both to be impermissible.*

Explanation: (That/other.) In all cases, demarcating oxen from non-oxen makes two. If something lacks the basis,* it is not it.

A74

Canon: Disputation/argument/distinction-drawing is contending over that/other. Winning in disputation is fitting.

Explanation: (Disputation*/argument/distinction-drawing.) One calls it 'ox', one calls it 'non-ox'; this is contending over that/other. These do not both fit. Not both fitting, surely one does not fit. Not like fitting 'hound'.

A75

Canon: To act for the sake of/to take as an end is to weigh one's desires, having reached the limit of one's knowledge.

Explanation: (Act for the sake of/have as an end.) Desiring to cut off one's finger, if one's knowledge does not know the harm, this is one's knowledge being at fault. If, one's knowledge considering it and overlooking none of the harm in it, one still desires to cut it off, then one removes it.*

This is like eating dried meat. The benefit or harm of the flavour being unknown, if one desires it and tastes the flavour, this is not taking what one is unsure about as a basis for stopping what one desires.

The benefit or harm of what is beyond the wall being unknowable in advance, supposing that by going there one gets money, then if one does not go there, this is taking what one is unsure about as a basis for stopping what one desires.*

Observing the pattern of 'acting for the sake of something is weighing one's desires, having reached the limit of one's knowledge', eating the dried meat is not knowledge, and cutting off one's finger is not ignorance. When what one acts for the sake of and what one does not act for the sake of render each other unsure, this is failing to plan.

A76*

Canon: To end/finish. To complete, to eliminate.

Explanation: (End/finish.) Of making a coat, to complete. Of curing an illness, to eliminate.

A77

Canon: To employ/cause. To say. The cause.*

Explanation: (Employ/cause.) To order is to say. It is not necessarily completed/brought about.* Dampness is a cause. It depends on the completion of what it brings about.*

A78

Canon: Names. All-reaching, kind, personal.*

Explanation: Names. 'Thing' is an all-reaching name. Any object must take this name. Naming it 'horse' is a kind name. For what is similar to the object, one must use this name. Naming him 'John' is a personal name. This name stops in this object.* When sounds are uttered by speakers, they all consist of names.* Like surname and style-name.

A79

Canon: Saying/asserting. Transferring, mentioning, applying.*

Explanation: (Saying/asserting.) Linking 'dog' and 'hound' is naming.* 'Dog', 'hound' is mentioning. Scolding a dog is applying.*

A80

Canon: Knowing. By hearsay, by explanation, personal.* Names, objects, matching, acting.*

Explanation: (Knowing.) Receiving it when passed on is 'by hearsay'. Distance does not obstruct is 'by explanation'.* Observing it oneself is 'personal'. That by which we say/assert is names. What we say/assert about is objects. Names and objects mating is matching.* Proceeding with intent is acting.

A81

Canon: Hearing. Passed along, in person.*

Explanation: (Hearing.) Someone informs one of it is 'passed on'. Observing it oneself is 'personal'.

A82

Canon: Seeing. Units/parts, all.*

Explanation: (Seeing.) Only one is a unit/part. Two are all.

A83

Canon: Matching/uniting. Exact/direct, appropriate/fitting, surely/definitely.*

Explanation: (Matching/uniting.) Standing side by side, the opposite or coinciding, intent and achievement—these are exact/direct. What John is deemed to be—this is fitting/appropriate. Without that, it surely does not exist—this is surely/definitely. As to the sages, use them but do not treat them as definite/for sure. As to what is definite/for sure, it is permissible to not doubt. Converses, apply both without being one-sided.*

A84

Canon: Desire/want/be about to. Direct/exact, weighing benefits, about to. Detesting. Direct/exact, weighing harms.*

Explanation: (None.)

A85

Canon: Make/do/become/deem. Preserve, eliminate, exchange, dissolve, order/manage, transform.*

Explanation: [Omitted.]

A86

Canon: Same. Identity/overlap/doubling, unit/part, united, kind.*

Explanation: (Same.) Two names for one object is the same in being identical/overlapping/doubling. Not being external to a whole is the same in being parts [of the same thing]. Both together in a room is the same in being united. Having that by which they're the same is the same in being the same kind.

A87

Canon: Different. Two, not parts, not united, not of a kind.

Explanation: (Different.) Two surely being different is being two. Not connected or belonging is not being parts. Not being in the same place is not being united. Not having something the same is being different kinds.

A88–A92* [Omitted.]

A93*

Canon: Agreement is not one/identical in benefit and use.

Explanation: (Agreement.) When going beyond the wall, the circle stops. Of what follows from or excludes each other, knowing beforehand that something is 'this' is permissible/possible. The five colours, long and short, before and after, light and heavy—cite what is held.

A94

Canon: Submit to what is held . . . if there is a devious turn, then seek the reason for it.

Explanation: (Submit.) If it is difficult to establish a statement, yet one must establish it . . . then seek the model by which [the opponent?] holds [his assertion?].*

A95

Canon: If the model is the same, then observe what is the same in it.*

Explanation: (Model.) Select what is the same and observe devious turns.

A96

Canon: If the model is different, then observe what is appropriate in it.

Explanation: (Model.) Select this and choose that, ask about reasons and observe what is appropriate. On the basis of a person's having something black or something not black, settle 'black person', and on the basis of one's caring about people or not caring about people, settle 'caring about people'. Of these, which is appropriate?*

A97

Canon: Settle the basis in order to separate ways.*

Explanation: (Settle/stop.) If the other side mentions/cites what is so as grounds for taking this one to be so, then mention/cite what is not so and ask about it. Like the sage having features that are not/wrong without not being a sage.*

A98

Canon: Exact is having nothing that is not it.*

158 *The Essential* Mòzǐ

Explanation: (Exact.) . . . When there is an explanation [to support doing so], one goes beyond the agreement that the object matches [the model]—like a circle being nowhere straight—and when there is no explanation [to support doing so], one uses the agreement . . .*

B1

Canon: Settle the kind in order to let the other* proceed. Explained by:* sameness.

Explanation: (Settle/stop.) The other side takes something being so of this one as grounds for explaining/contending that this kind is so. I take something being not so of this one as grounds for doubting this kind is so.*

B2

Canon: Calling/asserting/saying . . . the difficulty of extending kinds. Explained by: [settling the scope of the kind as?] larger or smaller and things all being so.*

Explanation: (Calling/asserting/saying.) If four footed, is it a beast? If a living thing, is it a bird? Things all being so and [the scope being] larger or smaller.* If, this one being so, this kind is surely so, then all are milu deer.*

B3* [Omitted.]

B4

Canon: They cannot be partially removed yet are two.* Explained by: seeing and coming into view, one and two, breadth and length.

Explanation: (Not.) Seeing and coming into view are separate [?]. One and two do not fill each other. Breadth and length are hard-white.*

B5 [Omitted.]

B6

Canon: Different kinds are not comparable. Explained by: measuring/amount.*

Explanation: (Different.) Wood and night, which is longer? Knowledge and grain, which is more? Noble rank, parents, conduct, or a price, which is more valuable? A milu deer or a crane, which is higher? . . .

B7

Canon: Part being removed, there is no reduction. Explained by: the reason/cause.

Explanation: (Part.) There is no change in their being together as one.*

B8

Canon: Borrowing [names] surely leads to perversity/contradiction.* Explained by: not being so.

Explanation: (Borrowing.) In borrowing [names], the thing must be not [the kind normally referred to by that name], only then do we borrow [a name]. Borrowing 'crane' for dogs, it's like being surnamed 'Crane'.*

B9

Canon: That by which things are so, and that by which we know them, and that by which we make others know them are not necessarily the same. Explained by: illness.

Explanation: (Things.) Something injures it is it's being so. Seeing it is knowing. Informing them is making them know.

B10

Canon: Doubt. Explained by: accident, following, encountering, passing.*

Explanation: (Doubt.) Encountering fog, one takes a person to be an ox; someone staying in a cottage is cold in the summer—accident.* Lifting something light or dropping something heavy is not having strength; shaving wood along the grain is not skill—like stone and feathers—following.* Whether the fighter's collapse was from drinking wine or from the noon sun, this cannot be known—encountering.* Is it knowledge? Or is it taking what has already ended to be so?—having passed.*

B11

Canon: United together or one thing, in one case compound, in the other not. Explained by: demarcating.*

Explanation: (None.)

B12

Canon: Demarcated things form one unit/part.* Explained by: together as one and being this.

Explanation: (Demarcated.) 'Together as one' is like oxen and horses being four-footed. 'Being this' is fitting 'ox' or 'horse'. Counting oxen and counting horses, oxen and horses are two. Counting oxen and horses, oxen and horses are one. Like counting fingers, the fingers are five but the five are one.*

B13

Canon: Space moves somewhere. Explained by: growth.

Explanation: (Space.) In growing one moves, yet there is a place one is located in space.*

B14

Canon: Space and duration are not hard-white. Explained by . . . [missing text].

Explanation: (Space.) South and north are present both in the morning and in the evening. Space moves with duration.*

B15

Canon: The durationless and space are hard-white. Explained by: the cause/basis.

Explanation: (Durationless.) When hard combines with white they must fill each other.*

B16

Canon: Locating it where it is so or yet to be so. Explained by: at this [time].

Explanation: (Locating.) Yao is good at governing—this is from the present standpoint locating it in the past.* If from a past standpoint one located it in the present, then Yao is not able to govern.*

B17–B29* [Omitted.]

B30*

Canon: In buying, there is no such thing as too expensive. Explained by: the converse of the price.

Explanation: (Buying.) Coin and grain are each other's price. If the coin is light, then the grain is not expensive; if the coin is heavy, then the grain is not exchanged.* The king's coin not altering but the grain for sale altering, if the harvest alters the grain for sale, the harvest alters the coin.* Like selling off children.*

B31

Canon: The price being appropriate, it sells. Explained by: all.

Explanation: (Price.) 'All' is completely removing that by which it doesn't sell.* Removing that by which it doesn't sell, it sells for exactly the right price.* Whether the price is appropriate or not corresponds exactly to whether people desire it or not. Like the people of a defeated state selling off houses and marrying off daughters.

B32

Canon: Without an explanation, one fears. Explained by: it not being sure.

Explanation: (Without.) One's son serving in the army, one cannot take it as sure whether he is dead or alive. Hearing of a battle, again one cannot take it as sure that he is alive. If previously one did not fear, now one fears.

B33 [Omitted.]

B34

Canon: It's perverse to hold that knowing whether one knows it or not is enough for practical use. Explained by: lacking the basis.

Explanation: (Knowledge.) When discoursing on it, if it's not the case that one knows it, one lacks the basis.*

B35

Canon: Saying that in disputation there is no winning surely does not fit [the facts]. Explained by: disputation.

Explanation: (Saying/asserting.) The things something is called are either the same or different. In a case when they're the same, one side calls it 'dog', the other calls it 'hound'; in a case when they're different, one side calls it 'ox', the other calls it 'horse'.* Both not winning, this is not disputation. Disputation is when one side calls it 'this', the other calls it 'not', and the one that fits wins.*

B36

Canon: Deferring in everything is impermissible. Explained by: the start.

Explanation: (Nothing.) The start is the time before the deferring person yields the wine to the other person. It cannot be deferred.*

B37

Canon: In one thing, there is something known and there is something not known. Explained by: being present in it.

Explanation: (In.) The stone is one. Hard and white are two that are located in the stone. So it is permissible that there be something known in it and something not known in it.*

B38 [Omitted.]

B39

Canon: What one knows but cannot point to. Explained by: spring, a runaway servant, dogs and hounds, something missing.*

Explanation: (What.) Spring—its tendencies inherently cannot be pointed out. A runaway servant—not knowing his location. Dogs and hounds—not knowing their name. What is missing—cleverness cannot make them two.

B40

Canon: Knowing dogs while oneself saying one doesn't know hounds is an error. Explained by: identity/overlap/doubling.

Explanation: (Knowing.) If knowing dogs is identical to/overlaps with knowing hounds, then it's an error. If not identical/overlapping, then it's not an error.*

B41

Canon: Connect the thought/intention and only then reply. Explained by: not knowing what he refers to.*

Explanation. (Connect.) The questioner says, 'Do you know borogoves?'* Respond to him, saying, 'What does "borogove" refer to?' If he says, 'Borogoves are birds', then you know them. If you do not ask what 'borogove' refers to and directly respond that you don't know them, this is an error. Moreover, in responding you must respond to the timing of the question, as when the response is long. Among responses there are deep and shallow . . .

B42* [Omitted.]

B43

Canon: The five processes have no regular pattern of overcoming each other.* Explained by: what fits the situation.

Explanation: (Five.) . . . When fire melts metal, it's that the fire is larger; when metal outlasts the charcoal, it's that the amount of metal is greater. . . .

B44

Canon: Whether lacking desires and dislikes is an advantage or a loss. Explained by: what fits the situation.

Explanation: (Lacking.) Desires and dislikes injure life and reduce one's lifespan—if one takes this as grounds to advocate reducing connections to things, who is this caring about? Eating too much, one desires not to have some of it, as it can injure one. Like how wine affects people. Yet if wise people's care is directed at benefiting others, then although wise they do not control it.*

B45

Canon: There being a loss poses no obstacle. Explained by: surplus.

Explanation: (Loss.) Those who've eaten their fill discarding the surplus poses no obstacle to their having enough, though it could interfere with their being full [?].* Like an injured milu deer missing a haunch.* Moreover, there are cases of gaining an advantage only after first suffering a loss. Like how severe malaria affects malaria.*

B46

Canon: Knowing but not by means of the five routes. Explained by: duration.

Explanation: (Knowing.) The knower sees by means of the eye and the eye sees by means of the fire but the fire does not see. If one could know only by means of the five routes, then after a duration knowledge would cease to fit the facts. Seeing by means of the eye is like seeing by means of the fire.*

B47

Canon: Fire is hot.* Explained by . . .

Explanation: (Fire.) If we say fire is hot, it's not taking the fire's heat to be something we possess. Like looking at the sun.

B48

Canon: Knowing what one doesn't know. Explained by: using the name to select it.

Explanation: (Knowing.) If we mix what someone knows and what he doesn't know and ask him, then he must say, 'This is what I know; this is what I don't know.' Being able both to select some things and to reject others, this is knowing both of them.*

B49

Canon: Absence/not-existence/nothing does not necessarily depend on presence/existence/something. Explained by: what's referred to.

Explanation: (Absence.) If there is none of it, first there was some and then not. As to there being no cases of the sky falling, there were none and there are none.*

B50 [Omitted.]

B51

Canon: What is about to be so cannot be corrected, yet this poses no obstacle to applying effort. Explained by: what fits the situation.

Explanation: (About to be.) What is about to be so must be so; what is about to end must end; as to what is about to end only after applying effort, it must end only after applying effort.*

B52 [Omitted.]

B53

Canon: The sage-king Yáo's being an exemplar arises in the present yet is located in the past, these being different times.* Explained by: what's taken as an exemplar* being two.

Explanation: (Yáo.) . . . cranes,* in some cases one uses names to show people; in some cases one uses objects to show people. Mentioning/citing one's friend as a wealthy merchant, this is using names to show people. Pointing to this as a crane, this is using objects to show people. Yáo's being an exemplar, this spoken sound is in the present, while the object taken as an exemplar is located in the past . . .*

B54

Canon: Dogs are hounds, yet 'killing dogs is not killing hounds' is permissible. Explained by: identity/overlap/doubling.

Explanation: (Dogs.) Dogs are hounds. Calling it 'killing hounds' is permissible. Like two haunches.*

B55, B56 [Omitted.]

B57

Canon: Taking pillars to be round, in what one takes it to be one knows beforehand. Explained by: the thought/intention.

Explanation: (Taking.) The pillars being round, on seeing them, they're unchanged from the thought, because we know beforehand the form that is intended/thought. If the pillars are lighter than catalpa wood, this feature is indeterminate in the thought/intention.*

B58

Canon: The thought/intention of hammers can't be known in advance. Explained by: being usable, going beyond a match.

Explanation: (Hammer.) Anvil and hammer both being used to work on shoes—this is 'being usable'. Completing embroidered shoes goes beyond the hammer, just as completing a hammer goes beyond embroidered shoes—this is 'going beyond a match'.*

B59 [Omitted.]

B60

Canon: If one hoes only by half at a time, then one doesn't move.* Explained by: the tip/starting point.

Explanation: (Not.) Advancing by hoeing half is taking from the front. If we take from the front, the centre doesn't make half; it is still the starting point.* If we take from the front and back, the starting point is the centre.* If hoeing must be by half, there being nothing remaining that isn't half, one cannot hoe.

B61 [Omitted.]

B62 [Omitted.]

B63

Canon: Space, in advancing there's no getting nearer to it. Explained by: covering/spreading.

Explanation: (Space.) Demarcating it, one cannot mention/cite only one part—that is space. Someone advancing through it first covers the near and then covers the far.*

B64

Canon: Travelling a distance takes up duration. Explained by: at first and later.

Explanation: (Travelling.) Someone travelling must first be near and only later far. Far or near is distance. At first and later is duration. People travelling a distance must take up duration.

B65

Canon: The relating to each other of things that are one with a model is complete. Like the matching each other of squares. Explained by: squares.

Explanation: (One.) The square features being complete, each being like the model but different, some wood and some stone, poses no obstacle to their square shape matching each other. The features being complete—like square—things are each so.*

B66

Canon: By wild mentioning/citing, one cannot know differences. Explained by: having.

Explanation: (Wild.) Although oxen and horses are different, it is impermissible to use oxen having teeth and horses having tails to explain that oxen are not horses. These they both have; it's not that one side has them and one side lacks them. To say, 'Oxen and horses are not of a kind', and appeal to oxen having horns and horses lacking horns, in this the kinds are not the same. If you mention/cite oxen having horns and horses lacking horns, and take this to be [how] the kinds are not the same, this is wild mentioning/citing, like oxen having teeth and horses having tails.*

B67

Canon. Deeming impermissible oxen-and-horses being non-oxen and deeming it permissible are the same.* Explained by: whole/aggregate.

Explanation. (Not.) If it's permissible that, some being non-oxen, they are non-oxen, then it's permissible that, some being non-oxen and some oxen, they are oxen.* Therefore, if saying 'oxen-and-horses are non-oxen' is not permissible and 'oxen-and-horses are oxen' is not permissible, then treating one [of those two claims] as permissible and the other as impermissible and so saying ' "oxen-and-horses are oxen" is not permissible' is also impermissible. Moreover, if, oxen not being two and horses not being two, oxen-and-horses are two, then without oxen being non-oxen or horses being non-horses, there's no difficulty in oxen-and-horses being non-oxen and non-horses.

B68

Canon: Reversing 'that' and 'this' is the same as deeming them 'that' and 'this'. Explained by: difference.*

Explanation: (That.) For those who correct names to reverse 'that' and 'this' is permissible. If their deeming that 'that' stops in that or this 'this' stops in this, reversing 'that' and 'this' is impermissible.* If that is to be 'this', reversing 'that' and 'this' is indeed permissible. 'That' and 'this' stopping in that and this, if in this case they are reversed, then that is also about to be this [and this is also about to be that (?)].*

B69 [Omitted.]

B70

Canon: Hearing that what you don't know is like what you know, you know both. Explaining by: informing.

Explanation: (Hearing.) What's outside is what one knows; what's in the room is what one doesn't know. Someone says, 'The colour of the one in the room is like the colour of this.' This is what one doesn't know being like what one knows. It is like, 'white or black, which fits? This is like its colour.' What is like white must be white. Now knowing its colour is like white, thus one knows it's white. As to names, one uses what people understand to correct what they don't know, not what they don't know to cast doubt on what they understand. It's like using a measured foot to measure a length one doesn't know.* Outside is personal knowledge; in the room is knowledge by explanation.*

B71

Canon: Deeming statements all perverse is perverse. Explained by: his statement.

Explanation: (Deeming.) Perverse is impermissible. If this person's statement is permissible—this is not perverse—then this is there being [some statement that's] permissible. If this person's statement is impermissible, then deeming it to fit the facts is surely injudicious.*

B72

Canon: Taking it to be just what I call it. If it's not the name, this is impermissible. Explained by: the converse.

Explanation: (Being.) It's permissible/possible to call this 'crane', but still it's not a crane. Calling both that and this 'this' is impermissible.* One making assertions mustn't take things to be whatever he calls them. If the other nevertheless takes it to be whatever he calls it, then my calling does not proceed. If the other does not take it to be what he calls it, then it does not proceed.*

B73

Canon: The limitless/infinite poses no obstacle to all-inclusiveness.* Explained by: filling or not.

Explanation: (Lacking.) [Objection:] If the south has a limit, then it can be covered. If it is limitless/infinite, then it can't be covered. Whether it has a limit or not can't yet be known, so whether it can be covered or not can't yet be known. Whether or not people fill it can't yet be known, and whether or not people can all be covered also can't yet be known, so it is perverse to take it as sure that it's possible to care for all people.*
[Reply:] If people do not fill the limitless, then people have a limit. Covering all of what has a limit presents no difficulty. If people do fill the limitless, then the limitless can all be covered. Covering all of the limitless presents no difficulty.

B74

Canon: Not knowing their number yet knowing they are all covered. Explained by: the one who asks.

Explanation: (Not.) Not knowing their number, if one asks, 'How do we know one's caring about the people covers them all?' some have been left out of what one asks about. If asking about people covers them all, then caring about the people asked about covers them all.* It's like not knowing their number, yet knowing that caring about them covers them all. There is no difficulty.

B75

Canon: Not knowing where they are located poses no obstacle to caring about them. Explained by: someone who has lost a child.*

Explanation: (None.)

B76

Canon: Benevolence and righteousness being deemed external and internal is perverse.* Explained by: matching up on a face.*

Explanation: (Benevolence.) Benevolence is caring; righteousness is benefiting. Caring and benefiting are this; those who are cared about and benefited are that. Caring and benefiting are not internal or external to each other; those cared about and benefited are also not internal or external to each other. To deem benevolence internal and righteousness external is to cite caring and those benefited. This is wild citing.* Like the left eye looking out and the right eye taking in.*

B77

Canon: The advantages of learning/study. Explained by: those who reject it.

Explanation. (Learning/study.) They take it that others don't know that learning/study is of no advantage, so they inform them. This is making them know that learning/study is of no advantage. This is teaching. If they take learning/study to be of no advantage, then teaching is perverse.*

B78

Canon: Whether rejection is permissible is not determined by how many or few there are. Explained by: it being rejectable.

Explanation: (Rejection.) In sorting out whether rejection is permissible, if there are good grounds to support rejecting it, then even if there are many rejections, one's rejecting it is right. If the grounds do not support rejecting it, then even if there are few rejections, it is wrong. Now if one asserts that it's impermissible for there to be many rejections, this is like using long to sort out short.*

B79

Canon: Rejecting rejection is perverse. Explained by: not rejecting it.*

Explanation: (Rejection.) Not rejecting one's own rejection, this is not rejecting rejection. Whether one's rejecting something can be rejected or not, [either way] this is not rejecting rejection.*

B80

Canon: Whether things are extreme. Explained by: like this.

Explanation: (Things.) The extreme in length, the extreme in shortness—none are longer than this, none are shorter than this. As to this being this, other than this, nothing is more extreme than this.*

B81

Canon: Selecting [what is] below in order to seek being above. Explained by: marshes.

Explanation: (Selecting.) High and low are measured by whether they are good or not good. Not like mountains and marshes. If dwelling below is better than dwelling above, then below is actually above.*

B82 [Omitted.]

BOOK 44

THE 'GREATER SELECTION'

44.1 Heaven cares about people less than the sage cares about people. It benefits people more than the sage benefits people. Great men care about commoners less than commoners care about great men. They benefit commoners more than commoners benefit great men. (44/1–2)

44.2 Deeming John one's kin and caring about him is not caring about one's kin. Deeming John one's kin and benefiting him is not benefiting one's kin.* Deeming music beneficial to one's son and desiring it for him is caring about one's son. Deeming music beneficial to one's son and seeking it for him is not benefiting one's son.* (44/2–4)

44.3a Among what are taken as units/parts, weighing the light and heavy is called weighing.* Weighing the wrong such that it comes out right and condemning the wrong such that it comes out wrong are 'by weighing' and 'exact'.* Cutting off a finger to save a wrist is selecting the greater among benefits or selecting the lesser among harms. Selecting the lesser among harms is not selecting harm; it is selecting benefit. What one selects is something controlled by others. When one encounters robbers, cutting off one's finger to save one's life is benefit. One's encountering robbers is harm.* Cutting off a finger and cutting off a wrist / . . . * (44/4–7)

44.3b . . . / If the benefit to the world is equal, there are no grounds for choosing one over the other. Life and death—if the benefit is the same, there are no grounds for choosing one over the other.

Killing one person to save the world is not killing one person to benefit the world. Killing oneself to save the world, this is killing oneself to benefit the world. (44/7–8)

44.3c Among affairs and conduct, weighing the light and heavy is called seeking. Seeking to do something is not / . . . / selecting the lesser among harms / . . . / Seeking to be righteous is not being righteous.* (44/8–9)

. . .

44.5 Selecting the greater among benefits is not something one is forced to do. Selecting the lesser among harms is something one is forced to do.* Selecting from among what doesn't exist yet, this is selecting the greater among benefits. Relinquishing from among what already exists, this is selecting the lesser among harms.* (44/12–13)

44.6 Benefiting more those whom righteousness permits benefiting more and less those whom righteousness permits benefiting less is called 'relation ranking'.* The virtuous in conduct, rulers, the elderly, and parents—these are those one benefits more. Benefiting the elderly more, one does not benefit the young less. If the kinship is closer, benefit more; if the kinship is more distant, benefit less. No matter how distant the kinship, it still falls within the scope of righteousness. If the kinship is close, do not treat them according to their conduct but do observe their conduct. (44/13–15)

. . .

44.8 Caring about people/others does not exclude oneself; oneself is among those cared about. Oneself being among those cared about, care is applied to oneself. Caring about oneself according to relation ranking is caring about people/others.* (44/17)

. . .

44.10 . . . Promoting benefit to a greater or lesser extent without promoting benefit according to relation ranking is acting for oneself* . . . (44/20)

. . .

44.12 . . . Benefiting more does not exclude oneself. As to care, there is neither more nor less . . . (44/21–2)

44.13 For there to be some Qín horse is for there to be some horse. This is knowing the horse of someone coming.* (44/22–3)

44.14 Care about a heavily populated era and care about a scarcely populated one are equal; to inclusively care about them is for it to be equal. Care about a previous era and care about a later one are identical to care about people of the present era. (44/23–4)

44.15 People's ghosts are not people. One's brother's ghost is one's brother. (44/24)

. . .

44.18 The round of a small round thing is the same as the round of a large round thing. The not reaching of not reaching a measured foot and the not reaching of not reaching a thousand *lǐ* are not different. As to their not reaching being the same, it refers to far and near. (44/26–7)

44.19 . . . Thinking of a pillar is not thinking of wood; it is thinking of the wood of this pillar. Thinking of a person's finger is not thinking of a person. Thinking of one's hunting catch is thinking of game. Intent and achievement cannot be taken to follow from each other . . . (44/27–8)

. . .

44.22 . . . names and objects. As to names and objects, one does not treat names as surely applying [to objects].* Supposing this stone is white, smash this stone and all of it is the same as white. But although this stone is big, it is not all the same as big.* In these cases, there is something that determines what to call it.

As to things named on the basis of shape and features, one must know this is such-and-such, only then can one know such-and-such.* As to things that cannot be named on the basis of shape and features,* even if one does not know this is such-and-such, it's possible to know such-and-such. All things named on the basis of residence or movement, if they have entered among them, they are all this. If they leave, on that basis they are not.* As to all things named on the basis of residence or movement, such as district and village names, 'Qí' and 'Jīng',* these are all such things. As to all things named on the basis of shape and features, such as mountains, hills, houses, and shrines, these are all such things . . . (44/33–6)

44.23 The same in being identical/doubled, the same in being together, the same in being connected, the same in being the same kind—the same in taking the same name.

The same in being segregated together, the same in being associated, the same in being this, the same in being so—the same in having the same root.

There is being different in being not-this and there is being different in being not-so.

There are differences that are deemed the same and what is deemed the same that is different.*

The first is called this and so; the second is called this and not-so; the third is called shifting; the fourth is called forced. (44/36–9)
. . .

44.25 . . . The caring about others that is caring about Jane is produced by considering Jane's benefit, not by considering John's benefit. Yet the caring about others that is caring about John is just the caring about others that is caring about Jane. If the world benefited from eliminating care about them, one could not eliminate it . . . Though as high-ranking as the Son of Heaven, he benefits others no more than a commoner does.

Two sons serving their parents, one encounters good fortune, one encounters misfortune, their parents being equal, it's not that the first son's conduct is more advantageous. External circumstances cannot make our benefit to parents greater.

If by John's death the world were harmed, we would look after John a myriad times more, but our caring about John would not be greater.* (44/42–6)

44.26 Tall people's being the same as short people is their features being the same, so they are the same. A finger's being a person and a head's being a person are different. The parts of a person's body are not one in their features, so they are different. A *jiāng* sword and a *tǐng* sword are different. Swords are named on the basis of shape and features. Their shape is not the same, so they are different.

The wood of willow-wood and the wood of peach-wood are the same.

All things not named on the basis of citing amount or number, if they are smashed, they are all this thing.* So a person's finger is not a person, but this person's finger is this person. One side of a square is not a square, but one side of a square piece of wood is that square piece of wood. (44/46–9)

44.27 . . . [Expressions?]* arise on the basis of reasons, develop on the basis of patterns, and proceed on the basis of kinds.* To establish expressions without understanding what they arise from is reckless. Now without *dào* people have nothing to proceed by. Even if they have strong legs, without understanding *dào* they are sure to run into difficulty. Now as to expressions proceeding on the basis of kinds, if one establishes expressions* without understanding the relevant kinds, one will surely have difficulty. So* . . . (44/49–51)

44.28* . . . The sage acts for the sake of the world . . . One long-lived, one short-lived, their benefit to the world is equal . . . Caring about them equally, select and kill one person among them . . . All cases of promoting benefit and eliminating harm . . . That not acting for one's own sake can be learned . . . Caring about others is not for praise . . . Caring about others' parents as one cares about one's parents . . . Inclusive care for all is equal, care for each one is equal . . . (44/52–7)

BOOK 45

THE 'LESSER SELECTION'

45.1a As to disputation,* by it we clarify the divisions between what is this and not and judge the guidelines of order and disorder; clarify places of sameness and difference and examine the patterns of names and objects; settle benefit and harm and resolve doubt. Only then can we lay out what is so of the myriad things and sort out parallels in groups of statements. (45/1–2)

45.1b By names, mention objects. By expressions, put across thoughts. By explanations, present reasons.* Select and propose on the basis of kinds.* Having it oneself, one doesn't condemn it in others. Lacking it oneself, one doesn't seek it in others.* (45/2–3)

45.1c Some is not all. Supposing is when it's now not so. Emulating is making a model for it.* What's emulated is what's made the model for it. So if something matches in emulating, it's this/right. If it doesn't match in emulating, it's not. This is emulating. (45/3–4)

45.1d Analogy is mentioning other things and using them to clarify it. 'Paralleling' is placing expressions side by side and jointly proceeding. 'Pulling' is saying, 'You are so, how is it that I alone cannot be so?' 'Pushing' is, on the basis that what they don't accept is the same as what they do accept, proposing it.*

'This is like what's been said' is being the same. 'How could I say that?' is being different. (45/4–6)

45.1e Things have respects in which they are the same, yet it doesn't follow that they are completely the same. Parallels between expressions are correct only up to a point. When things are so, there is that by which they are so. Their being so is the same, but that by which they are so isn't necessarily the same. When people accept things, there is that by which they accept them. Their accepting them is the same, but that by which they accept them isn't necessarily the same. Thus expressions in analogies, paralleling, pulling, and pushing become different as they proceed, become dangerous as they change direction, fail when taken too far, and leave their roots as they flow, and so one cannot fail to be cautious and cannot invariably use them.

So statements have many methods, separate kinds have different reasons/causes, and so one cannot look at only one side.* (45/7–10)

45.2a As to things, some are this and so, some are this but not so, some are not this but so,* some are in one case comprehensive and in one case not comprehensive, some are in one case this and in one case not.* (45/10–11)

45.2b White horses are horses; riding white horses is riding horses. Black horses are horses; riding black horses is riding horses. Jane is a person; caring about Jane is caring about people. John is a person; caring about John is caring about people. These are cases of 'this and so'.* (45/12–13)

45.2c Jane's parents are people; Jane's serving her parents isn't serving people.* Her brother is a handsome man; caring about her brother isn't caring about a handsome man. Carts are wood; riding carts isn't riding wood. Boats are wood; entering boats isn't entering wood. Robber-people are people; there being many robbers isn't there being many people. There being no robbers isn't there being no people.*

How do we clarify it?

Detesting there being many robbers isn't detesting there being many people. Desiring there be no robbers isn't desiring there be no people. All the world accompany each other in together deeming these right.

If it's like this, then although robber-people are people, caring about robbers isn't caring about people, not caring about robbers isn't not caring about people, and killing robber-people isn't killing people. There's no difficulty in this. These cases and those previous ones are the same kind. The world accepts those without condemning themselves; the Mohists accept these but the world condemns them. Is there any other reason for it than what's called 'clogged up inside and closed off outside', such that their hearts have no space within? They are clogged up inside and cannot be released. These are cases of 'this but not so'. (45/13–19).

45.2d Moreover, reading books isn't books; liking reading books is liking books. Cockfights aren't gamecocks; liking cockfighting is liking gamecocks. Being about to fall into a well isn't falling into a well; stopping someone about to fall into a well is stopping someone from falling into a well. Being about to go out the door isn't going out the door; stopping someone about to go out the door is stopping someone from going out the door.

If it's like this, then being about to die young isn't dying young; stopping someone from being about to die young is stopping someone from dying young. Holding there is fate isn't fate; condemning holding there is fate is condemning fate.*

There's no difficulty in this. These cases and those previous ones are the same kind. The world accepts those without condemning themselves; the Mohists accept these but the world condemns them for a crime. Is there any other reason for it than what's called 'clogged up inside and closed off outside', such that their hearts have no space within? They are clogged up inside and cannot be released. These are cases of 'not this but so'.* (45/19–23)

45.2e Caring about people requires comprehensively caring about people and only then does it count as caring about people. Not caring about people doesn't require comprehensively not caring about people; if one doesn't comprehensively care about them, on this basis one counts as not caring about people. Riding horses doesn't require comprehensively riding horses and only then counts as riding horses; if one rides any horse, on this basis one counts as riding horses. When it comes to not riding horses, it requires comprehensively not riding horses and only then counts as not riding horses. These are examples of 'in one case comprehensive and in one case not comprehensive'.* (45/23–5)

45.2f If one lives within a state, then one counts as living in the state. Owning a house within a state, one doesn't count as owning the state.

The fruit of peach trees is peaches, but the fruit of brambles isn't brambles.

Asking about a person's illness is asking about a person; detesting a person's illness isn't detesting a person.

A person's ghost isn't a person; your elder brother's ghost is your elder brother. Sacrificing to a person's ghost isn't sacrificing to a person; sacrificing to your elder brother's ghost is sacrificing to your elder brother.

If this horse's eyes are blind, we say this horse is blind. This horse's eyes are big, but we don't say this horse is big.

If this ox's hair is brown, we say this ox is brown. This ox's hairs being many, we don't say this ox is many.

One horse is horse. Two horses are horse. Horses have four feet—this is one horse and four feet, not two horses and four feet. Horses, some white—this is two horses with one being white, not one horse with part being white.

These are examples of 'in one case this and in one case not'. (45/25–30)

PART V
THE DIALOGUES

. . .

46.3 Zhì Túyú and Xiàn Zǐshuò* asked of our master Mòzǐ, 'In practising righteousness, what is the greatest duty?'

Our master Mòzǐ said, 'It is analogous to building an earthen wall. Those capable of building the frame, build; those capable of filling in the earth, fill it in; those capable of shovelling up the earth, shovel it; and then the wall is completed. Practising righteousness is like this. Those capable of discussing and disputing, discuss and dispute; those capable of explaining documents, explain documents; those capable of undertaking tasks, undertake tasks; and then the work of righteousness is accomplished.' (46/10–12)

46.4 Wūmǎzǐ* said to our master Mòzǐ, 'You inclusively care about all the world, but as yet there's no benefit. I don't care about all the world, but as yet there's no injury. Neither result having arrived, why do you deem you alone right and me wrong?'

Our master Mòzǐ said, 'Now suppose there is something burning here. One person carries water to pour on it, one person holds burning fuel to add to the fire. Neither result having arrived, which of the two people do you value more?'

Wūmǎzǐ said, 'I deem the intention of the one carrying water right and the intention of the one holding fire wrong.'

Our master Mòzǐ said, 'I too deem my intention right and your intention wrong.' (46/12–15)

. . .

46.6 Wūmǎzǐ said to our master Mòzǐ, 'As to your practising righteousness, people don't see and assist you, the ghosts don't see and reward you, yet you do it. You're mad.'

Our master Mòzǐ said, 'Now suppose you had two servants here. One of them works when he sees you and doesn't work when he doesn't see you. One of them works when he sees you and also works when he doesn't see you. Which of these two people do you value more?'

Wūmǎzǐ said, 'I value the one who works when he sees me and also works when he doesn't see me.'

Our master Mòzǐ said, 'That being so, then this is you too valuing madness.' (46/18–22)

46.7 A follower of Zǐ Xià* asked our master Mòzǐ, 'Do gentlemen have fights?'*

Our master Mòzǐ said, 'Gentlemen don't have fights.'

The follower of Zǐ Xià said, 'Even dogs and pigs have fights. How can there be officers who don't have fights?'

Our master Mòzǐ said, 'That hurts! In your statements, you cite from the sage-kings Tāng and Wén, while in your conduct, you draw analogies to dogs and pigs. That hurts!' (46/22–4)

46.8 Wūmǎzǐ said to our master Mòzǐ, 'To set aside people of today to praise the former kings, this is to praise rotten bones. It's analogous to a carpenter who knows rotten wood but not living wood.'

Our master Mòzǐ said, 'That by which the world lives is through the teachings of the way of the former kings. Now to praise the former kings, this is to praise that by which the world lives. Failing to praise what is praiseworthy is not benevolence.' (46/24–6)

46.9 Our master Mòzǐ said, 'The jade of Mr Hé, the pearl of the Lord of Suí, the nine precious cauldrons—these are what the various lords call excellent treasures. Can they enrich the state, increase the population, order punishments and government, and secure the altars of soil and grain? I say, they cannot. The purpose of valuing excellent treasures is that they can benefit. Yet the jade of Mr Hé, the pearl of the Lord of Suí, and the nine precious cauldrons cannot benefit people. These are not the world's excellent treasures.

'Now if one uses righteousness to govern a state, the population will surely increase, punishments and government will surely be in order, and the altars of soil and grain will surely be secure. The purpose of valuing excellent treasures is that they can benefit the people, and righteousness can benefit people. So I say, righteousness is the most excellent treasure in the world.' (46/26–30)

46.10 Duke Zǐgāo of Shè asked Confucius about governing, saying, 'Those good at governing, what are they like?'

Confucius replied, 'Those good at governing, the distant are attracted to them, and old relationships are renewed.'*

Our master Mòzǐ heard it and said, 'Duke Zǐgāo of Shè failed to get what he asked about, and Confucius too failed to find the proper response. How could Duke Zǐgāo of Shè not know that, as for those good at governing, the distant are attracted to them, and the old are renewed? He asked what the means of accomplishing this is like. Don't use what people don't know to tell them; use what they do know to tell them.* So Duke Zǐgāo of Shè failed to get what he asked about, and Confucius too failed to find the proper response.' (46/30–4)

46.11 Our master Mòzǐ said to Lord Wén of Lǔyáng,* 'When great states attack small states, it's analogous to children playing horse. When children play horse, they use their feet until they're weary. Now when great states attack small states, for those attacked, farmers don't get to plough and women don't get to weave; they take defence as their task. For those who attack others, farmers also don't get to plough and women don't get to weave; they take attacking as their task. So when great states attack small states, it's analogous to children playing horse.'* (46/34–7)

46.12 Our master Mòzǐ said, 'Statements adequate to repeatedly guide conduct, make them regular. Those not adequate to guide conduct, don't make them regular.* Making regular those not adequate to guide conduct, this is empty jabbering.' (46/37–8)

46.13 Our master Mòzǐ sent Guǎn Qián Aó to the state of Wèi to recommend Gāo Shízǐ.* The Lord of Wèi paid Gāo an extremely rich salary and installed him as minister. Gāo Shízǐ went to court three times and inevitably finished all he had to state, but none of his statements were put into practice. He left and went to Qí. He met with our master Mòzǐ and said, 'Because of you, Sir, the Lord of Wèi paid me an extremely rich salary and installed me as minister. I went to court three times and inevitably finished all I had to state, but none of my statements were put into practice. Hence I left him. Won't the Lord of Wèi deem me mad?'

Our master Mòzǐ said, 'If leaving was the way, what hurt is it to be accused of madness? In antiquity, Duke Dàn of Zhōu condemned Guān Shū, resigned as one of the three dukes, and went east to dwell in Shāng Yǎn. People all called him mad, but later generations cite his virtue and praise his name to this day. Moreover, I have heard, being righteous is not a matter of avoiding defamation and seeking acclaim. If leaving was the way, what hurt is it to be accused of madness?'

Gāo Shízǐ said, 'In leaving him, how dare I not follow the way? In the past, you, Sir, made a statement, "When the way is absent from the world, a benevolent officer doesn't stay in a rich position." Now, the Lord of Wèi lacking the way, were I to covet his salary and title, this would be for me to dishonestly live off others' provisions.'

Our master Mòzǐ was pleased and summoned Master Qínzǐ,* saying, 'Listen to this! As for turning one's back on righteousness to pursue a salary, I often hear of it, but turning one's back on salary to pursue righteousness, only in Gāo Shízǐ have I seen it.' (46/38–46)

46.14 Our master Mòzǐ said, 'The gentlemen of the age, if they are poor and you call them wealthy, they get angry; if they lack righteousness and you call them righteous, they are pleased. How is this not perverse?!' (46/46)

. . .

46.17 Gōng Mèngzǐ* said, 'The gentleman doesn't initiate. He transmits, that's all.'*

Our master Mòzǐ said, 'Not so. The most ungentlemanly people, what is good of antiquity they don't transmit, what is good today they don't initiate. The second most ungentlemanly, what is good of antiquity they don't transmit, but if they themselves have something good, they initiate it, as they desire good things to issue from them. Now to transmit but not initiate, this is no different from someone who dislikes transmitting but does initiate. I take it that what is good of antiquity, transmit it, and what is good today, initiate it, since I desire to increase the amount of good.' (46/49–52)

46.18 Wūmǎzǐ said to our master Mòzǐ, 'I am different from you. I cannot care inclusively. I care about the people of Zōu more than the people of Yuè, care about the people of Lǔ more than the people of Zōu, care about the people of my hometown more than the people of Lǔ, care about my clansmen more than the people of my hometown, care about my parents more than my clansmen, and care about myself more than my parents, deeming each case closer to me.*

'If you hit me, it hurts; if you hit them, it doesn't hurt me. Why would I not resist what hurts but instead resist what doesn't hurt? So, for me, there is killing others to benefit myself; there is no killing myself to benefit others.'

Our master Mòzǐ said, 'Your norm* [of righteousness], will you conceal it? Or will you tell it to others?'

Wūmǎzǐ said, 'Why would I conceal my norm? I will tell it to others.'

Our master Mòzǐ said, 'That being so, then if one person is pleased with you,* one person desires to kill you to benefit himself; if ten people are pleased with you, ten people desire to kill you to benefit themselves; if all the world are pleased with you, all the world desires to kill you to benefit themselves. If one person is displeased with you, one person desires to kill you, taking you to be spreading an inauspicious statement.* If ten people are displeased with you, ten people desire to kill you, taking you to be spreading an inauspicious statement. If all the world are displeased with you, all the world desires to kill you, taking you to be spreading an inauspicious statement. This is what's called "What passes from your own mouth is what takes your life." '

Our master Mòzǐ said, 'How is your statement beneficial? Making statements without any benefit, this is empty jabbering.' (46/52–60)

46.19 Our master Mòzǐ said to Lord Wén of Lǔyáng, 'Now suppose there is a person here whose sheep, oxen, and other livestock are so plentiful that he hires others to butcher and cook them, and there's so much food it can't all be finished. Seeing someone making cakes, he rushes to steal them, saying, "Give them to me to eat." I wonder, is it that day and night he just can't get enough food? Or that he has kleptomania?'

Lord Wén of Lǔyáng said, 'He has kleptomania.'

Our master Mòzǐ said, 'Of the fields within the four borders of Chǔ, there's so much wild, overgrown land that it can't all be developed; there're so many thousands of vacant villages that they can't all be populated. Yet on seeing the empty regions of Sòng and Zhèng, Chǔ rushed to steal them. Is this different from that?'

Lord Wén of Lǔyáng said, 'This is like that. Chǔ really has kleptomania.'* (46/60–3)

. . .

BOOK 47

VALUING RIGHTEOUSNESS

47.1 Our master Mòzǐ said, 'Of the myriad things, none are more valuable than righteousness. Now suppose we say to someone, "I'll give you a hat and shoes but chop off your hands and feet, will you do it?" Surely he wouldn't do it. Why? It's because a hat and shoes are not as valuable as hands and feet. Again, suppose we say, "I'll give you the world but take your life, will you do it?" Surely he wouldn't do it. Why? It's because the world is not as valuable as one's life. Yet people kill each other fighting over a single statement.* This is valuing righteousness more than one's life. So I say, of the myriad things, none are more valuable than righteousness.' (47/1–3)

47.2 Travelling from Lǔ to Qí, our master Mòzǐ met an old acquaintance, who said to our master Mòzǐ, 'Now in the world no one practises righteousness. You alone make yourself suffer to practise righteousness. It'd be better if you quit.'

Our master Mòzǐ said, 'Now suppose there is a man here who has ten sons. One ploughs the fields while nine sit around. Then the one who ploughs the fields could not but work even more urgently. Why? It's because those who eat are many, while those who plough are few. Now if in the world no one practises righteousness, you should encourage me. Why stop me?' (47/3–6)

. . .

47.4 Our master Mòzǐ said, 'In all statements and all actions, what is beneficial to Heaven, ghosts, and the common people, do it. In all statements and all actions, what is harmful to Heaven, ghosts, and the common people, reject it. In all statements and all actions, what conforms to the sage-kings of the three dynasties, Yáo, Shùn, Yǔ, Tāng, Wén, and Wǔ, do it. In all statements and all actions, what conforms to the tyrants of the three dynasties, Jié, Zhōu, Yōu, and Lì, reject it.' (47/16–18)

47.5 Our master Mòzǐ said, 'Statements adequate to change conduct, make them regular. Those not adequate to change conduct, don't make them regular. Making regular those not adequate to change conduct, this is empty jabbering.'* (47/18–19)

47.6 Our master Mòzǐ said, 'You must eliminate the six biases. When silent, ponder; when speaking, instruct; when acting, work. Make these three alternate and surely you will be a sage. You must eliminate happiness and eliminate anger, eliminate joy and eliminate sorrow, eliminate fondness and eliminate dislike, and use benevolence and righteousness. Your hands, feet, mouth, nose, and ears undertaking righteousness, surely you will be a sage.' (47/19–20)

47.7 Our master Mòzǐ said to several disciples, 'If you [attempt to] practise righteousness but are unable, you must not abandon the way. To give an analogy, a carpenter who saws a straight edge but is unable doesn't abandon the marking line.' (47/20–1)

47.8 Our master Mòzǐ said, 'The gentlemen of the age, employ them as butcher of a hound or a hog, and if they are unable, they refuse it; employ them as minister of a state, and though unable, they do it. How is this not perverse?!' (47/21–3)

47.9 Our master Mòzǐ said, 'Now the blind say, "What's bright is white, what's dark is black." Even the clear-sighted have no grounds for changing this. But collect white and black things together and make the blind select from among them, and they cannot know. So when I say the blind don't know white and black, it's not by their naming, it's by their selecting.*

'Now as to how the gentlemen of the world name benevolence, even the sage-kings Yǔ and Tāng have no basis for changing it. But collect benevolent and unbenevolent things together and make the gentlemen of the world select from among them, and they cannot know. So when I say the gentlemen of the world don't know benevolence, it's not by their naming, it's by their selecting.' (47/23–6)

47.10 Our master Mòzǐ said, 'The officers of today in using their persons are less careful than a merchant using a piece of money. In using money, the merchant dares not exchange it carelessly. He surely chooses good items. The officers of today in using their persons, on the other hand, are not so. Whatever their intention desires, they do it. In serious cases, they are subject to punishment. In minor cases, they are condemned and disgraced. So officers in using their

persons are not as careful as a merchant using a bit of money.'
(47/26–8)

47.11 Our master Mòzǐ said, 'The gentlemen of the age desire to build up their righteousness, yet if you help them cultivate themselves, they're indignant. This is like desiring to build a wall, yet if others help you construct it, getting indignant. How is it not perverse?!' (47/29–30)

47.12 Our master Mòzǐ said, 'The ancient sage-kings desired to transmit their way to later generations. Thus they wrote it on bamboo and silk and engraved it on metal and stone to transmit it to their sons and grandsons in later generations, desiring that their sons and grandsons in later generations would take it as a model. Now to hear the teachings left by the former kings without practising them, this is to discard the heritage of the former kings.' (47/31–2)

. . .

47.14 Our master Mòzǐ said to Gōngliáng Huánzǐ,* 'Wèi is a small state, situated between Qí and Jìn, like a poor family situated between two wealthy families. If a poor family emulates wealthy families' many expenditures on clothing and food, its speedy ruin is certain. Now inspecting your house, we find hundreds of decorated carriages, hundreds of grain-fed horses, and hundreds of women clothed in finery. If we took the cost of decorating the carriages and feeding the horses and the resources needed for the fine clothing and used them to maintain soldiers, surely there would be more than a thousand men. If there were a crisis, you could station several hundred in the front and several hundred in the rear. Compared with stationing several hundred women in the front and rear, which would be more secure? I take it that would be less secure than the soldiers.' (47/36–40)

. . .

47.16 Our master Mòzǐ said, 'The gentlemen of the age hold the righteous officer in less regard than a grain bearer. Now suppose there is a man here bearing grain who is resting by the roadside and desires to get up but is unable. Gentlemen seeing him, whether old or young, noble or lowly, would surely help him up. Why? I say, it's righteous. Now gentlemen who practise righteousness carry on the way of the former kings and expound it to them [the gentlemen of the age], but not only are they not pleased to practise it, they even then denounce it. So this is the gentlemen of the age holding the righteous officer in less regard than a grain bearer.' (47/43–6)

47.17 Our master Mòzǐ said, 'The merchants go to the four corners of the world, buying and selling at double or quintuple the price. Despite the difficulties of passes and bridges and the dangers of robbers and thieves, they inevitably do it. Now if officers sit and make statements about righteousness, there are no difficulties of passes and bridges, no dangers of robbers and thieves. This produces doubling and quintupling beyond calculation.* Yet they don't do it. So officers' calculation of benefit is less discerning than merchants'.' (47/46–8)

. . .

47.19 Our master Mòzǐ said, 'My statements are adequate to use. To set aside these statements and change one's thoughts, this is like abandoning one's harvest to scavenge for scattered grain. Using others' statements to deem my statements wrong,* this is like throwing eggs against a rock. Use up all the eggs in the world, and the rock is still here. It's indestructible.' (47/53–5) not only are these not pleased to praise, furthermore they denounce it. So this is the entire blame of the world, being the righteousness which less regard him as even lo the he [...]

11.1? Our master Mozi said [...] I go to the four corners of the world, to rise and affairs of virtues or quintuple the pros. Deemed to be able where of praise and virtue, and the denom [...]

48.3 Gōng Mèngzǐ came to see our master Mòzǐ wearing a ceremonial hat, carrying an official's tablet, and dressed in Erudites' robes, and said, 'Does the gentleman attend first to his attire and only then to his conduct? Or does he attend to his conduct and only then to his attire?'

Our master Mòzǐ said, 'Conduct doesn't lie in attire.'

Gōng Mèngzǐ said, 'How do you know this is so?'

Our master Mòzǐ said, 'In the past, Duke Huán of Qí put his state in order wearing a high hat and wide belt, with a gold sword and wooden shield, and his state was in order. In the past, Duke Wén of Jìn put his state in order wearing garments of rough cloth and a sheepskin coat, with his sword in a plain leather belt, and his state was in order. In the past, King Zhuāng of Chǔ put his state in order wearing a fancy hat with a tassel and an elaborate robe with a wide gown, and his state was in order. In the past, King Gōu Jiàn of Yuè put his state in order with his hair cut short and tattoos on his body, and his state was in order. These four rulers, their attire was different, but their conduct was nonetheless one and the same.* By this I know conduct doesn't lie in attire.'

Gōng Mèngzǐ said, 'Excellent! I have heard it, "One who delays the good is inauspicious." Please, may I set aside my tablet, change my hat, and come again to see you, Sir?'

Our master Mòzǐ said, 'Please meet with me as you are. If you must set aside your tablet and change your hat before seeing me, then conduct does lie in attire after all.' (48/15–22)

48.4 Gōng Mèngzǐ said, 'The gentleman must be ancient in his speech and attire, only then can he be benevolent.'*

Our master Mòzǐ said, 'In the past, Fèi Zhòng, high minister for King Zhòu of Shāng, was the most vicious person in the world, while Jīzǐ and Wēizǐ were the most sagely people in the world. These spoke the same speech,* but some were benevolent, some unbenevolent. Duke Dàn of Zhōu was the most sagely person in the world, Guān

Shū was the most vicious person in the world. These wore the same attire, but one was benevolent, one unbenevolent. That being so, then benevolence doesn't lie in ancient attire and ancient speech. Moreover, you emulate the Zhōu without emulating the Xià; your antiquity is not ancient.'* (48/22–5)

48.5 Gōng Mèngzǐ said to our master Mòzǐ, 'As to the ranks of the former sage-kings, the most sagely were established as Son of Heaven, the next established as high ministers. Now Confucius was learned in the odes and documents, discerning in ceremony and righteousness, and thoroughly familiar with the myriad things. If Confucius were made a sage-king, how could he not be made the Son of Heaven?!'

Our master Mòzǐ said, 'Now the wise must honour Heaven and serve the ghosts, care about others and moderate the use of resources. Combining these constitutes wisdom.* Now you say, "Confucius was learned in the odes and documents, discerning in ceremony and righteousness, and thoroughly familiar with the myriad things" and say he could have been the Son of Heaven. This is counting the teeth on someone else's tally and taking oneself to be wealthy.'* (48/25–8)

48.6 Gōng Mèngzǐ said, 'Poverty or wealth and longevity or early death are fixed by Heaven and cannot be decreased or increased.'* He also said, 'The gentleman must study.'

Our master Mòzǐ said, 'Instructing people to study while holding there is fate, this is like commanding people to wrap up their hair while taking away their hat.'* (48/28–30)

. . .

48.8 Our master Mòzǐ said to Gōng Mèngzǐ, 'According to the mourning ceremonies, when a ruler or parent, wife, or eldest son dies, for three years mourning clothes are worn. When an elder uncle, younger uncle, or brother dies, it's one year. For a clansman, it's five months. For aunts, sisters, maternal uncles, and nephews on one's sister's side, there is mourning of several months. If there are some intervals between mourning, you Erudites recite three hundred odes, strum music for three hundred odes, sing to three hundred odes, and dance to three hundred odes. If we use your statements,* what days do gentlemen attend to government, what days do commoners undertake work?'

Gōng Mèngzǐ said, 'If the state is in disorder, order it; if it is in order, perform ceremonies and music. If the state is poor, undertake work; if the state is wealthy, perform ceremonies and music.'

Our master Mòzǐ said, 'As to the state's being in order, we put it in order, and so it is in order.* If putting it in order is abandoned, then order in the state is also abandoned. As to the state's wealth, we work and so it is wealthy. If work is abandoned, the state's wealth is also abandoned. So even if a state is orderly, only if we encourage order without cease will things be acceptable. Now you say, "If the state is in order, perform ceremonies and music, if in disorder, order it." This is analogous to drilling a well for water only after choking on food or seeking a doctor only after dying. The ancient tyrants of the three dynasties, Jié, Zhòu, Yōu, and Lì, indulged in song and music and neglected their people. Hence their bodies were mutilated and executed and their states were ruined, all from following this way.' (48/33–40)

48.9 Gōng Mèngzǐ said, 'There are no ghosts and spirits.' He also said, 'The gentleman must study sacrificial ceremonies.' Our master Mòzǐ said, 'To hold there are no ghosts yet study sacrificial ceremonies, this is like studying guest ceremonies when there are no guests. This is like making a fishnet when there are no fish.' (48/40–2)

48.10 Gōng Mèngzǐ said to our master Mòzǐ, 'You deem three years of mourning wrong. Your three days of mourning are also wrong.'

Our master Mòzǐ said, 'On the basis of three years of mourning, you deem three days of mourning wrong. This is like being naked yet calling someone who lifts their robe indecorous.' (48/42–3)

. . .

48.12 Gōng Mèngzǐ said, 'Three years of mourning emulates a baby's attachment to its parents.'*

Our master Mòzǐ said, 'Now a baby knows only to be attached to its parents and that's all. Unable to find its parents, it cries without cease. What is the reason for this? It's the height of ignorance. That being so, then how is the knowledge of the Erudites any better than a baby's?!' (48/44–6)

. . .

48.14 Our master Mòzǐ said to Chéngzǐ,* 'The way of the Erudites includes four policies that are each enough to ruin the world.*

'The Erudites deem Heaven unseeing and the ghosts inanimate, displeasing Heaven and the ghosts. This is enough to ruin the world.

'Again, they conduct rich burials and prolonged mourning, with multiple inner and outer coffins and many layers of shrouds, and their funeral processions are like moving house. For three years they cry and weep, until they cannot stand without support or walk without a cane, their ears hear nothing, and their eyes see nothing. This is enough to ruin the world.

'Again, they sing to strings and dance to drums, practising songs and music. This is enough to ruin the world.

'Again, they deem that fate exists, holding that poverty or wealth, longevity or early death, order or disorder, security or danger have fixed limits that cannot be decreased or increased.* If superiors practise this, they will surely not attend to government; if subordinates practise it, they will surely not undertake work. This is enough to ruin the world.'

Chéngzǐ said, 'You go too far, Sir, in defaming the Erudites!'

Our master Mòzǐ said, 'If the Erudites indeed don't have four policies such as these and I state that they do, this is defaming them. Now if the Erudites indeed have these four policies and I state them, it's not defaming them, it's reporting what I've heard.'. . . (48/49–55)

48.15 Our master Mòzǐ engaged in disputation with Chéngzǐ and cited Confucius. Chéngzǐ said, 'You deem the Erudites wrong.* Why cite Confucius?'

Our master Mòzǐ said, 'This is something that indeed fits the facts and can't be changed. Now when birds learn about the hazard of heat and drought, they fly high; when fish hear about the hazard of heat and drought they swim deep. In these cases, even if the sage-kings Yǔ and Tāng were planning for them, surely they'd be unable to change anything.* Fish and birds can be called ignorant, but in some cases Yǔ and Tāng still go along with them. Now should I never cite Confucius?' (48/58–61)

. . .

48.18 A person who came to study with our master Mòzǐ said to him, 'Sir, you take ghosts and spirits to be seeing and knowing,* able to bless people or curse them with misfortune. Those who do good, they bless; those who do vicious things, they curse. Now I have served you, Sir, a long time, yet blessings have not come. Could it be that some of your statements are mistaken? Or that the ghosts and spirits are unseeing? Why do I not get blessings?'

Our master Mòzǐ said, 'Even though you have not got blessings, how is it that my statements are mistaken, and how is it that the ghosts and spirits are unseeing? Surely you have heard about there being a punishment for concealing a fugitive?'

He replied, 'I haven't heard about it.'

Our master Mòzǐ said, 'Now suppose there is a person here who is ten times more virtuous than you. Are you able to praise him ten times while praising yourself only once?'

He replied, 'I'm unable.'

'Suppose there is a man here who is a hundred times more virtuous than you. Are you able to praise his goodness your whole life, without praising yourself even once?'

He replied, 'I'm unable.'

Our master Mòzǐ said, 'Even someone who conceals just one person commits a crime. Now what you conceal is as much as this—you're committing a heavy crime.* What blessings could you seek?!' (48/69–76)

48.19 Our master Mòzǐ had an illness. Diē Bí entered and asked, 'Sir, you take the ghosts and spirits to be seeing and able to bring misfortune or blessings. Those who do good, they reward; those who do bad, they punish. Now you, Sir, are a sage. Why do you have an illness? Could it be that some of your statements are mistaken? Or that the ghosts and spirits are unseeing and unknowing?'

Our master Mòzǐ said, 'Even supposing I have an illness, how is it that they are unseeing? People can catch an illness in many ways. Some get ill from the cold or heat, some from exhaustion. If there are a hundred doors and you close one of them, how is it that a robber has no way in?'* (48/76–9)

48.20 Some disciples reported to our master Mòzǐ that they wished to study archery. Our master Mòzǐ said, 'You cannot. Now the wise* surely measure what their strength is capable of achieving and undertake it. Even the finest soldiers in the state cannot fight while holding someone up.* Now you are not the finest soldiers in the state. How could you be capable of both completing your studies and mastering archery?!' (48/79–81)

. . .

49.1 The Lord of Lǔ said to our master Mòzǐ, 'I fear that Qí will attack me. Can this be prevented?'

Our master Mòzǐ said, 'Yes. In the past, the sage-kings of the three dynasties, Yǔ, Tāng, Wén, and Wǔ, were feudal lords of only a hundred *lǐ*,* but they expounded loyalty and their conduct was righteous, and so they gained the world.* The tyrants of the three dynasties, Jié, Zhòu, Yōu, and Lì, incited enmity and resentment and their conduct was vicious, and so they lost the world.

'I hope your Lordship may honour Heaven and serve the ghosts above, care about and benefit the common people below, richly prepare furs and coin, make your remarks humble, urgently pay respects to the lords of neighbouring states, and lead your state to serve Qí—then trouble can be prevented. Other than this, there's really nothing that can be done.' (49/1–4)

. . .

49.4 Lord Wén of Lǔ Yáng was about to attack Zhèng. Our master Mòzǐ heard about it and stopped him, saying to Lord Wén, 'Now suppose within the four borders of Lǔ Yáng large cities attacked the small cities and great clans assaulted the small clans, killing their people and taking their oxen, horses, dogs, swine, bolts of silk, grain, and goods. What would that be like?'

Lord Wén of Lǔ Yáng said, 'Within the four borders of Lǔ Yáng, all are my subjects. Now if large cities attacked the small cities and great clans assaulted the small clans, seizing their goods, then I would surely punish them heavily.'

Our master Mòzǐ said, 'Now Heaven inclusively possesses all the world just as your Lordship possesses the territory within your four borders. Now you mobilize an army to attack Zhèng. Could Heaven's punishment not come?'

Lord Wén of Lǔ Yáng said, 'Sir, why stop me from attacking Zhèng? My attacking Zhèng follows Heaven's intent. For three generations, the people of Zhèng have murdered their ruler. Heaven has punished them, causing three years of scarcity. I will assist Heaven in punishing them.'

Our master Mòzǐ said, 'For three generations, the people of Zhèng have murdered their ruler and Heaven has punished them, causing three years of scarcity. Heaven's punishment is sufficient. Yet now you deploy your army to attack Zhèng, saying, "My attacking Zhèng follows Heaven's intent." By analogy, suppose there is a man here whose son is hale and hearty but worthless, so his father whips him with a bamboo cane. The father of the neighbouring family then beats him with a wooden staff, saying, "My beating him is following his father's intent." How is this not perverse?!' (49/12–20)

49.5 Our master Mòzǐ said to Lord Wén of Lǔyáng, '[The rulers of today] attack neighbouring states, kill their people, take their oxen and horses, grain, and goods, and then write their deeds on bamboo and silk, engrave them on metal and stone, and inscribe them on bells and cauldrons to pass down to their sons and grandsons in later generations, saying, "No one has as much as I." Now suppose commoners were similarly to attack neighbouring families, kill their people, seize their dogs and swine, food, and clothing,* and similarly write their deeds on bamboo and silk and inscribe them on vessels and dishes to pass down to their sons and grandsons in later generations, saying, "No one has as much as I." How could this be acceptable?'

Lord Wén of Lǔ Yáng said, 'That being so, then if I look at things on the basis of your statement, what all the world calls acceptable is not necessarily so.' (49/20–4)

49.6 Our master Mòzǐ said to Lord Wén of Lǔyáng, 'The gentlemen of the age all know the little things but don't know the big things. Suppose there is a man here, if he steals a hound or hog, they call him unbenevolent, but if he steals a state or a city, they deem him righteous. It's analogous to seeing a small amount of white and calling it white, yet seeing a large amount of white and calling it black. Thus the gentlemen of the age know the little things but don't know the big things—this is what this statement refers to.'* (49/24–6)

49.7 Lord Wén of Lǔyáng said to our master Mòzǐ, 'South of Chǔ there is a country Qiáo where they eat people. In their country, when the eldest son is born, they chop him up and eat him, calling this "advantageous to the younger brothers". If the meat is delicious, they offer some to their ruler. If the ruler is pleased, he rewards the father. How is this not a vile custom?!'*

Our master Mòzǐ said, 'Even the customs of the central states are also like this. Killing the father and rewarding the son,* how is this different from eating the son and rewarding the father?! If we don't use benevolence and righteousness, on what grounds do we deem the barbarians wrong for eating their sons?' (49/26–30)

. . .

49.12 Among the country people south of Lǔ there was one Wú Lǜ. In the winter, he made pottery, in the summer, he ploughed the fields. He compared himself to the sage-king Shùn. Our master Mòzǐ heard about him and went to meet him.

Wú Lǜ said to our master Mòzǐ, 'Just be righteous, that's all. What's the use of making statements about it?'*

Our master Mòzǐ said, 'What you call righteous, does it too involve those who have strength labouring for others, those who have resources sharing them with others?'

Wú Lǜ said, 'It does.'

Our master Mòzǐ said, 'I have calculated it. I considered ploughing in order to feed the people of the world. Even if successful, however, this amounts to just a single farmer's ploughing. Divide it among all the world, and people cannot get even one pint of grain each. Even if in this way they do manage to get one pint of grain, it can be seen that this cannot satisfy all the hungry people in the world.

'I considered weaving to clothe the people of the world. Even if successful, however, this amounts to just a single woman's weaving. Divide it among all the world, and people cannot get even one foot of cloth each. Even if in this way they do manage to get one foot of cloth, it can be seen that this cannot warm all the cold people in the world.

'I considered donning tough armour, wielding a sharp sword, and rescuing the various lords from troubles. Even if successful, however, this amounts to just a single soldier's fighting. It can be seen that a single soldier's fighting cannot defend against an entire army.

'I take it that none of these is as good as reciting the way of the former kings and seeking their explanations; mastering the statements of the sages and examining their remarks; above, persuading kings, dukes, and great men, and, below, persuading commoners and the man in the street. If kings, dukes, and great men put my statements to use, the state will surely be in order. If commoners and the man in the street put my statements to use, their conduct will surely be refined. So I take it that although I don't plough to feed the hungry or weave to clothe the cold, my accomplishments are more worthy than someone who ploughs to feed them or weaves to clothe them. So I take it that even though I don't plough or weave, my accomplishments are worthier than ploughing and weaving.'

Wú Lù said to our master Mòzǐ, 'Just be righteous, that's all. What's the use of making statements about it?'

Our master Mòzǐ said, 'Suppose the world did not know how to plough. Whose accomplishment would be greater, someone who teaches others to plough, or someone who ploughs by himself without teaching others to plough?'

Wú Lù said, 'The one who teaches others to plough, his accomplishment would be greater.'

Our master Mòzǐ said, 'Suppose we are attacking an unrighteous state. Whose accomplishment would be greater, someone who drums and encourages the masses to advance, or someone who doesn't drum and encourage the masses to advance, but advances by himself?'

Wú Lù said, 'The one who drums and encourages the masses to advance, his accomplishment would be greater.'

Our master Mòzǐ said, 'The commoners and men in the street of the world knowing little of righteousness, the accomplishment of someone who teaches the world about righteousness is also greater. Why not make statements about it? If I succeed in drumming people to advance toward righteousness, then how could my righteousness not advance further?!' (49/40–54)

. . .

49.14 Our master Mòzǐ visited Wèi Yuè, who said: 'Having been granted an audience with the rulers of the four corners of the world, what would you expound first?'

Our master Mòzǐ said, 'Whenever you enter a state, you must select a priority to work on. If the state is in disorder, expound "promoting the worthy" and "identifying upward"; if the state is impoverished, expound "moderation in use" and "moderation in burial"; if the state overindulges in musical entertainment, expound "condemning music" and "condemning fate"; if the state is dissolute and indecorous, expound "honouring Heaven" and "serving ghosts"; if the state is devoted to aggression and conquest, expound "inclusive care" and "condemning aggression". So I say, select a priority to work on.' (49/61–4)

49.15 Our master Mòzǐ recommended Cáo Gōngzǐ for a position in Sòng. After three years he returned, saw our master Mòzǐ, and said, 'When I first came to study with you, I wore a rough hemp coat and ate soup of grasses and leaves. If I got some in the morning, I got none in the evening, and I had nothing to offer in sacrifice to the ghosts and spirits. Now through your teachings, Sir, my household is better off than at first. Having a better-off household, I meticulously offer sacrifices to the ghosts and spirits. However, many people in my household died, my livestock don't breed, and I've been swamped with illnesses. I'm not convinced your way is usable.'

Our master Mòzǐ said, 'Not so. Now the ghosts and spirits desire much from people. They desire people in positions of high rank and salary to yield them to those more worthy and those with many resources to share them with the poor. How could the ghosts and spirits desire only to grab the sacrificial food you offer them? Now you hold a position of high rank and salary and don't yield it to the more worthy, this is one inauspicious thing. You have many resources and don't share them with the poor, this is a second inauspicious thing. Now you serve the ghosts and spirits merely by offering sacrifices, yet you say, "Where do illnesses come from?" This is like closing one door among a hundred and saying, "Where do robbers come in?"* You're like this, yet you seek blessings from ghosts who fault you—how could this be acceptable?!' (49/64–71)

. . .

49.22 Gōngshūzǐ said to our master Mòzǐ, 'Before I saw you, I desired to take Sòng.* Since I saw you, were someone to give me Sòng unrighteously, I wouldn't accept it.'

Our master Mòzǐ said, 'Before I saw you, you desired to take Sòng. Since I saw you, were someone to give you Sòng unrighteously, you wouldn't accept it. This is my giving you Sòng. If you strive to practise righteousness, I will yet give you the whole world.' (49/94–7)

BOOK 50
GŌNGSHŪ

50.1 Gōngshū Bān built cloud-ladder machines* for Chǔ with which to attack Sòng.* Our master Mòzǐ heard about it and, starting from Qí,* walked ten days and ten nights to arrive in Yǐng.* He met Gōngshū Bān.

Gōngshū Bān said, 'Sir, what commands do you have for me to carry out?'*

Our master Mòzǐ said, 'In the north there is a person who humiliated me. I wish to have you kill him.'

Gōngshū Bān was displeased.

Our master Mòzǐ said, 'Please let me offer you ten pieces of gold.'

Gōngshū Bān said, 'My norm of righteousness is certainly not to kill people.'

Our master Mòzǐ stood up, bowed twice, and said, 'Please let me explain. From the north, I heard that you made ladders to attack Sòng. What crime has Sòng committed?! The state of Jīng* has a surplus of land but a shortage of people. Killing what's in shortage to fight for what's in surplus cannot be called wisdom.* Sòng is innocent yet you attack it—this cannot be called benevolence. To know something yet not strive for it cannot be called loyalty.* To strive for something yet not succeed cannot be called strength. Your norm of righteousness is not to kill few, yet you would kill many—this cannot be called knowing kinds.'*

Gōngshū Bān was convinced.

Our master Mòzǐ said, 'So, why not stop the attack?'

Gōngshū Bān said, 'It's not possible. I have already stated it to the king.'

Our master Mòzǐ said, 'Why not present me to the king?'

Gōngshū Bān said, 'Agreed.' (50/1–7)

50.2 Our master Mòzǐ saw the king and said, 'Now suppose there is a person here who sets aside his fine carriage, as his neighbour has a broken cart and he desires to steal it. He sets aside his embroidered finery, as his neighbour has a rough hemp coat and he desires to steal it. He sets aside his grain and meat, as his neighbour has some chaff and dregs and he desires to steal them. What kind of person is this?'

The King said, 'Surely he is a kleptomaniac.'*

Our master Mòzǐ said, 'The territory of Jīng is five thousand *lǐ* square; the territory of Sòng is five hundred *lǐ* square. This is like the relation between a fine carriage and a broken cart. Jīng has Yún Mèng, full of rhinoceroses and milu deer,* while the Yángzǐ and Hàn rivers are the richest in the world in fish, tortoises, and crocodiles; Sòng is said to lack pheasants, rabbits, and foxes. This is like the relation between grain and meat and chaff and dregs. Jīng has tall pines, catalpa, camphor, and oak; Sòng has no tall trees. This is like the relation between embroidered finery and a rough hemp coat. Your subject takes the King's officials' attacking Sòng to be of the same kind as this.* I see the great King will surely injure righteousness to no gain.'

The King said, 'Excellent! However, Gōngshū Bān has made the cloud-ladders for me. We must take Sòng.' (50/7–13)

50.3 Thereupon the King received Gōngshū Bān. Our master Mòzǐ untied his belt to make a city wall and used sticks as machines.* Gōngshū Bān tried nine different ways of setting up his machines to attack the city wall, and our master Mòzǐ repelled him nine times. Gōngshū Bān's attack machines were all used up, while our master Mòzǐ had defences to spare.

Gōngshū Bān yielded and said, 'I know how to repel you, but I won't state it.'

Our master Mòzǐ also said, 'I know how you would repel me, but I won't state it.'

The King of Chǔ asked the reason.

Our master Mòzǐ said, 'Gōngshūzǐ's intention is simply that he desires to kill me. If he kills me, no one can defend Sòng and he can attack. However, my disciple Qín Gǔlí and three hundred others are already equipped with my defence devices and await the Chǔ raiders on the walls of Sòng. Even if you kill me, you cannot cut them off.'

The King of Chǔ said, 'Excellent! I request that we not attack Sòng.' (50/13–18)

50.4 Our master Mòzǐ returned home. As he passed Sòng, it rained. He sought shelter in the city gate, but the gatekeepers did not let him in. So it's said, 'Those who handle things with the efficacy of spirits, the masses of people don't know their achievements; those who contend in the light, the masses of people know them.'* (50/18–19)

EXPLANATORY NOTES

Throughout the translation, the section numbers are the translator's. The traditional Chinese text is not divided into paragraphs. The section numbers generally correspond to what seem to be shifts in topic.

The index numbers at the end of each section give the chapter and line numbers in *A Concordance to Mo Tzu*, Harvard-Yenching Sinological Index series, Supplement no. 21 (Cambridge, MA: Harvard University Press, 1956). These indices can be used to locate the Chinese text of the paragraph through the concordance search tool at the Chinese Text Project (https://ctext.org/mozi), edited by Donald Sturgeon.

PART I: MISCELLANEOUS ESSAYS

The translation omits books 1 to 3. Book 3, 'On Dyeing', is an anecdote about Mòzǐ that appears also in *The Annals of Lǚ Bùwéi*. Books 1 and 2, 'Kinship with Officers' and 'Cultivating Oneself', are of marginal interest to Mohist thought.

BOOK 4: MODELS AND STANDARDS

5 *Our master Mòzǐ*: the Mohists' distinctive way of referring to their founding teacher. The phrase can be literally rendered as 'our master, Master Mò'.

officers: shì 士, an elite class of educated men, including military officers, minor aristocracy, gentry, landowners, and scholars, whose education, status, or other qualifications make them fit candidates for government or military posts. The *shì* rank above commoners but below the aristocracy; in some contexts, *shì* is a near synonym of *jūnzǐ* 君子, 'gentleman'. Mòzǐ himself and his more educated followers would have been *shì*. Since *shì* was originally a military rank similar to 'knight', the translation renders it as 'officers'.

make squares . . . compass: two examples of models to which Mohist writers return repeatedly are the wheelwright's compass, used to check whether a wheel is true, and the carpenter's set square, used to check whether a corner is square.

flat surfaces with the level: inserting a fifth model, missing from the text, to agree with the mention of five models in the next line.

models: fǎ 法, a general term for explicit standards used in guidance and evaluation. Models include weights and measures, tools such as the set square and compass, role models, instructions, and laws or paradigmatic legal judgements. The same word, *fǎ*, is used both as a noun and as a verb, meaning to emulate or model on something.

order: one of the Mohists' basic values and central topics of discussion. The word for 'order', zhì 治, can also be interpreted as to govern, control, or manage. The text often mentions ordering the world or the people, referring to governing them and bringing them to good order.

5 *Heaven*: tiān 天, also 'the sky'; the highest deity recognized by the Mohists.

6 *Yǔ, Tāng, Wén, and Wǔ*: four of the six ancient sage-kings (shèngwáng 聖王) the Mohists regularly cite as moral and political exemplars. See 'shèngwáng' in the Glossary.

Son of Heaven: tiānzǐ 天子, the name for the highest leader or overlord of all the various rulers of states.

Jié, Zhòu, Yōu, and Lì: the four ancient tyrants the Mohists cite as examples of malicious, unscrupulous rulers. See 'tyrants' in the Glossary.

BOOK 5: SEVEN TROUBLES

8 *models*. fǎ 法, here probably refers to laws or to paradigmatic legal adjudications, which were considered a type of model or standard. The point is that the ruler capriciously rewrites the laws.

altars to the spirits: an important responsibility of a ruler was to venerate the spirits of soil and grain at shrines devoted to them in the capital. By synecdoche, 'the altars of soil and grain' refers to the state itself. The altars being lost or toppled refers to the state being overthrown.

Wherever these seven troubles . . . disaster: it is unclear whether Mòzǐ's speech ends here or is intended to include the succeeding paragraphs, which do not directly continue the themes of the opening paragraph.

the five grains: probably rice, wheat, soybeans, and two varieties of millet.

9 *How could it . . . way*: the people become stingy and mean only because they face hardship.

go back to the timing: correct the timing of planting and harvesting.

go back to use: moderate the use of resources.

'*Yǔ had seven years . . . drought*': Yǔ was a sage-king of the Xià dynasty renowned for ambitious engineering projects that ameliorated chronic flooding. Tāng was a sage-king of Yīn dynasty, also known as the Shāng dynasty, who supposedly distributed money to the drought-stricken poor.

they: the unscrupulous rulers of the day.

10 *Zhōu*: the third of the 'three dynasties', after the Xià and Shāng, that the Mohists draw on for historical examples.

'*A state without . . . children*': any state without three years' worth of food supplies risks collapse; any family without three years' worth of supplies risks being forced to abandon or sell their children.

BOOK 6: AVOIDING EXCESS

This book is a concise summary of the doctrines in books 20 and 21. The first paragraph, for instance, corresponds to doctrines presented in §20.1 and §21.7.

11 *palaces*: in the *Mòzǐ* refers not only to a royal palace but to any large or elaborate building. In §8.3, the enclosed courtyard home of a wealthy man is called a 'palace'.

model: the concept of a model overlaps those of a method, standard, or specification.

If city walls . . . people: this paragraph and the next seem misplaced.

well ordered: that is, well governed or in good order.

the people are . . . order: alternatively, the people are difficult to govern.

12 *model for making clothing*: compare §21.4.

the endeavour . . . world: a sage-king could succeed in the endeavour of becoming the benevolent hegemon of all the world.

13 *ate only plain foods . . . other*: they ate only wild plants and did not live together in agriculture-based communities.

boats and carts: compare §21.5.

14 *all of these five*: housing, clothing, food and drink, transportation, and sexual relations.

BOOK 7: THREE DISPUTATIONS

15 *Chéng Fán*: commentators suggest Chéng was a student of both Mòzǐ and the Erudites. He also appears in the Dialogues.

music of jars and pots: ceramic instruments that were drummed.

16 *Eating is beneficial . . . all*: knowing enough to eat when hungry is such minimal know-how that it doesn't count as having knowledge or wisdom. Similarly, the sage-kings' music was so minimal as to not count as having music. As book 32 makes clear, by 'music', the Mohists refer primarily to large-scale orchestral and dance performances held in a special theatre, accompanied by a banquet. Hence Mòzǐ can allow that the sage-kings played a few songs without regarding it as a contradiction to also claim they did not 'have music'.

PART II: THE TRIADS

BOOKS 8–10: PROMOTING THE WORTHY

The title can also be interpreted as 'honouring' the worthy. Since the main theme is not merely honouring the worthy but elevating them to government posts, the translation renders the title 'promoting the worthy'.

19 *stated*: the use of 'stated' (*yán* 言) instead of simply 'said' (*yuē* 曰) probably marks what follows as having the status of a recognized teaching or pronouncement from Mòzǐ.

punishments and government: shorthand for legal and administrative affairs, including the content and application of statutes and edicts and the policies and management of state institutions.

'Nowadays kings, dukes . . . detest': compare §35.1.

208 *Explanatory Notes*

19 *What is the reason for this?*: it is unclear whether this question is part of Mòzǐ's statement. Throughout the translation, I will punctuate as a quoted statement only when the text makes it reasonably clear that the content is to be construed as Mòzǐ's speech. (Some passages may defensibly be interpreted as Mòzǐ's speech even when not punctuated that way.) The Triads frequently employ the device of having an unnamed narrator pose questions for Mòzǐ to answer or explain the reasons for Mòzǐ's statements.

unable to govern . . . capable: alternatively, 'unable to implement promoting the worthy and employing the capable as government policy'. In Mohist writing, often the same phrase can be interpreted as 'to govern by doing x', 'to take x as a basis for governing', or 'to adopt x as official government policy'.

officers: shì 士, an educated elite class of men suitable to be military or civil service officers.

[We] say: here and in many contexts throughout the Triads, no speaker is specified for the verb yuē 曰 ('say'). The attribution to a subject, such as 'we', 'I', or 'he', is the translator's, indicated in square brackets.

20 *Superiors employed . . . method*: people were employed and their service evaluated by a single criterion, moral righteousness.

[They] said, 'If . . . them': compare §9.4.

21 *'Elevate public righteousness . . . resentment'*: apparently a well-known saying.

nine realms: a name for the nine divisions of the territory of the ancient Chinese peoples.

So in antiquity . . . submitted: these examples allude to a series of legends about power being invested in capable people of humble origins. The sage-king Yáo discovered the talents of Shùn, his eventual successor, and promoted him to a position of authority. The sage-king Yú employed Bó Yì as a high official to assist him in flood control projects. Yī Yǐn was a cook whom the sage-king Tāng elevated to high office. Hóng Yāo and Tài Diān began as gamekeepers and rose to become great men in King Wén's government. Compare §§9.6b and 10.3.

22 *The noble and wise . . . disorder*: compare §27.1a. Alternatively, 'noble' versus 'lowly' can be interpreted as 'exalted' versus 'base' or 'common', while 'wise' versus 'foolish' can be interpreted as 'knowledgeable' versus 'ignorant'. 'Wise' (here zhì zhě 智者) is literally 'those of knowledge' or 'the knowledgeable'.

order: zhì 治, also referring to governing and managing.

punishments and models: 'punishments' refers to the content and the application of the penal code. 'Models' here probably refers to laws or to prototype legal adjudications.

fish weirs: large fish traps built by placing stakes in a river or in tidal waters.

23 *ploughing and sowing . . . crops*: presumably the worthies are supervising this labour, not performing it themselves.

When worthies order . . . eat: compare §§25.3a, 32.7b, and 37.3.

entering to defend . . . powerful: defensive and punitive warfare, respectively—entering a city to defend it from a siege and going abroad on a punitive expedition against an aggressor. See book 19.

Three Foundations: alternatively, the 'Three Roots' or the 'Three Fundamentals'.

[We] say . . . them: compare §8.4.

An ode says: as their rhetoric and doctrines developed, the Mohists came to think it crucial not only to appeal to the deeds of the legendary sage-kings but to cite ancient texts in support of their views. Another example in this book is §9.6a. Readers will notice many further examples in other books.

24 *to emulate ancient . . . capable*: alternatively, to interact with people by adopting this as a government policy.

If kings, dukes . . . vicious: the short-sighted rulers appoint unworthy candidates to high posts, thus praising and rewarding the unworthy. Their praise and rewards do not go to genuinely worthy people, while their punishments do not go to genuinely vicious people.

25 *If rewards don't . . . this*: compare §35.4.

All this is . . . things: the demand for analogical consistency between how we handle small-scale matters and how we handle large-scale ones is a recurring theme in the *Mòzǐ*. Compare §§10.2, 26.1, 27.2a, 28.1a, 28.5b, and 49.6.

ordering: this paragraph and the next illustrate how the Mohists' concept of 'good order' (*zhì* 治) overlaps with 'managing' and 'governing'. For consistency, the translation uses the word 'order', but the text reads more smoothly if 'ordering' here is construed as 'managing'.

the occupant of . . . it: they give the person a high-status, high-paying job merely because they admire his looks.

26 *Knowledge*: for the Mohists refers not only to knowledge of facts but to know-how and wisdom.

those statements above: that is, the statements in §§9.2, 9.3, and 9.4.

my statements here: the statements in §§9.5a and 9.5b.

distant years: an alternative interpretation is that this may refer to the title of a lost text. The corresponding phrase in §10.4 similarly could refer to a saying established over many years or to the title of an otherwise unknown text.

In antiquity, Shùn . . . world: compare §8.5. This section introduces a further legend, the story of Fù Yuè the wall-layer who was elevated to high office by Wǔ Dīng, a ruler of the Shāng. See too §10.3.

27 *Thus Heaven and . . . day*: to the Mohists, the worst possible outcome in life is for one's name to be eternally reviled and one's descendants cut off, so that no kin remain to offer sacrifices in honour of one's ghost.

27 *punishments.*...: the text continues with several further historical examples and citations from ancient documents.

29 *models*: most likely laws or prototype legal judgements.

adopted to govern the world: or 'adopted as government policy throughout the world'.

previously: since this is the first paragraph in book 10, it is unclear what 'previously' refers to. Perhaps it refers to Mòzǐ's standing practice of valuing the way of the sage-kings.

30 *By this I know . . . things*: compare §§9.5b, 26.1, 27.2a, 28.1a, 28.5b, and 49.6.

they will ruin the resource: that is, they will ruin a valuable asset.

31 *Thus as to how . . . world*: compare §9.6b.

bamboo and silk: documents were written either on sheets of silk or on thin strips of bamboo bound together with thread.

What should you consider . . . this: this sentence has been translated to follow the idiosyncratic interpretation given in the next several lines of the text, which diverges from how the sentence is usually read.

32 *In the documents . . . is so*: it is unclear whether the text is citing a traditional saying or the title of an otherwise unknown document.

[They] say: no speaker is specified for the three instances of *yuē* 曰 ('say') in this section.

knowledgeable: alternatively, 'knowing' or 'wise'.

33 *superior*: in moral qualities.

BOOKS 11–13: IDENTIFYING UPWARD

The title of the next three books, *shàng tóng* 尚同, can be interpreted in several ways. Taking *shàng* (promote, exalt) as a verb and *tóng* (same, similar) as its object gives an interpretation along the lines of 'promoting identity' or 'exalting conformity'. This interpretation reflects the books' themes and parallels the syntax of the similar title of books 8–10, 'Promoting the Worthy' (*shàng xián* 尚賢). Alternatively, taking *shàng* (up, above) as an adverb and *tóng* (same, similar) as a verb gives 'upwardly conforming' or 'identifying upward'. Since the text repeatedly uses *shàng tóng* (sometimes written 上同) to refer to conforming to or identifying with superiors, the latter interpretation seems better justified. Part of the meaning of *shàng tóng* is being the same (*tóng*) as or emulating superiors. Beyond this, the text repeatedly contrasts *shàng tóng* with 'aligning below' (*xià bǐ* 下比), or 'subordinates' allying together against their superiors. *Shàng tóng* thus implies not merely agreeing with and emulating superiors but identifying with them. 'Identifying upward' hence seems a fitting translation.

34 *"People have different . . . righteousness"*: each person had a 'different righteousness'—different people all applied different norms concerning what they considered righteous or proper.

Hence people deemed . . . wrong: alternatively, 'people approved their norm and condemned others' norms, so in interacting they condemned each other'. 'Right' (*shì* 是) and 'wrong' (*fēi* 非) can be used as verbs (to deem right, to deem wrong) referring to the attitudes of approving or condemning. One's norms of righteousness are understood to be norms for distinguishing right from wrong or approving some actions and condemning others.

Son of Heaven: the supreme ruler.

Son of Heaven was established: in the Chinese text, many sentences in this paragraph have no grammatical subject, leaving it unspecified who selects the Son of Heaven and other leaders. For this reason, the translation uses the passive voice and leaves several participles dangling. Compare §§12.2 and 13.2.

35 *What superiors deem . . . wrong*: alternatively, 'what superiors approve, all must approve; what superiors condemn, all must condemn'.

36 *Thus the village head . . . order*: compare §§12.4 and 13.4.

If the common people . . . Heaven: compare §§12.5 and 13.4.

the five punishments: tattooing the face, cutting off the nose, chopping off the foot, castration, and death.

'The ancient sage-kings . . . superiors': compare §12.7a.

37 *the people lacked . . . righteousness*: compare §§11.2 and 13.2.

40 *five grains . . . six livestock*: the five grains are probably rice, wheat, soybeans, and two varieties of millet. The six livestock are horses, oxen, sheep, pigs, dogs, and fowl.

Now having identified . . . Heaven: compare §§11.5 and 13.4.

entering to defend . . . victorious: as in §9.3, these are references to defensive and punitive war.

41 *the Miáo tribes*: a foreign tribe who lived to the south, between modern Hunan and Jiangxi.

teaches: the word used is *dào* (way), so an alternative translation might be, 'The way of the "Penal Code of Lü" is. . . .'

The Miáo people . . . execution: the text of the quotation is uncertain and the translation is tentative. The punishments are mutilating corporal punishments. Supposedly, the Miáo applied them so viciously that they amounted to five ways of torturing offenders to death.

models: laws or prototype cases used as a basis for legal adjudication.

teaches: again, this word could also be interpreted as 'the way of the document is. . . .'

to assist in ordering . . . calm: to assist in achieving peace and order throughout all under Heaven (all the world).

the Lord on High: the high god Dì of the Shāng dynasty, whom the Mohists continue to venerate. Mohist writings partly distinguish Dì from Heaven but also partly conflate them. See 'Shàng Dì' in the Glossary.

42 *those the masses condemn*: alternatively, those they deem wrong.

"*People dwell together in masses*": people live together as a community.

If people are praised . . . them: compare §13.3.

were able to apply . . . leaders: some commentators suggest revising this sentence to read 'were able to govern by identifying upward' or 'were able to apply identifying upward as a government policy'.

the facts about . . . communicated: the actual situation among those governing and among their subjects was reliably communicated both ways. The word for facts, *qíng* 情, refers also to attitudes and feelings, so an implication is that rulers and subjects are both aware of the other party's views.

43 *lǐ*: slightly over 400 metres or about a quarter of a mile.

seeing and hearing are spirit-like: they are magically effective, like the powers of a spirit.

that they were able . . . upward: or 'that they were able to adopt identifying upward as a government policy'.

punishments and government: again, the legal system and state administration.

44 *the wise*: alternatively, 'the knowledgeable'.

If superiors in governing . . . wrong: the facts, *qíng* 情, include people's attitudes and feelings, and 'what the people have done good or wrong' can also be construed as 'what the people deem good or wrong'. So an alternative interpretation is that rulers are informed about people's attitudes or win their emotional identification, and so they understand what the people approve or condemn.

the common people were persons: they were each their own person. Commoners—literally, the 'hundred surnames'—were each their own master, not subjects of a lord or ruler.

45 *they chose a worthy . . . Heaven*: compare §§11.2 and 12.2. Only this version specifies who chose the Son of Heaven.

it was to distinguish. . . . brightness: the text may be faulty, so the interpretation is tentative. The sentence is a variant of that quoted in §12.7b, which has 'ordering Heaven's calm'. One interpretation is that Heaven's brightness is Heaven's bright way.

46 *Nowadays why are . . . different*: compare §12.7c.

48 *it's this way . . . refers*: that is, this is an apt description of the way of governing by identifying upward to a unified norm of righteousness. The description is a variant of a statement attributed to the 'former kings' in a portion of §9.7 not translated here.

49 *superior*: a reference to virtue, not rank.

BOOKS 14–16: INCLUSIVE CARE

Book 14, 'Inclusive Care (I)', is one of only three books in the Triads (the others being books 17 and 20) that do not begin with a pronouncement attributed to

Mòzǐ. It and book 20 are organized similarly, with a discussion of the policies or ways of the sage, followed by a concluding slogan attributed to Mòzǐ. These are likely to be among the earliest Mohist writings. The concluding line is a promising candidate for a direct quotation from the historical Mòzǐ.

50 *How could putting . . . so*: how could it be the sole exception to this pattern?

52 *benevolent person*: in this context, perhaps specifically political leaders.

tasks: in this context, perhaps affairs of state.

53 *the benevolent deem it wrong*: alternatively, the benevolent condemn or reject it. Compare §16.1a.

the model of . . . benefiting each other: the doctrine of 'inclusive care' is considered a model (*fǎ* 法) by which to guide action, with two parts. Everyone is to include or combine (*jiān* 兼) one another within the scope of those we care about, and we are to interact (*jiāo* 交) with one another in ways that benefit both sides. The phrasing suggests that inclusive care is a standing attitude toward everyone that produces mutually beneficial actions when we interact with others. Since the model specifies that the benefit is mutual, inclusive care is not purely altruistic.

'*Thus if the various . . . it*': compare §16.1b.

the most difficult . . . world: compare §16.6.

55 *Yet now the officers . . . river*: compare §16.4.

56 *is it "inclusion" . . . "exclusion"*: is it including others within the scope of our care and benefit, or excluding them—dividing them off from—the scope of our care and benefit?

'*If we try to . . . wrong*': compare §15.1b.

57 *it issues from this method*: alternatively, 'it issues from this direction'—that is, this line of argument. Compare §15.1c.

adopting it as government policy: alternatively, 'adopting it as a norm of correctness'.

how can it possibly be used: the issue is whether it can be applied beneficially as a social practice. 'Use' is the third of the Mohists' three standards for evaluating a statement or teaching as right or wrong, beneficial or harmful. See §§35.1, 36.1, 37.1.

58 *would deem it wrong*: alternatively, would 'reject' or 'condemn' it.

Thus the statement . . . this: the text emphasizes the pairing of statements (*yán* 言) and conduct (*xíng* 行)—words and deeds, theory and practice—because the statements or teachings one endorses are expected to guide and correspond to one's actions or conduct.

high officers: officers of high ideals, not high rank.

Bā, Yuè, Qí, or Jīng: four distant places.

59 *deem it wrong*: alternatively, 'condemn it' or 'reject it'.

60 *it's like picking . . . river*: compare §15.3.

61 '*Might it fail . . . devotion*': compare §31.7a.

do you take . . . correct: alternatively, do you take them to be ignorant and inadequate to serve as a standard of correctness?

Offer me a peach . . . plum: a peach tree quickly bears fruit; a plum tree takes longer, but the fruit is more valuable. Small acts of generosity may bring the giver greater rewards in the long term.

62 *Might it be . . . done*: compare §15.2. The phrasing of this objection is similar to that in §16.4. The difference is that this section addresses whether inclusive care is too difficult for a community to practise, while §16.4 addresses whether it is even physically possible.

63 *If one practises inclusion . . . fraternal*: this is the most complete list in the *Mòzǐ* of the relational virtues—virtues associated with excellent performance of what the Mohists take to be the three core pairs of relational social roles: ruler and subject, who are expected to be generous and loyal, respectively; father and son, who are to be paternally kind and filially devoted; and elder and younger brother. Younger brothers are to show fraternal devotion; the virtue associated with elder brothers is variously described as being amicable, respectful, good, and peaceful or harmonious.

BOOKS 17–19: CONDEMNING AGGRESSION

64 *they deem him wrong*: alternatively, they condemn him.

Now suppose a person . . . himself: compare §28.5b.

65 *Now suppose there . . . 'white'*: compare §§28.5c and 49.6.

Now when someone . . . unrighteousness: compare the discussion of knowing the little things but not the big ones in §§9.5b, 10.2, 27.2, 28.1a, 28.5b, and 49.6.

66 *faulty. . .*: there appears to be a lacuna in the text, as this opening remark is incomplete.

ghosts and spirits . . . descendants: the ancestral ghosts lose the heirs of their family line and thus have no direct descendants to preside over sacrifices venerating them.

67 *discard what's in shortage . . . surplus*: compare §§19.4 and 50.1.

Governing like this . . . state: pursuing military aggression as a government policy runs contrary to the proper duties or business of the state.

one cannot deem them wrong: alternatively, one cannot condemn or reject them.

not practising medicine: to count as practising medicine competently, the doctor must heal patients reliably, not heal only a tiny percentage. Compare §19.6.

68 *Sòng and Lǔ*: after his defeat of Chǔ, these two states pledged allegiance to him.

70 *reality*: shí 實, stuff, facts, objects.

the blind being . . . names: compare §47.9. The blind can make correct statements using the names 'white' and 'black' but when presented with white and black things cannot distinguish them.

the way of the wise: alternatively, the way of those who possess knowledge.

§19.1a . . . 19.2b: the discussion in §19.1–2 is only weakly coherent and does not directly mention the purported topic of the book. These paragraphs provide a particularly clear example of the composite nature of many of the books. For all we know, they could represent an unknown ancient editor's work in progress.

doctrine of great states: presumably, the doctrine that great states should strive to expand their territory through military conquest.

71 *They inevitably all muster . . . animals*: compare §28.5a.

ghosts: ancestral ghosts are harmed because their descendants can no longer venerate them—some are dead, others lack the resources for sacrifices or have fled their homes, leaving the ancestral altars behind.

The gentlemen . . . foot soldiers: these three levels seem to refer to officers from the social elite, officers from common families, and foot soldiers, perhaps including forced labourers.

72 *common people abandon their duties*: they leave their normal vocations to join the military campaign.

to lose what's . . . surplus: compare §§18.3 and 50.1.

in order to deem . . . wrong: alternatively, in order to refute or condemn Mòzǐ.

These men were all . . . this: since the sage-kings themselves engaged in military aggression, how can aggression be wrong?

You have not examined . . . them: that is, you have not understood the basis for drawing distinctions between normatively relevant kinds, or different types of things or conduct. See too §50.1 and books 44–5.

"punishment": the wars of the sage-kings were not unrighteous wars of aggression but righteous punitive wars. In places, the text uses the same word, *gōng* 攻, for both the unjust attacks it condemns and the purportedly just wars of the sage-kings. For clarity, the translation uses 'aggression' for unjust warfare in contexts where the contrast is stressed.

Heaven again issued . . . mandate: the preceding story, omitted here, recounts how Heaven used supernatural portents, such as a visit from a spirit with the face of a person and the body of a bird, to signal its mandate for the sage-king Yǔ to subjugate the disorderly Miáo tribes and bring peace to the world.

73 *Yīn Bào*: Wú Yùjiāng suggests Yīn Bào ('Dark Violence') is the name of a spirit sent to assist in defeating Xià.

this is how . . . Jié: the ensuing passage, omitted here, relates the parallel story of how, again through supernatural omens, Heaven mandated that King Wén of the Zhōu dynasty conquer the tyrant Zhòu of the Shāng dynasty.

73 *four states stand alone*: a rhetorical exaggeration. Probably more than a dozen states existed at the time the text was written, of which the four mentioned were among the most powerful.

  a good doctor: compare §18.4.

74 *The world . . . horse*: see §46.11. All the world are exhausted, like children who have been skipping around on a hobby horse all day.

  matchless: invincible and unopposed by any enemy.

  not knowing . . . the world: they fail to recognize that the major priority in benefiting the world is to refrain from aggression and apply resources more productively.

BOOKS 20–1: MODERATION IN USE

The third book of this triad is lost. 'Moderation in Use (II)' is one of only three books in the Triads (the others are books 14 and 17) that does not begin with a pronouncement attributed to Mòzǐ. It and book 14 are organized similarly, with a discussion of the policies or ways of the sage, followed by a concluding slogan attributed to Mòzǐ. These may be among the earliest Mohist texts.

75 *they*: presumably referring to the sages.

  five weapons: most likely the sword, bow, spear, halberd, and lance.

76 *In all cases . . . benefit*: compare this paragraph with book 6, 'Avoiding Excess'.

  Taking the average . . . late: the average of 20 and 40 years of age—that is, 30.

  Yet [things are] . . . this: leaders don't enforce this policy.

  men and women . . . time: thus preventing them from having offspring.

78 *'Enough to satisfy . . . lands'*: compare §6.3.

  dark greyish-blue: the colour mentioned is likely a dark, slightly greyish shade of cyan. It is the same colour the Confucian *Analects* §10.6 states the gentleman does not use to decorate his clothing.

  in summer, wear linen . . . stop: compare §6.2.

79 *Carts . . . the benefit of boats*: compare §6.4.

  'Three layers of shrouds . . . grieving': compare §25.4.

  palaces: any large, elaborate building, not only royal palaces.

  'Build them such . . . stop': compare §6.1.

BOOK 25: MODERATION IN BURIAL

The first two books of this triad are lost.

80 *if their people . . . order*: if their family or clan is small, he tries to have more children; if the family or clan is disrupted by troubles, he seeks to resolve them.

81 *three benefits*: wealth, population, and social order, as presented in §25.1. Promulgating a policy to see whether it is beneficial is an application of the third of the three standards introduced in §35.2.

make people deem it wrong: alternatively, make them condemn it.

Moreover, from antiquity . . . so: the text may be faulty here, as this short paragraph coheres with neither the preceding nor the following paragraphs. The question it raises is dropped and the topic changes.

82 *the attendants buried alive . . . people*: these remarks refer to the practice of funerary human sacrifice, in which up to hundreds of an aristocrat's attendants would be buried along with him so that they could continue to serve him in the afterlife. The practice is said to have been widespread until banned by Duke Xiàn of Qín 秦獻公 in 384 BC.

mourners must wail . . . cane: mourners were expected to eat only a thin, austere diet, to wear poor, inadequate clothing, and to live in rough, uncomfortable conditions. The aim was partly to make themselves appear sick from grief, partly to display that they were too anguished to enjoy the comforts of normal food, clothing, and housing. Appearing ill and weak from mourning was considered ethically admirable, so those who considered themselves of good moral fibre sought to present themselves as extremely sick and weak. 'Superior officers' refers to officers of superior moral virtue, not high rank.

they cannot go to court . . . weaving: compare §§9.3, 32.7b, and 37.3.

84 *unfraternal younger brothers . . . brothers*: younger brothers lacking the virtue of fraternal devotion will resent their elder brothers when the latter are unable to help them.

take attacking and . . . world: alternatively, 'attempt to govern the world by attacking and annexing'.

85 *'A coffin three inches . . . interactions'*: compare §§21.6 and 25.8.

86 *the three kings were . . . burials*: given their wealth, the expense of a rich burial was not a worry for them. Their burials were simple because they considered this the proper model or norm for burials.

Previously: see §25.2a.

87 *it's like fitting . . . together*: it matches them perfectly.

deeming their habits . . . righteous: they assume their existing habits must be the most convenient or appropriate way and their customs must be righteous.

When their eldest son . . . righteousness: compare §49.7.

88 *'A coffin three inches . . . parents'*: compare §§21.6 and 25.4.

BOOKS 26–8: HEAVEN'S INTENT

89 *know the little things . . . big things*: compare §§9.5b, 10.2, 27.2a, 28.1a, 28.5b, and 49.6.

90 *righteousness is [good] government*: righteousness coincides with orderly or proper governance. Compare §§27.1a and 28.1b.

Lord on High . . . Heaven: this paragraph illustrates how the Mohists conceive of the relationship between the Lord on High (the Shāng dynasty ancestor-deity) and Heaven (the Zhōu deity, whom the Mohists revere).

Heaven and the Lord on High are spoken of as two distinct entities, yet offering sacrifices to the Lord and the ghosts and spirits is either a means of or counts as part of the same activity as praying to Heaven for blessings.

91 *Heaven's intention*: the text sometimes refers to Heaven's intent (*zhì* 志), as in the title of the chapter, sometimes to Heaven's intention (*yì* 意).

shining light on them: since Heaven is also the sky, it shines light on all its people.

92 *people who eat grain*: settled, agricultural societies, which the Chinese considered superior to nomadic tribes.

Heaven possesses the townspeople: compare §4.3. All the cities and states of the world are 'Heaven's towns', so all people are its townspeople.

wheelwright's having a compass . . . square: compare §27.3a and §28.4.

94 *foolish and lowly . . . noble and wise*: as in §9.1, the contrast between the wise and the foolish can also be interpreted as one between the knowledgeable and the ignorant, while that between the noble and the lowly can be interpreted as one between the exalted and the common.

'Righteousness is good government': compare §§26.3 and 28.1b.

People must be noble . . . lowly: compare §9.1.

97 *understanding the little things . . . things*: compare §§9.5b, 10.2, 26.1, 28.1a, 28.5b, and 49.6.

98 *Heaven's virtue*: a virtue or potency that aligns with Heaven's intent.

99 *being a criminal to Heaven*: violating Heaven's intent and so committing crimes against it.

Zhòu was insolent . . . him: slightly different versions of this passage appear in §§27.2d, 35.5, and 36.4. Zhòu neglects his ancestors and duties on the grounds that he already holds the mandate of Heaven and thus is fated to rule. *Mìng* 命, the word rendered here as 'mandate', can also be interpreted as 'fate'. In §35.5 and §36.4, the corresponding line reads 'my people have *mìng*', implying that his people's destiny is fated and nothing he does will change it.

he defied Heaven's intention . . . known: compare §28.3.

100 *wheelwright's having a compass . . . square*: compare §26.7 and §28.4.

it is like dividing . . . white: given this clear criterion, distinguishing benevolent from unbenevolent conduct is as easy as distinguishing black from white.

101 *all understand . . . the big things*: compare §§9.5b, 10.2, 26.1, 27.2, 28.5b, and 49.6.

How do we know it is so?: the issue of what Heaven desires seems to be adopted from §26.2. However, having followed §26.2 in raising the question of how we know Heaven desires righteousness, the text here drops the question without answering it. The next several lines jump first to a claim about order from §26.2 and then to the topic of §26.3, about how righteousness requires that superiors govern subordinates.

Righteousness is [good] government: alternatively, the sentence can be interpreted as 'righteousness is correctness'. 'Govern' (*zhèng* 政) and 'correct' (*zhèng* 正) are homophones, and the graph for the latter is sometimes used as a loan for the former. This section uses the graph for 'correct' in the same context that §26.3 and §27.1a use that for 'govern'. Conceptually, governing was seen as a matter of correcting people so as to put them in good order. Hence each instance of 'govern' or 'government' in this paragraph can also plausibly be read as 'correct' or 'correctness'.

subordinates governing superiors: alternatively, 'subordinates correcting superiors'.

102 *commoners don't get . . . them*: alternatively, 'commoners don't get to deem whatever they please correct. There are officers to correct them.'

righteousness turns out . . . Heaven: in this paragraph, the discussion jumps abruptly from an argument based on §26.2 and §26.3 to the conclusion of §27.1a, without having introduced the issue of what righteousness issues from.

103 *Heaven inclusively accepts . . . world*: like §26.3, this paragraph illustrates the vague relationship between Heaven and the Lord on High. That people all over the world sacrifice to the Lord on High and the ghosts and spirits of the natural landscape is considered evidence that Heaven accepts offerings from all people. Heaven as an overarching nature deity seems to incorporate other deities and spirits, such that revering them counts as revering Heaven and their actions are by extension Heaven's actions.

people who eat grain: settled, agricultural civilizations.

the worthy surely reward . . . vicious: the text appeals to how the worthy reward the good and punish the vicious, but the examples it gives are of Heaven rewarding the sage-kings and punishing the tyrants.

models: by parallelism with the remarks about the tyrants that follow, it appears that several lines of text may be missing here.

104 *To follow inclusion . . . force*: alternatively, to follow inclusion as a way is 'to take righteousness to be correct', and to follow exclusion is 'to take force to be correct'.

they oppose Heaven's intention: compare §27.2d.

wheelwright has the compass . . . round: compare §26.7 and §27.3a.

105 *they muster their sharpest . . . animals*: compare §19.3.

not knowing the big things: compare §§17.2 and 49.5.

knowing the little things: compare §§9.5b, 10.2, 26.1, 27.2a, 28.1a, and 49.6.

a person here . . . possession: compare §17.1.

107 *sweet and bitter*: compare §§17.2 and 49.6.

This. . .: the text is faulty here and several words may have dropped out.

BOOK 31: UNDERSTANDING GHOSTS

The first two books in this triad are lost. The title of the triad is ambiguous. Typically in the *Mòzǐ* the word *míng* 明 used as a transitive verb refers to understanding or being clear about something. By extension, it can sometimes be interpreted as 'to explain' or 'to clarify'. Since it is used this way in the text (§§31.1a, 31.8), I have translated it as 'understanding'. 'Clarifying' is another defensible interpretation, and the related phrase *míng chá* 明察 (clearly examine) is used twice (§§31.1b, 31.2). *Míng* can also be used as a noun to refer to the keen sightedness or sentience of ghosts and by extension as a putative verb to refer to treating ghosts as sentient. This use of *míng* might suggest an interpretation of the title as, roughly, 'treating ghosts as sentient' or 'sentient ghosts'. However, this verbal use of *míng* does not occur in the text of book 31.

108 *the world lost righteousness . . . force*: alternatively, 'the world neglected righteousness, and the various lords took force to be correct'.

109 *reality*: shí 實, also 'stuff' or 'objects'; the facts or what is really present. The *Mòzǐ* sometimes refers to what the masses hear and see as 'the reality of the masses' ears and eyes', sometimes as 'the facts (*qíng* 情) of the masses' ears and eyes'. The text is adducing one of the three models presented in §§35.1, 36.1, and 37.1.

If I die . . . knowing: if he dies yet remains sentient.

110 *this document*: the court annals of Zhōu.

explanation: shuō 說, an account, an explanation, or a piece of argumentation. The text goes on to present four similar ghost stories, each purportedly recorded in ancient documents, concluding in each case that 'looking at things on the basis of the explanation in this document, how can one doubt there are ghosts and spirits?'

superior officer or gentlemen . . . see: the common rabble are unreliable witnesses, not to be trusted by a gentleman.

deeds of the sage-kings: here the text invokes another of the three models.

divide up the sacrifices: after executing Zhòu, King Wǔ became responsible for maintaining the Yīn sacrificial rites. The 'inner' sacrifices were those in the Yīn ancestral shrine, which were to be performed by descendants with the same surname as the Yīn ancestors. The 'outer' sacrifices were to other spirits, such as those of the mountains and rivers. Supposedly, King Wǔ divided up the ritual duties because he assumed the Yīn ancestral ghosts indeed existed and would be angered if their sacrifices were not performed by their direct descendants.

that portions were fair: the resources of the state were equitably divided.

111 *this document*: no document was mentioned in the preceding paragraph. The text is inadvertently repeating the formula used to introduce the ghost stories in §31.3.

Yú Xià, Shāng, and Zhōu: the names of the dynasties, not the kings.

the ancient sage-kings . . . this: this paragraph aptly illustrates the centrality of the Mohists' religious beliefs within their worldview. Maintaining proper, respectful relations with the ghosts, spirits, and deities who rank above us in the cosmic sociopolitical hierarchy is of utmost importance.

every foot of silk . . . strips: texts were written on rolls of silk or on strips of bamboo stitched together with thread and rolled up to form scrolls, or 'bundles'.

112 *documents of the former kings*: another version of one of the three models: the documents of the sage-kings.

Shāng. . . .: the text continues with citations from documents of the Shāng and Xià dynasties that the writers regard as acknowledging or implying the existence of ghosts and spirits.

implement it . . . people: this is the third of the three models.

people. . . .: the next sentence of the text seems faulty, and a misplaced phrase has been omitted from the translation.

113 *this. . . .*: several garbled sentences have been omitted from the translation.

the keen sight . . . spirits: can be interpreted literally—their sharp eyesight— or figuratively, as referring to their sentience.

He ruined the achievements . . . High: the text of this sentence is faulty and the translation is tentative.

"bird formation" . . . "goose march": possibly military formations. 'Nine' may be a symbolic number. Each chariot was accompanied by a squad of twenty-five foot soldiers, but a force of 225 seems too small to conquer the Xià capital.

Tāng climbed Dàzàn . . . lands: the text is obscure and the translation tentative.

Tuīchǐ Dàxì: a famous warrior who served King Jié.

114 *this. . .*: the text goes on to relate a similar story of Heaven commanding King Wǔ to punish the cruel tyrant Zhòu.

'Might it fail . . . devotion': compare §16.5.

ghosts of Heaven: alternatively, 'sky ghosts'.

in fact: qíng 情 (here written 請), also 'actually' or 'genuinely'.

BOOK 32: CONDEMNING MUSIC

Only the first book of this triad survives. As the text makes clear, by 'music', the writers are referring specifically to extravagant performances involving large orchestras, expensive instruments, specially built and decorated facilities, and lavish banquets. The musical instruments involved could be elaborate and costly. A set of bronze bells unearthed from the tomb of Marquis Yǐ of Zēng 曾侯乙 (*c*.433 BC) in 1978 included sixty-four bells ranging from 2.4 to over 200 kilograms in weight.

116 *The task of benevolence*: this may be a scribal error for 'the task of the benevolent person', as in §16.1a.

117 *deem it wrong*: again, here and throughout the book, the connotation here overlaps that of 'condemn it', 'reject it', and 'refute it'.

119 *officers and gentlemen . . . not so*: that is, they take them to be incorrect.

   Kings, dukes . . . apportioned task: compare §§9.3, 25.3a, and 37.3.

120 *Their constant dancing . . . silk*: the text is faulty, so the translation is tentative.

   The Lord on High . . . him: Jié, the tyrant overthrown by Tāng.

   The nine realms are lost: the empire is lost. The nine realms are the nine divisions of the territory of the ancient Chinese peoples.

BOOKS 35–7: CONDEMNING FATALISM

Linguistic and contextual features strongly suggest that several passages in the three books of this triad have been dislocated and others have probably been lost. To produce a more thematically coherent text, I have tentatively moved several paragraphs from one book to another. I have placed §36.2 after §35.2 because it presents the only discussion of what people see and hear, the second of the three criteria mentioned in §35.1. Still, the terminology in §36.2 is different from that of §35.1, suggesting that this may not have been its original location. (Where §35.1 mentions 'the reality the common people's ears hear and eyes see', for example, §36.2a mentions 'the facts the people of the masses' ears hear and eyes see.) I have moved §35.3 to book 36 because it discusses the documents of the sage-kings, which are mentioned in §36.1 but not in §35.1. Finally, I have moved §35.4 to book 37 because it shares phrasing distinctive of the same stratum of Mohist writing. (See the Appendix for a related discussion.) Readers will notice that the relocated passages fit imperfectly with the preceding and succeeding paragraphs. Many textual questions about this triad remain unresolved.

121 *'Ancient kings, dukes . . . detested'*: compare §8.1.

   "If fated to be wealthy . . . is it": compare §§39.4, 48.6, and 48.14.

   one cannot fail . . . distinguish them: we must compare them to reliable criteria to distinguish or discriminate (*biàn* 辨) whether they are right or wrong, beneficial or harmful. In Mohist logic, evaluating or arguing for claims or doctrines was regarded as a process of 'distinguishing' them. 'Disputation' or 'dialectics' (*biàn* 辯) was seen as a process of examining how to draw distinctions properly.

   doctrine: *shuō* 說, clarifying something by explaining the grounds for it; by extension, a doctrine, a teaching, or an account. Alternatively, pronounced *shuì*, the same graph refers to persuading or expounding. In this context, the word could also be taken to refer back to how the fatalists 'persuaded kings, dukes, and great men', in which case we might translate, 'how do we clearly distinguish these people's persuasions/arguments [as right or wrong]?'

   sunrise and sunset . . . three markers: the analogy is to marking the directions of sunrise and sunset to determine the directions of east and west. The word rendered 'markers', *biǎo* 表, originally referred to gnomons or stakes planted in a line of three to record the positions of sunrise and sunset on the horizon. A handy alternative translation might be 'three indicators'. Making marks on a potter's wheel, or turntable, is useless, since as soon as the wheel turns the marks no longer point in the correct direction.

found it in the deeds . . . sage kings: alternatively, find a 'root' for it in the deeds of the ancient sage-kings.

122 *whether it confirms . . . people*: to test whether assertions or teachings are right or wrong, beneficial or harmful, we are to identify a foundation, or precedent, for them in the deeds of the sage-kings; check whether they have a source in the facts people observe, thus giving them an empirical basis; and confirm they are beneficial when applied in government policy and the legal system, thus establishing their practical utility. An acceptable statement must meet all three criteria. The Mohists apply these criteria regularly in many of their arguments, such as those on ghosts (see book 31, where all three are applied) and music (see book 32, where the observational criterion is dropped, since it is irrelevant).

three markers: compare §§36.1 and 37.1. The versions of the three criteria given in these three passages vary, and the terminology shifts from 'three markers' to 'three models'.

36.2a: I have placed §36.2a here because it presents the only discussion of what people see and hear, the second of the three markers mentioned in §35.1.

123 *ancient sage-kings elevated . . . fate*: compare §37.2a.

So the claims . . . not so: what they say is surely not the case.

statements: includes teachings and sayings.

tyrants of previous eras . . . them: compare §§36.4 and 37.2a.

Zhòu was insolent . . . him: slightly different versions of this passage appear in §§27.2d, 35.5, and 36.4.

the grounds by which . . . fate: alternatively, 'the grounds by which King Wǔ condemned Zhòu's holding that there is fate'.

124 *deem them wrong*: alternatively, 'condemn them' or 'reject them'.

125 *three models*: compare §§35.1 and 37.1. This version of the three models drops the references to what people see and hear and to checking whether statements prove beneficial when applied as a basis for state policy.

35.3: I have placed this section here because it discusses the documents of the sage-kings, which are mentioned in §36.1 but not in §35.1.

126 *Expounding . . . distress to the common people*: alternatively, 'delighting in the distress of the people'.

Now why do you . . . it: the translation of the last sentence is tentative, as the text may be faulty.

36.4: this subsection cites five passages from ancient texts to show, in the writers' view, that earlier leaders rejected the doctrine of fate or that events are 'fated by Heaven'. Because of textual problems, the translation omits three of the citations.

127 *'My fate was fixed . . . poor'*: compare this section with §37.2a and §35.5.

    Zhòu was insolent . . . him: slightly different versions of this passage appear in §§27.2d, 35.5, and 36.4.

    our master Mòzǐ deems it wrong: alternatively, he rejects it or he condemns it.

128 *masses' ears hear and eyes see*: presumably, book 37 originally contained a section discussing the importance of examining what the masses hear and see. If so, it is now lost. See §36.2a, which I have placed in book 35, for a rough idea of its likely content.

    observe it: observe whether acting on the statement brings benefit or harm.

    "three models": compare §§35.1 and 36.1.

    If anyone takes this . . . fate: compare §36.2b.

129 *'My fate was fixed . . . poor'*: compare this section with §§35.5 and 36.4.

130 *35.4*: I have placed this section here because it shares phrasing distinctive of the same textual stratum as other material in book 37.

    chief worshipper: a leader to preside over sacrificial rites in their honour.

    lǐ: roughly 400 metres.

131 *entering the home . . . denounce*: compare this section with §9.5a.

    Crown Prince Fā: another name for King Wǔ of the Zhōu dynasty, who with Heaven's blessing overthrew the tyrant Zhòu of the Yīn dynasty (the Shāng dynasty).

132 *the records of . . . dynasties*: the unabridged text quotes one document for each dynasty, two of which have been omitted here.

    bundles of ten strips or more: all documents of any significant length.

    none have it: none support the existence of fate.

    go to court early . . . negligent: compare §§9.3, 25.3a, and 32.7b.

133 *entering to defend . . . victorious*: as in §§9.3 and 12.6, these are references to defensive and punitive war.

    deem them wrong: alternatively, to condemn or reject them.

    statement: also teachings.

PART III: CONDEMNING THE ERUDITES

BOOK 39: CONDEMNING THE ERUDITES

There were originally two books entitled 'Condemning the Erudites', but only the second survives. 'Erudites' is a translation of *rú* 儒 (often translated as 'Confucians'), the Chinese word for the tradition represented by Confucius and his followers.

137 *'In treating kin . . . degrees'*: a paraphrase of a statement in the 'Doctrine of the Mean', §20. The 'methods' mentioned stipulate different treatment depending on the closeness of the kinship.

wife and eldest son . . . father: all are mourned for three years, contrary to the rule that the closer relation (the father) should be mourned longer.

fated by Heaven: tiān mìng 天命, identical to the phrase translated elsewhere as 'Heaven's mandate', referring to the commands the sage-kings received from Heaven to overthrow the tyrants and bring order to the world. See §19.5. The Mohists reject the doctrine that Heaven or other forces mandate the outcome of our actions, thus predetermining our fate. However, they endorse the traditional view that a leader's sanction to rule can be given or withdrawn by Heaven's mandate.

Failure or success . . . them: compare §§35.1, 48.6, and 48.14.

foundation: alternatively, they are contrary to the 'root' or 'fundamentals' of government.

138 *Managing several funerals . . . food*: as experts in ceremonial rites, the Erudites were often employed as funeral officiants.

speech and attire: the Erudites dressed in antique clothing and were fond of using archaic expressions and pronunciation. 'Speech' here is *yán* 言, the same word translated in the Triads as 'statements'. *Yán* may refer to pronouncements, sayings, teachings, or speech; here it may refer both to a style of speaking and to what is said. See too §48.4.

initiate: a version of *Analects* §7.1. Compare §46.17. The word for 'initiate' also refers to inventing.

helps put them into a cart: the translation is tentative. Another interpretation is that the gentleman helps the retreating enemy push their heavy carts.

140 *Yànzǐ*: Yàn Yīng, chief minister to three rulers of Qí. His views converged with the Mohists' in many respects, and they admired him accordingly. A collection of anecdotes about him is preserved in *The Annals of Yànzǐ*, which includes a version of this story (Outer Books, Part II, section 1).

When Confucius was . . . Chén: this is the Mohist version of a well-known story referenced in *Analects* §15.2.

soup of wild greens . . . in: the only food available was wild vegetables collected by Confucius's students.

141 *if his mat . . . eat it*: these are quotations from *Analects* §§10.8 and 10.9, indicating that Confucius was extremely fastidious about minor details of etiquette.

PART IV: THE DIALECTICS

A digital supplement in PDF format providing the full Chinese text and detailed textual notes for this part of the translation is available for download at http://www.mohistcanons.net.

BOOKS 40–3: THE CANONS AND EXPLANATIONS

145 *reason/cause*: gù 故 refers to both reasons and causes.

145 *Minor reason/cause . . . seeing*: a minor reason/cause is similar to a neces-
sary but not sufficient condition; a major reason/cause is similar to a sufficient condition. Any unit/part has a tip (a dimensionless starting point),
but the tip alone is not sufficient to constitute the unit/part. Something
coming into one's view is sufficient for one to see it.

Like one . . . foot: see A61. A pair of discrete items can count as a whole
or aggregate (*jiān* 兼); either member of the pair can count as a unit/part
(*tǐ* 體). A part of a continuous whole, such as the tip of a standard unit of
length, can also count as a unit/part. Any unit/part that itself has parts
can also be considered a whole—a hand is a unit/part of the body, while
the fingers are units/parts of the hand.

The knowing is the capacity: canons A3–A6 form a series on knowledge.

the knowing . . . eyesight: 'the knowing' is a cognitive capacity akin to the
awareness or the understanding. It is that by which we have knowledge
or awareness of things. If this capacity is functioning—if we are awake
or conscious—then we must know, in the sense that we must be aware of
something or other. By analogy, if we have normally functioning eyesight
and are awake, with eyes open, we see something or other. We might nevertheless lack knowledge in the sense of correct judgement, as our judgements about what we are aware of could be mistaken.

Considering: also 'thinking things through', depicted as an activity of cognitive 'seeking', analogous to trying to spy out or catch sight of something.
Unlike the awareness mentioned in A3, considering can fail to obtain what
is sought.

Knowing: using the capacity to know (introduced in A3) to acquire the
ability to correctly describe something. 'The knowing' of A3 is analogous
to the capacity of eyesight; knowing in A5 is analogous to correctly seeing
the features of something.

Knowledge: possessing knowledge or wisdom is being able to use one's
capacity for knowing (A3) to discourse on things—specifically, to sort
them into kinds—in such a way that one obviously knows them in the
sense explained in A5. To complete the extended analogy with vision,
whereas knowing in A5 is like seeing one thing or another, knowledge in
A6 is like having keen vision and thus seeing many things clearly.

146 *A7*: canons A7–A14 form a series on ethical topics.

Benevolence: not merely caring for humanity as a whole, but caring for
units/parts of humanity—that is, each individual. The type of care
required for benevolence is analogous to our care for ourselves. It is caring
for others for their own sake, not as means to our ends, as we might care
about a horse we use for work or transportation.

In intent . . . used: what is righteous is what benefits all the world. The
righteous person intends to take all the world as the 'portion' or 'share'
that he or she seeks to benefit, while being able to carry through on this
intent. However, a person can qualify as righteous even if circumstances

do not place the person in a position to follow through in actually benefiting all the world.

The noble being . . . sorting/ranking: various social ranks are treated differently, according to the appropriate way of sorting or grading them into kinds. With respect to each rank, there are more and less respectful ways of treating people.

What one does . . . robber: the explanation is obscure, and the translation is tentative. A passage in 'Heaven's Intent' (§28.3) uses the phrase 'fine name' in the context of applying terms of approbation to morally worthy conduct. The explanation might be implying that 'conduct' (*xíng* 行) refers to action as described without applying terms of praise, whereas reporting one's action in laudatory terms is devious. The point of the closing analogy is unclear; perhaps it alludes to misrepresenting robbery by giving it a fine name, as when a warlike ruler who conquers another state claims to be righteously bringing good order to the world.

The display of . . . garments: the graph rendered 'sincerity', *shí* 實 ('full, solid'), may originally have read *chéng* 誠, 'integrity'. The canon can be interpreted as stating that sincerity is honour, or, in line with the explanation, that it is the display of one's genuine attitudes. According to the explanation, sincerity involves an expression or display of intent and *qì* 氣 (breath, spirit) that enables others to know one. This manifestation of inward attitudes is unlike the tinkling of metal ornaments or look of jade jewellery, which may be only a hollow, outward show.

strongly: the correct reading and interpretation of the next word, 低, is obscure.

147 *Taking one's parents . . . succeed*: the filial take their parents as the 'portion' or 'share' that they seek to benefit, while indeed being able to benefit them. However, people can be filially devoted even if circumstances prevent them from successfully benefiting their parents.

A15–A18: the textual problems associated with these four canons on virtues such as shame, conscientiousness, honesty, and self-discipline are too thorny to attempt a translation here. Canons A19 and A20, on responsibility and courage, may be part of the same series.

A21: canons A21 to A25 form a series on physiological and psychological concepts.

the knowing: the capacity introduced in A3. Life is explained as the joint presence of a physical form and the capacity for knowing. This account either overlooks plant life or attributes knowing to it.

Omitted: many of the explanations from A22 to A39 are damaged or missing.

Sleep is . . . knowing: when one is asleep, the capacity for knowing or awareness (canon A3) does not know or is not aware of anything—it does not connect with or contact anything (A5).

Dreaming is sleeping . . . so: the dreamer takes things to be thus and so, although in fact they may not be so.

148 *Our affairs having . . . south*: the text here may be damaged or incomplete, and the point is obscure.

To mention . . . objects: in early texts, the verb *nǐ* 擬 followed by a direct object typically refers to emulating or imitating that object. According to A31, then, in using a name to mention something, we are emulating or modelling that thing by means of the name, which functions as a model for the thing referred to. In the case of names of kinds, which apply to things because of their similarity to other things of that kind, using the name as a model informs listeners that the thing is similar to other things of that kind.

object: *shí* 實, 'reality', 'stuff', the standard term in early Chinese logical and semantic theories for the things that names refer to. *Shí* can refer to persons and animals, inanimate objects, kinds, facts, or situations. It can be used as a countable or uncountable noun. The underlying or core connotation associated with *shí* is that of being solid or full; it can be helpful to think of *shí* as 'stuff'.

utter mentions: to speak or to state something is to use a series of words to mention objects, as explained in A31. It is thus to 'utter mentions'.

149 *A34*: A34–A38 form a series on political concepts.

It does not . . . clothing: the explanation is obscure and may be incomplete.

Superiors repaying . . . merit: the explanation may be damaged, as it merely repeats the canon.

Superiors repaying . . . crimes: the explanation may be damaged, as it merely repeats the canon.

A39: A39–A51 form a series devoted to logical and metaphysical concepts.

They are two . . . ruler: two different people can be the same in seeing the same pillar or serving the same ruler.

150 *A limit is . . . foot*: marking off standard units of length with a ruler, we come to a place with insufficient space to mark off another length.

durationless: an instant. References to time may be to parts of it that have duration or that are instantaneous. 'Starting' refers to the instant at which some period of time begins.

A47: can be divided into two parts, A and B. Part A consists of two apparently misplaced graphs, 大益, with no context and no obvious connection to the text preceding or following them. They are omitted here.

To circle around: the translation is tentative, as the meaning of the binome 楨柢 is obscure.

151 *A demarcated hollow . . . constant*: the translation is highly tentative and omits an obscure phrase, possibly a parenthetical gloss, from the middle of the explanation. The text might refer to the rotation of a circular object.

Durationless non-staying . . . 'non-horse': alternatively, 'durationless non-staying is when something fits "oxen are not horses"…Non-staying with duration is when something fits "horses are not horses".' Still another alternative is, 'durationless non-staying coincides with "oxen are non-horses". Non-staying with duration coincides with "horses are non-horses".'

Non-staying with . . . 'non-horse': all 'staying' or 'being fixed' in something has duration. There are two types of 'non-staying': non-staying that is durationless, or instantaneous, and non-staying that persists for some duration. Non-staying that is instantaneous is illustrated by the relation between oxen and 'non-horse', which like the term 'ox' can 'stay' or be 'fixed' in oxen. Since staying requires duration, if we consider only a durationless instant, the term 'non-horse' does not stay in oxen. However, for any duration beyond an instant, 'non-horse' does stay in oxen, since oxen are not horses. Non-staying with duration is illustrated by the relation between horses and 'non-horse'. 'Non-horse' never stays in horses, since they are not non-horses and 'horses are non-horses' is a contradiction. To help explain the idea of a durationless instant, the text gives the example of a person (or, according to some interpreters, an arrow) passing a pillar—an event of very short duration, although not actually instantaneous. This event contrasts with walking over a bridge, which has a longer duration.

Like younger brother . . . case: the first sentence of the explanation is too obscure to justify translation. The example of younger or elder brother illustrates the notion of being 'surely the case' in that for any pair of brothers, one must be elder, one younger. One thing being so, the other not so illustrates being 'not surely the case'. Of two horses, for example, it is not necessarily the case that one is black and the other not black. Both might be black or neither. The example of 'this or not' being surely the case alludes to a version of the law of excluded middle. For any kind of thing, such as horses, it is surely the case that any one animal is either 'this' (a horse) or not.

A52: canons A52–A69 form a series on geometry.

Centre is the same length: the point seems to be that the centre is the location from which the length in two or more directions is the same.

dimensionless: a geometric point.

152 *The compass draws*: the meaning of the next graph, 攴, is obscure.

Square is four . . . balancing: the translation is tentative, as the meaning of 譁 is obscure.

The set square shows: the meaning of the next graph, 攴, is obscure.

Two is measured . . . one: the two foot lengths both depart from one central point, in opposite directions without overlapping, so the total length is two feet.

This is not . . . anything: the tip does not overlap anything, so it is not the same as anything (?). The explanation is obscure and may be damaged.

It refers to the flanked: the remainder of the explanation is obscure.

A lintel . . . empty: the meaning of the graph 繼 is obscure and the translation is speculative. Possibly the graph refers to a header or lintel running across the top of two columns and thus corresponding to the gap between them.

153 _measured foot . . . two_: if a measured foot is filled by something, then anywhere along it we find 'two', the measured length and the object or stuff filling it.

Hard-white: alternatively, 'as hard is to white'; appears to have been a technical term for features that can be compresent or mutually pervasive, as colour and shape or colour and texture. A stone can be both hard and white in the same location at the same time. Hard and white are thus not mutually exclusive. By contrast, a stone cannot be both hard and soft or both black and white in the same place at the same time.

Not each other . . . other: if two things are not one another—as white and black are not one another—then they exclude one another. Something's being white excludes its being black.

Of a measured . . . other: two sequential measured foot lengths touch at their tips and so coincide at only one point, not their entire length. A tip is a dimensionless point, so two tips can fully coincide. A tip that touches a measured foot does so only at the tip of the foot, so the tip is fully covered but the foot is not. Features such as texture and colour can fully coincide, as when every part of a stone is both hard and white, but units/parts cannot, just as the tip of a measured foot does not cover the whole foot.

It is possible . . . tip: the translation is tentative. Normally, 比 would refer to laying things side by side to compare them, as the different pipes of a panpipe are arranged side by side. Here, however, the term seems to refer specifically to measuring against each other two different, overlapping lengths lying along the same line, starting from the same point. Part of the longer length coincides with the shorter one and part extends beyond it. This relation between two lengths contrasts with that described in A69.

It is possible . . . dimensionless: by contrast with the overlapping lengths of A68, this canon describes two adjacent lengths along the same line. The endpoint of the first is the starting point of the second, so the adjacent lengths do not coincide but meet at only one point. As the explanation states, this relation is possible only because the endpoint and starting point are dimensionless.

A model is . . . so: alternatively, a model is what something is like and thereby is so. To determine whether something is _x_, we compare it to a model (_fǎ_) for _x_ to see whether they are similar. If they are, the thing is 'so', namely _x_. To determine whether something is circular, for example, we compare it to a circular object, check it with a compass, or gauge it against the thought or intention associated with a circle (such as the thought that a circle is nowhere straight—A98—or is a line everywhere equidistant from a centrepoint—A58). See too A71. Canons A70–A74 form a series presenting major concepts in dialectics or argumentation, including models, similarity, explanation, distinctions, and disputation or distinction-drawing.

Thought / intention . . . three: to determine whether something is *x*, we compare it to a model of *x* to see whether they are relevantly similar. Models can be exemplars, tools, or thoughts (that is, what one has in mind).

The match / duplicate . . . so: alternatively, it is the aspect or feature of something that is so. Since the surrounding canons treat technical terms relevant to disputation, we would expect A71 to do so as well. Instead, its first graph is 佴 ('duplicate', 'second'), a word that has already appeared in A15, where it may be a variant for 恥 ('shame'), and is never used again in the dialectical texts. Thus, 佴 may be an error or an obscure variant for another graph more pertinent to argumentation. Unfortunately, if this is indeed the case, there is little or no evidence for any hypothesis about the identity of the original graph. Graham conjectures it was 因 (criterion, basis), written with a 'person' radical 亻, a proposal that coheres well with the use of 因 in contexts such as canon A97. However, the conjectured graph occurs nowhere else in the canons—not even in A97—and so the case for this emendation is weak. Moreover, known archaic graphs for 耳 do not closely resemble those for 因. Another possibility is that the graph could have been 仵 or 伍, graphs that in A98, B58, and B76 are associated with the notion of things matching up or aligning with each other as counterparts.

154 *Explanations*: *shuō* 說, in Mohist logic, the analogue of what we would call an argument, a justification, or a piece of reasoning. See §45.1b.

that / other . . . impermissible: for any two terms that stand in the relation of 'this' versus 'that / other', such as 'oxen' and 'non-oxen', it cannot be the case that when asserted of something, both are impermissible (or, equivalently, that neither is permissible). 'Permissible' refers to it being possible to correctly assert a term of something without violating logical and semantic norms.

basis: *yǐ* 以, the features by which we distinguish what is some kind of thing from what is not, such as the features that distinguish oxen from non-oxen. This is the same word that in A86 is translated 'that by which' things are the same.

Disputation: *biàn* 辯, the early Chinese term for dialectical discussion, debate, or argumentation, which is seen as centring on the activity of drawing distinctions. Disputation is understood as contending over which of two contradictory terms applies to something—whether the thing is 'this' or 'that / other'. A disputation is won by the side who asserts a term that 'fits' the thing under consideration. The explanation gives an example of disputing whether some animal is an ox or not. Implicitly applying the law of non-contradiction, the explanation states that the terms 'ox' and 'non-ox' cannot 'both fit' the animal. Applying a version of the law of excluded middle, it then points out that exactly one of the terms 'ox' and 'non-ox' must fit. This case is unlike that of the terms 'dog' and 'hound', both of which can fit the same animal. See too B35.

If, one's knowledge . . . it: what one takes as ends or acts for the sake of is determined not only by one's knowledge but by what one desires. One might act for the sake of cutting off one's finger even if fully informed about the harm involved.

154 *This is like . . . desires*: the dried meat has a distinctive flavour that we are unsure we will like. Having reached the limit of our knowledge about the flavour, we still desire to try it, and we proceed to act toward that end. This is a case in which the limits of our knowledge, and the ensuing uncertainty, do not change our ends—our desire to try the meat. We are similarly unsure about whether a trip beyond the wall will be profitable, as we might encounter robbers or other hazards. If we decide not to go, this is a case in which the limits of our knowledge about the benefits and harms leads us to 'stop' our original desire for money.

155 *A76*: canons A76–A87 list different types or aspects of various things or words. In A76 we have two respects in which things may end or finish.

To employ / cause . . . name: one can employ people or cause them to act by telling them to do something. A physical cause can also cause something to happen.

To order is . . . about: an order is not necessarily carried out successfully.

It depends on . . . about: whatever is caused, such as an illness, must come about before the cause, such as dampness, can be identified as such.

Names . . . personal: three types of names. Canons A78–A79 treat the use of names or words. See too A31–A32.

Naming it 'horse' . . . object: there may be an implied contrast between personal names, which 'stop' in one thing, and kind names, which 'proceed' to all things of the kind. See B72.

When sounds are . . . names: speech consists of names.

Transferring, mentioning, applying: three types or aspects of speech.

Linking 'dog' . . . naming: it is unclear why the explanation refers to 'naming' while the canon refers to 'transferring'. Possibly this is a scribal error, the more common word 命 being substituted for the uncommon technical term 移. Possibly in this context the two terms are synonymous.

'Dog', 'hound' . . . applying: 'naming' or 'transferring' is linking two words together, as when we say 'Dogs are hounds'. Mentioning or 'bringing up' is using a name such as 'dog' or 'hound' to talk about something. (See A31–A32.) 'Applying' is using a term of approval or disapproval of something, as when we scold a dog by calling him 'bad'. In the Triads, 'applying' is used to refer to applying terms of praise to the sage-kings and condemnation to the tyrants.

By hearsay . . . personal: these are three sources of knowledge. On the latter two, see B70.

Names, objects, matching, acting: these are four objects or kinds of knowledge. One may know names, objects, how to match the two, and how to act. On knowledge, see too A3–A6.

Distance does not . . . explanation: the example is obscure. The point may be that distance is no obstacle to obtaining knowledge by explanation. According to B70, an example of such knowledge is knowing the colour of an unseen object in another room when told it is the same colour as an object one can see. Location would be irrelevant to such knowledge.

Names and objects . . . matching: names are correctly matched with their standard referents.

Hearing. Passed . . . person: hearing something or hearing about it may be either first-hand or second-hand.

156 *Seeing . . . all*: seeing something may be seeing part (as when seeing one member of a pair) or all (as when seeing both members of the pair).

Exact . . . definitely: three respects in which things may match or conform.

Standing . . . one-sided: the explanation presents several difficult textual and interpretive problems and the translation is tentative. Regarding the 'exact', see canon A98. Regarding the 'appropriate' or 'fitting', see A96.

Desire . . . weighing harms: the canon lists two respects in which one can desire or dislike something: either directly (as when we simply want something) or after evaluating benefits and harms (as when we do not want something but prefer it as the lesser of two harms). The third item listed for desire, 'about to', refers to the grammatical use of the graph 欲 in Classical Chinese to indicate future action.

Make . . . transform: the canon gives six respects in which the verb *wéi* 為 can be used. The explanation gives examples for each of the six, but several of these raise difficult textual problems.

Same. Identity . . . kind: A86 presents four respects in which things can be considered 'the same', A87 four corresponding respects in which things can be different.

157 *A88–A92*: canon A88 has extensive textual problems. Canons A89–A92 are four sentences, all lacking corresponding explanations, which are unlike all the other canons in format. They appear to be the content of a single bamboo strip that was mistakenly incorporated into the text from a different source.

A93: canons A93 to B1, and possibly B2, appear to form a series giving practical advice about how to proceed in disputation (*biàn*), explained in A74 as disputing what is 'that' versus 'this', such as non-oxen versus oxen. These canons present many interpretive challenges, beginning with the details of A93. The canon and explanation are obscure and the interpretation is provisional. The point seems to be that in disputation, the two sides' agreement may have different consequences, and thus be useful in different ways, depending on what is agreed. The explanation seems to present three types of cases. One is terms such as 'circle', whose application 'stops' in circular objects. Agreement that something is a circle settles the object's shape. The second is terms that follow from or exclude each other. The text gives no example, but perhaps it is referring to pairs of terms such as 'ox' and 'non-ox' or 'ox' and 'horse'. In the case of such pairs, agreement about which of the two is 'this/right' with respect to the object under consideration is enough for us to judge what is 'this' or 'not'. The third is terms that are relative to context. To dispute whether something is long or short, for example, we need to know what standard of length the opponent is applying. In such cases, we can agree on a relevant standard by citing a claim the opponent holds.

157 *If it is . . . assertion*: textual problems render the translation extremely tentative. A relatively clear implication is that disputers should seek to identify the grounds or model on the basis of which an opponent maintains some assertion.

If the model . . . it: two disputers are arguing over whether something is correctly deemed *x* or non-*x*. One side proposes a model—an exemplar—of *x* (see A70). If the model is the same as the thing under discussion, observe what is the same and watch for tricky shifts in how the opponent applies the term '*x*'.

Select this and . . . appropriate: if the model is not exactly the same as the thing under discussion, pick out various features of the thing and ask about the reasons for deeming something *x* in order to determine which features are appropriate for comparing to the model and thus judging whether the thing counts as *x*. For example, is 'black person' applied on the basis of hair colour or skin colour? If a person cares about some people but not all, does she qualify as 'caring about people', according to the doctrine of inclusive care? (It is unclear why the text uses 'black person' as an example and whether it is referring to a person of African descent or a person whose skin is dark from the sun.)

Settle the basis . . . ways: of the various ways of distinguishing what is or is not *x*, fix the basis or grounds relevant in the context under discussion. For example, the basis might be the form or shape of the thing (what determines whether it is an ox or a horse) or its place of origin (a Qín horse versus a Chǔ horse). It might be skin colour (what determines whether a person is a 'black person'). Or it might be whether a person's caring about others is all-inclusive or partly exclusive (what determines whether the person practises inclusive care).

If the other . . . sage: the point of the canon is that certain features are the basis by which to distinguish whether something is *x* or not. As an illustration, not all of a sage's features must be 'this/right'. Some may be 'not' (thus falling short of sageliness?) without disqualifying the sage from being a sage.

Exact is having . . . it: canon A83 implies that things can match a model either exactly or by what is 'appropriate/fitting'. A96 indicates that appropriate/fitting refers to the relevant part of something, as when skin colour is used to judge whether a person is a black person. Presumably, the point of A98 is that something matches a model exactly when it has no features that do not match the model.

158 *When there is . . . agreement*: interpretation of the explanation is conjectural because the meaning of the phrase *wǔ nuò* 五諾 is obscure. I tentatively follow Graham in reading 五 as 伍, equivalent to 仵, 'matching up as counterparts', and I take 諾 to refer, as implied in A93, to an agreement between two sides about how to apply some term in disputation. Since the canon seems to concern cases in which something matches a model exactly, I provisionally interpret *wǔ nuò* to refer to agreement between two sides that something matches a model exactly. The point of the explanation might then be that if two sides agree that an object matches the model, they apply this agreement in continuing their disputation. However, they can also go beyond the agreement if an explanation (a justification) is available to support further assertions that follow from the agreement, as the assertion that a thing is nowhere straight follows from the agreement that it matches the model for a circle.

other: the graph 人 ('others') may be faulty, so the translation is tentative. Following Sūn, many editors emend to 之 'it'. A likely hypothesis is that the text refers to settling what kind of object the other party is referring to, so as to allow the other's use of kind terms to 'proceed' to refer to all members of the kind. The aim would be to determine whether the terms are used in a semantically and logically 'permissible' way.

Explained by: beginning with B1, most canons end with the formula 'explained by. . .', which summarizes the theme of the corresponding explanation.

The other side . . . so: with reference to a particular exemplar, the two sides discuss which features are 'the same' among all members of the kind. They thus 'settle' what the kind under discussion is. The translation takes 此 'this (here)' to refer the exemplar and 是 'this (kind)' to refer to the kind of thing it is supposed to be an exemplar of.

Calling / asserting / saying . . . so: predication and disputation were regarded as based on analogically 'extending' to new cases our judgement as to what is or is not relevantly similar to a model or an exemplar (see A70) and thus is the same kind of thing. The process of extending similarity judgements is fraught with difficulty, as members of the same kind may not be the same in every respect, while members of different kinds may not be different in every respect. The text of the canon is so obscure that interpretation must be tentative, but it appears to offer two reasons for difficulty in extending kinds. First, some features, but not all, are shared by every thing of a kind. Second, because kinds may be larger or smaller in scope, two things may be similar in both falling under one kind without being similar in falling under another.

If four-footed . . . smaller: 'beast' refers specifically to four-footed animals, so it provides an example in which a single, identical feature is shared by every member of a kind. Every four-footed thing is a 'beast' and vice versa. Birds are living things, but not every living thing is a bird. One cannot invariably generalize from features of birds, a kind with a smaller scope, to those of living things, a kind with a larger scope, or vice versa.

158 *milu deer*: one cannot invariably generalize from features of an exemplar to
     claims about an entire kind, as it is not obvious from the exemplar which
     features are shared by all members of the kind. The milu deer is tradition-
     ally said to possess a mixture of features similar to those of other ani-
     mals—antlers like a deer, face like a horse, hooves like an ox, tail like
     a donkey—without actually being like any of these other kinds. (Hence its
     Chinese nickname, '*sìbúxiàng* 四不像' or 'four unalikes'.) The point of the
     closing metaphor may be that if all features of all particular exemplars
     were so of each kind they belong to, then all kinds would be a mishmash,
     as the milu is.

     B3: the many textual and interpretive problems in B3 put it beyond the
     scope of this discussion.

     two: typically, if something 'is two', it has two parts, one of which can be
     removed from the other. The canon addresses cases in which something is
     'two' yet has no part that can be removed.

     Breadth and length are hard-white: only the third example is clear: breadth
     and length are inseparable, as the hardness and whiteness of a hard, white
     stone are. So although breadth and length are two distinct features, nei-
     ther can be removed from the other. The other examples are obscure and
     the translation is tentative. Coming into view and seeing are distinct, but
     we cannot see a thing without it coming into view [?]. One and two do not
     wholly overlap, and thus are not identical, but we cannot have two without
     also having one [?].

     Different kinds . . . amount: different kinds of things may sometimes be
     incommensurable, as they lack any shared standard of measurement. For
     example, the length of a piece of wood (a physical dimension) is a different
     kind of length from the length of the night (a temporal one).

159 *together as one*: the text is obscure and any interpretation is tentative. B12
     uses 'together as one' to refer to oxen and horses—two different kinds of
     animals—being 'one' in having four feet. B7 may refer to a case in which,
     for example, the oxen and horses are removed from each other, but there is
     no reduction in the group of animals that are four-footed. If, as B12 sug-
     gests, the Mohists employ a mereological ontology, the implication may be
     that a mereological whole need not be spatially contiguous. Part can be
     removed without changing the relation of the items as 'together as one' in
     sharing some feature.

     perversity/contradiction: two frequently used terms of semantic and logical
     evaluation in the canons are *kě* 可, 'permissible' or 'admissible', and *bèi* 誖,
     'perverse', 'confused', or 'contradictory'. Assertions or patterns of word
     use that are 'permissible' are those that observe relevant semantic and
     logical norms, among them semantic and logical consistency. Assertions
     that are not permissible are 'perverse'.

     Borrowing 'crane' . . . 'Crane': a 'borrowed' name is a name (presumably
     a kind name or general term) used ad hoc to refer to something it does not
     normally denote, as when a speaker for some reason refers to a dog or dogs

as 'cranes'. By definition, things referred to by a borrowed name are 'not so', or not part of the normal extension of that name. The text suggests that such unorthodox uses of names are similar to having a surname that in other contexts functions as a general term. For example, we can refer to the members of a family as the 'Cranes' without assuming or implying they are actually a group of birds. Nevertheless, B8 contends that borrowed names inevitably generate perversity or contradiction, since in the end the objects of which they are used are 'not so' or 'not this'—they are actually not similar to the kind of object associated with that name. See too B72.

accident, following, encountering, passing: these are four types of potential sources of doubt. The four amount to accidental circumstances, inconclusive evidence, coincidental causes or causal overdetermination, and transience. Interpretation of the details in the explanation is tentative.

Encountering fog . . . accident: accidental, unexpected circumstances such as a dense fog or unseasonable weather can be grounds for doubting one's judgement of what one sees or whether one will be warm enough.

Lifting something light . . . following: following along with things provides insufficient evidence as to whether one can perform a task and thus gives grounds for doubt. That one can perform an easy task such as lifting a light weight or shaving along the grain is insufficient grounds to confirm one is strong or skilled. The parenthetical illustration 'like stone and feathers' seems to refer to the first of the two examples, lifting something light and dropping something heavy.

Whether the fighter's . . . encountering: 'encountering' seems to refer to multiple, coincidental factors and thus to causal overdetermination as a source of doubt. Different factors could each explain the fighter's collapse. Since we cannot know which was decisive, we have grounds to doubt claims that one or the other was.

having passed: transience as a source of doubt. Circumstances may change, rendering what we correctly took to be the case no longer so.

United together . . . demarcating: this canon forms a pair with B12. Things can be demarcated conceptually from other things either by using a term for one kind of thing, such as 'oxen' or 'horses', or by joining together more than one kind of thing using a compound term, such as 'boys and girls', 'fruits and vegetables', or 牛馬 'oxen and horses'.

one unit/part: any group of things demarcated from other things can be regarded as a single unit/part, a compound whole.

160 *'Together as one' . . . one*: different kinds of things can be grouped together and treated as one, as oxen and horses are one in being four-footed. Things can also be demarcated from other things on the grounds that they are 'this', or the same kind, as when we separate oxen from other animals or horses from other animals. We can count oxen and horses as two kinds of things, or we can group them together and treat them as one whole.

Classical Chinese nouns typically do not mark number, so the same word, *zhǐ* 指, can refer to each of the five individual fingers on a hand or to all the fingers as one. Instead of conceiving of demarcated groups of things as forming sets or collections, the Mohists conceive of them as forming larger or smaller parts and wholes. Canon B12 suggests that the Mohists likely employ a mereological ontology.

160 *In growing one . . . space*: canons B13 to B16, on space and time, are challenging to interpret, and the translation is accordingly tentative. The gist of B13 seems to be that space or extension moves along with things within it as they endure, since as things grow and move they remain located in space.

South and north . . . duration: this canon presents the crux of the Mohist conception of space and time, which they conceptualize as duration. Space and duration, they contend, are not 'as-hard-to-white', or mutually pervasive (see A66). The reason is that at any instant, all of space is present but not all of duration is. Things that are 'as-hard-to-white' must 'fill each other' or be everywhere compresent within the region where they are located. Since not all of duration is always and everywhere present, duration and space are not mutually pervasive in the required sense. Obviously, however, spatial relations such as north versus south are present at different times. The Mohist explanation is that space moves with duration, so it is present at one instant and then present again at later instants.

fill each other: duration is not mutually pervasive with space, but the durationless or instantaneous is, because it and space 'fill each other'. They are present together everywhere, albeit only for an instant.

Yao is good . . . past: compare B53.

Yao is not able to govern: perhaps because he would no longer be present, or perhaps because his methods of government would no longer be applicable (?).

B17–B29: this long series of canons on optics and mechanics presents interpretive issues that are beyond the scope of this book.

B30: canons B30–B31 are two historically remarkable discussions of economics, expressing a grasp of how supply and demand determine prices that anticipates discussions in Thomas Aquinas (1225–74), Ibn Taymiyyah (1263–1328), and John Locke (1632–1704) by well over a millennium. A comparable early Western source may be Xenophon of Athens (430–354 BC), although Xenophon may not articulate the relations between supply and demand as clearly as the Mohists do.

If the coin is . . . exchanged: if the amount of coin asked by the seller is light, the grain is not expensive; if the seller demands a heavy price, the buyer refuses the exchange.

161 *if the harvest . . . coin*: by changing the supply of grain for sale, the harvest changes the value of the king's coin.

Like selling off children: this final parenthetical remark seems out of place and may belong with the parenthetical remark at the end of B31.

'All' is completely . . . sell: that is, removing all reasons it does not sell, including an excessively high price.

it sells for . . . price: alternatively, 'selling sets the right price'.

When discoursing on . . . basis: the text rebuts the view that, since no one can know everything, for practical purposes what is important is being able to distinguish whether we do or do not know something. This view might reflect the statement in book 2 of the *Zhuāngzǐ* that 'knowing that stops at what it doesn't know is the ultimate'. Canon A6 tied knowledge to the ability to discourse on things reliably—specifically, to sort them into the proper kinds. B34 explains that if we do not know something, we lack the basis or means for discoursing on it. Hence in practice knowing merely that we do not know something is less useful than actually knowing it.

The things something . . . 'horse': the terms the two sides assert of something may refer to the same things or different things. 'Dog' and 'hound' apply to the same animals ('dog' and 'hound' are the Mohists' standard example of two names for the same thing). 'Horse' and 'ox' apply to different animals. In both sorts of cases, it is possible that neither of the terms fits the object under consideration, which might be neither a dog, nor a horse, nor an ox.

Both not winning . . . wins: canon B35 may be a response to a passage in book 2 of the *Zhuangzi* that questions whether either side can ever definitively win a distinction-drawing disputation (*biàn*): 'Suppose you and I were to dispute, and you win over me, I do not win over you. Are you indeed right and am I indeed wrong?' The Mohist response is that cases in which the terms the two sides assert of something both fail to fit it are not 'disputation', properly speaking (see A74). Disputation consists in disputing which of two opposite terms—*x* or non-*x*—fits the thing under consideration. Logically, by the laws of excluded middle and non-contradiction, exactly one of the terms must fit and thus one side must 'win'.

162 *The start is . . . deferred*: deference is a prominent virtue in Ruist ethics. Canon B36 argues that one cannot consistently practise deference in all situations. The explanation is obscure, but the idea may be that the deferring person must take the initiative to start the process of yielding the wine to others, allowing them to drink first. The deferring person must take this first step and cannot defer it. So one cannot defer in everything. Compare the argument in this canon with those of B71, B77, and B79.

The stone is . . . it: to know something about a thing is not to know everything about it. It is possible to know some aspects of a thing (such as the kind of thing it is, or its colour) while not knowing others (such as its texture). The canon may be aimed at deflecting the sophism that since knowing about the hardness or whiteness of a stone is different from knowing about the stone, the hardness or whiteness and the stone are different things.

162 *What one knows . . . missing*: the canon refutes the view that to know some-
     thing is to be able to point it out. Spring, a season, is not something that
     can be pointed to. One can know a runaway servant but be unable to point
     him out because his location is unknown. Knowing about dogs is knowing
     about hounds, but someone who knows only the name 'dog' will know
     about hounds without being able to point them out. In disputation, if two
     things, such as oxen and horses, do not form two opposing kinds, as oxen
     and non-oxen do, one can know this without being able to point to the
     missing alternatives.

     If knowing dogs . . . error: 'dog' and 'hound' are the standard example of
     two names for the same object (see A86). (The exact relation between the
     extension of the two terms is unclear. One possibility is that 'hound' 犬
     referred to mature canines, 'dog' 狗 to pups. Both are mentioned in the
     Mòzǐ as being slaughtered for their meat and as being offered as sacrifices.
     However, only hounds, not dogs, appear in typical lists of animals fattened
     for sacrifice to Heaven.) If knowing dogs is identical to knowing hounds,
     then it is a mistake to say one knows dogs but not hounds. Perhaps, if one
     does not know the two names refer to the same animals, then knowing
     hounds is not identical to knowing dogs; in this case, it would not be an
     error to claim to know one but not the other. See B54.

     Connect the thought . . . to: by identifying what a speaker's words refer to,
     we can understand the thought or intention the speaker expresses. The
     text is not presenting the Lockean view that words have meaning because
     they are the outward signs of ideas in the head, which provide their content.
     Rather, the Mohist view is that words can be used to communicate thoughts
     or intentions—what the speaker has in mind—once both speaker and
     hearer know what they refer to. See §45.1b.

     borogoves: the text uses an unknown, nonce graph that we are expected not
     to recognize.

     B42: the text of this canon is badly damaged.

163 *The five processes . . . other*: canon B43 refers to the early proto-scientific
     doctrine of the five processes or phases (sometimes called the five elem-
     ents) and the cyclical relation between them. The canon rejects the pre-
     vailing view that the five supposedly overcome each other according to
     a regular sequence—wood overcoming earth by parting it, earth overcom-
     ing water by damming it, water overcoming fire by extinguishing it, fire
     overcoming metal by melting it, metal overcoming wood by chopping it.
     The text of the explanation is damaged, but the intact fragment indicates
     that which phase overcomes which depends on the particular circum-
     stances. A large, long-burning fire will melt metal, but a large amount of
     metal will outlast a smaller fire. This rejection of the hasty generalizations
     offered by a simplistic, abstract model is informative as to the Mohists'
     implicit philosophy of natural science.

     Desires and dislikes . . . it: several passages in the *Dàodéjīng*, such as sec-
     tions 3 and 37, advocate reducing or eliminating desires. The antiwar

activists Sòng Xíng 宋鈃 and Yǐn Wén 尹文 contended that people's genuine desires are few and shallow. The Mohist response is that in some situations, as when avoiding excess food or alcohol, it may be advantageous not to desire something. In others, as when one cares about the benefit of other people, it may be better not to control such affective attitudes. The word translated 'wise' is *zhì*, the same word used in A6 to refer to knowledge. Intriguingly, this canon seems to treat *ài* 'care' as an affective attitude akin to desires and aversions.

though it could . . . full: the last clause is confusing and the translation is tentative.

Like an injured . . . haunch: the point of this remark is obscure. It may be that, despite its loss, a milu deer missing a haunch remains a milu [?].

Like how severe . . . malaria: suffering from malaria (a loss) can lead to immunity to malaria (a gain).

five routes . . . fire: the five routes are the five senses. The senses alone are not the only means of possessing knowledge, because knowledge endures after we have passed things and no longer perceive them. See A5. The explanation implies that the Mohists might affirm 'the eye does not see', one of the sophisms listed in book 33 of the *Zhuāngzǐ*.

Fire is hot: 'Fire is not hot' is among the sophisms listed in book 33 of the *Zhuāngzǐ*.

164 *If we mix . . . them*: the canon demystifies the seemingly contradictory idea that one can know what one doesn't know by explaining that it requires only that one be able to verbally identify things one doesn't know.

If there is . . . none: the canon may be criticizing the doctrine, found in section 2 of the *Dàodéjīng*, that *yǒu* 有 and *wú* 無 (existence and non-existence, presence and absence, something and nothing) are interdependent, such that they arise together and each cannot exist without the other. The Mohist response is that whether absence or non-existence depends on presence or existence is determined by what we are talking about. In the case of something originally present and now gone, absence depends on presence. In the case of something that never existed in the first place, it does not.

What is about . . . effort: this canon contributes to the Mohist rebuttal of fatalism. Logically, the Mohists acknowledge that what is about to be so or about to end must be so or must end, and hence these events cannot be changed. Yet what is about to be so or about to end might include events that will happen only if we exert effort. So the logical point about time does not entail that human effort is futile.

The sage-king . . . times: compare B16.

exemplar: following Graham in reading 義 as 儀, 'standard' or 'exemplar'.

cranes: some text appears to be missing from the beginning of the explanation.

in some cases . . . past: how can Yáo, who lived long ago, serve as a moral paragon today? Because by using 'names' to 'mention' objects we can 'show' others things that are not present, as when we mention our friend as an example of a wealthy merchant. Although we can no longer physically point to Yáo or his exemplary deeds, we can 'use names to show people' about him, what we say being in the present. What's taken as an exemplar is thus 'two', Yáo himself and the 'names' we use to speak of him.

165 *Dogs are hounds . . . haunches*: 'dogs' and 'hounds' are the standard example of two names for the same object, a relation the Mohists call 'overlap' or 'doubling' (A86, B40). 'Permissible' refers to assertions that could be semantically and logically correct in some situation. The content of B54 seems clear enough, but the reasoning is not, since the text seems to allow that two contradictory assertions could both be permissible. One interpretation might be that a speaker unaware that dogs are hounds could permissibly assert that killing dogs is not killing hounds, while a speaker who knows dogs are hounds could permissibly assert that killing dogs is killing hounds. Another possibility is that, although 'dog' and 'hound' were both names for canines, in some contexts 'killing hounds' and 'killing dogs' were indeed considered two distinct kinds of actions. (Perhaps 'killing dogs' was butchering common breeds for their meat, 'killing hounds' sacrificing rare breeds to the spirits. Compare §45.2c.) The parenthetical example is obscure, beyond the obvious point that haunches are two objects that can also be regarded as one object.

The pillars being . . . intention: canon B41 contends that before answering a question, we should first 'connect' our thought or intention with that of the questioner. If asked whether we know of *x*, we must first confirm what the questioner is referring to by '*x*'. B57 explains that because our thought/intention of something may specify some of its features, we can know of these in advance of perceiving the thing. For example, if we deem pillars round, then from our thought or intention of a pillar—from what we deem it to be like—we know a pillar's shape before seeing it, as the thought fixes the shape beforehand. However, the thought fixes only the relevant features of a thing, not all its features. The thought of a round pillar fixes its shape but not its weight or material. These remain indeterminate in the thought, so we do not know them beforehand.

Anvil and hammer . . . match: canon and explanation B58 are difficult but are included here to help fill out the Mohist conception of thought/intention (*yì*). This canon extends the topic of B57 with a contrasting example. B57 indicates that since we deem pillars round, our thought or intention specifies their shape while leaving features such as their weight indeterminate. B58 seems to imply that the thought of a hammer is similarly indeterminate. What speakers intend—what they have in mind—by 'hammer' can't be known in advance of their indicating a specific type of hammer. The canon and explanation give two reasons for this claim. Both are obscure, so our interpretation is strictly tentative. First, the features of hammers are determined by their being usable for some purpose. A cobbler's hammer is unlike a sledgehammer. Until the purpose is specified, we don't know what a speaker has in mind by 'hammer'. Second, unlike the example of a circle or square, there is no single model—nor any single purpose—that all hammers match up with exactly. Producing embroidered shoes obviously 'goes beyond' hammers in that it requires other tools as well; conversely, the Mohists contend, hammers also 'go beyond' shoemaking in that they too have other uses. Shoemaking and hammers do not 'match up as mates or counterparts' (*wǔ* 仵). The same goes for other types of hammers. So, unlike 'circle' or 'square', what someone intends by 'hammer' is not knowable without obtaining further details about the hammer in question.

If one hoes . . . move: the canon refers to a paradox of motion similar to Zeno's dichotomy or racetrack paradox. If we can move only in steps of one half the distance to be travelled, then—depending on how the paradox is formulated—either we can never reach our endpoint (since at each step, half of the distance remains to be covered) or never leave our starting point (since at each step, before reaching the halfway point, we must first cover half the distance there). In the scenario considered here, the hoeing of some length of a field proceeds only in steps of one half at a time. A related sophism is included among the claims of the disputers in book 33 of the *Zhuāngzǐ*.

Advancing by hoeing . . . point: originally the centre was halfway along the length. Since we have now hoed the front half, the point that was originally centre is now the tip—the starting point—of the remaining length.

If we take . . . centre: if we hoe both half the length in front of us and half the length behind us, we are already taking the centre as our starting point. We would then have two remaining lengths, one in front and one behind.

166 *Space, in advancing . . . far*: a tentative interpretation of the canon is that in advancing through space, there is no approaching its end, since, as the explanation states, the farther one advances, the more distant the area covered, without approaching any endpoint. The gist of the first sentence of the explanation seems to be that since space is infinitely vast, even if we demarcate two areas of it, we cannot successfully refer to only part or one side of it, as each part is itself infinitely vast.

The square features . . . so: for things to count as being similar and thus of the same kind, only the relevant features of the things must match the model (*fǎ* 法) for that kind. Other aspects of the things are irrelevant, as the material something is made of is irrelevant with respect to its shape being square.

Although oxen and . . . tails: to reliably identify the difference between two kinds, we must cite only features that all of one kind have and all of the other do not. Citing features that do not fulfil this criterion is 'wild' or 'crazy' citing. Although having horns is indeed a difference between cattle and horses, not all cattle have horns, so having horns is not a reliable feature for marking the difference between oxen and horses. (On 'wild' citing, see too B76.) B66 is the first of a cluster of canons dealing with language and distinctions. See too B67, B68, B71, and B72.

166 *Deeming impermissible . . . same*: there are the same grounds for denying that 'oxen-and-horses are non-oxen' can be a logically and semantically correct assertion as there are for accepting that it can be.

167 *If it's permissible . . . oxen*: the canon and explanation refer to the aggregate, or compound whole, of oxen and horses, 'oxen-and-horses'. Part of this whole consists of oxen, part consists of horses. The underlying issue is whether terms that are correctly applied to parts of a compound whole can also be applied to the whole itself. The explanation states that if, on the grounds that some parts of the aggregate are not oxen, it's permissible to assert 'oxen-and-horses are non-oxen', then on the parallel grounds that other parts are oxen, it's similarly permissible to assert that 'oxen-and-horses are oxen'. Indeed, as the explanation goes on to claim, one could even assert that 'oxen-and-horses are non-oxen and non-horses'. A consequence is that, depending on the term under discussion, a compound whole such as 'oxen-and-horses' may not be a fit object over which to undertake disputation as explained in A74.

Reversing 'that' and . . . difference: the translation of this canon and explanation is highly tentative, and alternative interpretations are plausible. The gist seems to be that how we use the pair of contrasting indexical pronouns 'that' and 'this'—what we refer to by them—can be reversed, provided the difference they mark between things is preserved. Having distinguished two different things as 'that' and 'this', we have equivalent grounds for swapping the indexicals and instead referring to the things as 'this' and 'that'. As long as both indexicals switch their referents as a pair, they continue to indicate the difference between the referents. I take the text to be using the phrase *bǐ cǐ* 彼此 (that/this) in several instances as a technical term for reversing the referents of 'that' and 'this'. Compare B68 with B72.

If their deeming . . . impermissible: if they insist that the indexical 'that' always refers to that thing (as a proper noun does; see A78) or 'this' always refers to this thing, and one or both of the two cannot be changed, then it is impermissible to deem this thing 'that'.

'That' and 'this' . . . that: it is impermissible—it violates norms of use—to hold the reference of one of 'that' or 'this' fixed and switch the reference of the other. Either both must switch or both must be held fixed.

It's like using . . . know: suppose someone does not know a thing's length. If we show her a ruler and indicate that the thing is one foot long, then she knows the length. Analogously, suppose she doesn't know what colour the thing is. If we tell her it is white, then she knows the colour. Words are like measuring tools or models (A31).

Outside is personal . . . explanation: on these two sources of knowledge, see A80.

168 *Perverse is impermissible . . . injudicious*: canon B71 refutes the view that all statements are perverse, a claim perhaps motivated by the thought that all statements fail to adequately guide us in following the way (*dào*). (Ideas

roughly resembling this view can be found in the *Dàodéjīng* and *Zhuāngzǐ*.) The Mohist argument is structured as a dilemma: the claim that all statements are perverse is itself either perverse or not. If it is, it can be ignored, since taking it to fit the facts would be injudicious. If it is not, then it itself is an example of a statement that is not perverse, so it is self-refuting. Compare B77 and B79.

Calling both that . . . impermissible: see B68.

It's permissible/possible . . . proceed: we can call dogs 'cranes', perhaps as a 'borrowed name' (see B8), perhaps as a given name. Still, they are not cranes. We cannot arbitrarily declare that two things normally referred to by converse terms, such as cranes and non-cranes, are both to be referred to by one of the terms. If another speaker insists on taking things to be whatever he calls them, then my calling them by their usual name will not 'proceed' in consistently picking out all and only things of the same kind. If the other speaker doesn't insist that the thing is indeed whatever he calls it—if, for example, he is merely using 'Crane' as a given name for a dog without suggesting that the dog is actually a kind of bird—then this is a one-off use that does not 'proceed' to other cases. B72 may be rebutting the view, associated with book 2 of the *Zhuāngzǐ*, that the distinctions underlying the use of names are radically conventional, such that we can take things to be whatever we call them, revising how we distinguish similarities between things as we go.

all-inclusiveness: canons B73, B74, and B75 form a series addressing potential logical problems facing the ethical doctrine of inclusive care.

If the south . . . people: the Mohists advocate all-inclusive care that covers all people, so they must hold that it is possible to care about all people. The objection is that it is perverse to assume for certain that it is possible to care about everyone, since we cannot know whether the totality of humanity can all be 'covered'. The Mohists respond with the quick dilemma that follows.

169 *Not knowing their number . . . all*: if we don't know the number of people who are to be cared about, can our inclusive care cover them all? The Mohist response is that since our question about them covers them all, our caring attitude can indeed cover them all.

Not knowing where . . . child: just as not knowing whether humanity is infinite or not knowing how many people there are does not present obstacles to caring about everyone, the Mohists claim that not knowing where people are located presents no obstacle. A parent who has lost a child cares about the child without knowing the child's location.

Benevolence and righteousness . . . perverse: *Mencius* 6A:4 depicts Gàozǐ advocating the view that benevolence is 'internal' and righteousness 'external'.

matching up on a face: as Graham suggests, this phrase may allude to the eye analogy in the explanation. *Wǔ* 仵 refers to comparable objects aligning or matching up with each other.

169 *wild citing*: see B66. The items cited do not reliably reflect actual differences or similarities between two things.

Like the left . . . in: we can describe the eyes as looking out on things or taking things in, but we cannot defensibly claim that one eye looks out while the other takes in. Caring and benefiting can be considered 'external' insofar as their recipients are others, or they can be considered 'internal' insofar as the caring and beneficent attitudes are ours. But we cannot defensibly claim that one is internal and the other external. Like the eyes, they must be treated in parallel, one being the match or counterpart of the other.

They take it . . . perverse: the text may be responding to ideas such as those presented in sections 19 and 20 of the *Dàodéjīng*, which advocate renouncing learning and discarding wisdom. The Mohists hold that to teach that learning is of no advantage is self-contradictory. Proponents advocate such a view only because they consider learning it beneficial. Compare this canon with B71 and B79.

if there are . . . short: the translation is tentative. The gist seems to be that whether a view should be rejected depends on the grounds for rejection, not on how many instances of rejecting it there are. This sort of case is unlike a relative comparison of short and long. If we are sorting out what is short and what long, and too many items of different lengths are deemed 'short', perhaps some of them should be relabelled 'long'.

170 *Rejecting rejection is . . . it*: canon B79 seems directed at a view, perhaps loosely associated with remarks in book 2 of the *Zhuāngzǐ*, that one can adopt the comprehensively tolerant stance of 'rejecting all rejections', or ceasing to deny or reject anything. The Mohist contention is that such a view is perverse or contradictory, since one cannot reject one's own rejection of views that do reject rival positions. Compare B71.

Not rejecting one's . . . rejection: if one's rejection of something stands, then one cannot consistently reject the activity of rejecting things. Conversely, if one's rejection does not stand, then the rejection itself is rejected, so again one cannot consistently reject the activity of rejecting things.

The extreme in . . . this: terms that express relative concepts, such as 'long' or 'short', admit of judgements of degree. Something can be the longest or the shortest. Terms that express whether something counts as a member of a certain kind do not admit of judgements of degree. Something either is or is not 'this'; no member of the kind is more extremely 'this' than any other.

then below is actually above: 'above' and 'below' carry the connotation of 'superior' and 'subordinate', so the last clause can also be read, 'subordinate is actually superior'. B81 may be responding to ideas such as those in section 61 of the *Dàodéjīng*, which advocate achieving success by seeking a subordinate position. The explanation contends that when 'above' and 'below' are used as evaluative terms—unlike when they are used to describe features of the physical landscape—whatever is considered good thereby counts as 'above' or 'superior'. Hence those who advocate adopting what is normally considered an inferior or a lower position are in fact treating it as the superior, and thus higher, position.

BOOK 44: THE 'GREATER SELECTION'

171 *Deeming John one's kin . . . kin*: alternatively, these two sentences could also be interpreted as 'caring about John on the grounds that he is one's kin is not caring about one's kin; benefiting John on the grounds that he is one's kin is not benefiting one's kin'. The point may be that inclusive care permits care and benefit for kin without this care and benefit counting as selfishly benefiting one's own.

Deeming music beneficial . . . son: because according to the Mohists music is not beneficial.

weighing: discretion or practical reasoning concerned with comparing what is 'lighter' or 'heavier'—more or less important—among the various factors relevant to evaluating some course of action. Here the discussion seems to focus on the ends for which we act.

'weighing' and 'exact': two types of practical judgements. The first is when, weighing relevant factors, we judge that something normally deemed wrong is nevertheless the least harmful course of action in a particular situation and so counts as right. The second is when, after considering something normally condemned as wrong, we reaffirm that in our situation it is indeed wrong. Compare canon A84.

Cutting off a finger . . . harm: the passage alludes to a scenario in which a traveller is waylaid by robbers, who force him to choose between sacrificing his finger or his hand, in one example, and between his finger and his life, in another. Consistent with the Mohist ethical *dào*, one decides what to do by weighing benefits and harms. Sacrificing one's finger is a harm, but in a situation that forces one to choose either a lighter or a heavier harm, selecting the lighter harm counts as selecting the greater benefit.

Cutting off a finger . . . wrist: the sentence appears to break off after the word 'wrist/arm', perhaps because the bamboo strip on which it was written broke at this point. The first sentence of §44.3b could be the second half of this sentence. However, given the context and further textual damage in ensuing sections, it seems more likely that the fragment 'selecting the lesser among harms' in §44.3c is part of the remainder of this sentence. §44.5 also seems to belong to the same discussion as §44.3a.

Among affairs and . . . righteous: this section appears to be assembled from three disjoint fragments.

Selecting the greater . . . do: one chooses the least harmful alternative only when forced to do so. Otherwise, we avoid harm altogether.

172 *Selecting from among . . . harms*: when choosing an end to pursue, one chooses what is most beneficial. When forced to give something up, one chooses the sacrifice that entails the least harm. This section appears to belong with §44.3a above.

172 *Benefiting more those . . . ranking*: Mohist ethics does not ask us to treat everyone equally. According to the norms of righteousness—norms that, according to the Mohists, best promote the benefit of all—we are permitted to do more for those with whom we have certain special relationships. This doctrine is called 'relation ranking'.

caring about people / others: the phrase *ài rén* 愛人 connotes both caring about others and caring about people. This section indicates that the moral ideal of all-inclusively caring about people is not selflessly altruistic. It includes caring about oneself, as part of the doctrine of relation ranking.

Promoting benefit to . . . oneself: by Mohist ethics, one should act for all, not only for oneself. If one benefits others more or less according to the norms of relation ranking, presumably this counts as acting for all. Violating those norms is acting for oneself.

For there to be . . . coming: if someone rides a Qín horse away from the state of Qín, by §44.22 it may no longer be a Qín horse, but it remains a horse. To know someone is coming on a Qín horse is to know they are coming on a horse. By implication, this fragment contradicts Gōngsūn Lóng's notorious claim that a white horse is not a horse.

173 *names and objects . . . objects*: alternatively, emending 名 to 合, this sentence can be interpreted as 'names and objects do not necessarily match'.

Supposing this stone . . . big: names do not apply to their referents under all conditions. If a large white stone is broken up, the name 'white' continues to apply to the bits, but the name 'large' no longer applies.

As to things . . . such-and-such: horses are an example of things named on the basis of their form or shape (*xíng* 形) and their looks or surface features (*mào* 貌). To know horses, one must know that this animal at hand is a horse. A person who does not know that 'horse' refers to this kind of animal does not know horses.

named on the basis of shape and features: things originating from the state of Qín are an example of something not named on the basis of shape or features. We can know that something is a Qín thing even if we do not know what exactly it is.

if they have entered . . . not: if something resides in Qín, it counts as 'this' with respect to the name 'Qín'—it is a Qín object. If it departs from Qín, it no longer takes the name 'Qín'.

'Qí' and 'Jīng': the names of two states.

There are differences . . . different: the translation is tentative.

174 *The caring about others . . . greater*: the translation of the entire section is tentative.

if they are smashed . . . thing: this point is illustrated by the example of the stone in §44.21. This paragraph and §44.21 may originally have belonged together.

Expressions: this section appears to be preceded by a lacuna, and the first sentence lacks a subject. A dangling instance of the word 'expressions' in an earlier section (omitted here) is a likely candidate for the subject of this sentence.

arise on the basis . . . kinds: compare section §45.1e.

expressions: roughly a synonym of 'statements'. It refers to utterances of indeterminate length expressing one's thoughts or intentions.

So: the text breaks off here.

175 *44.28*: this section lists thirteen short aphorisms, each associated with a brief explanatory analogy, such as 'the analogy lies in detesting harm'. The analogies are deeply obscure and their point cannot be reconstructed with confidence. The translation omits the analogies and several of the more mysterious aphorisms.

BOOK 45: THE 'LESSER SELECTION'

176 *disputation*: biàn 辯 (see canon A74) refers to discourse—often competitive—concerning how to draw distinctions correctly. Alternative translations include 'dialectics', 'distinguishing', and 'distinction-drawing'.

By names . . . reasons: these three units of disputation or discourse are explained functionally rather than structurally. Names are used to mention or refer to things. Expressions are strings of names used to express thoughts. These could be phrases, sentences, or series of sentences. Explanations are pieces of discourse that explain the reasons for the expressions one asserts.

Select and propose . . . kinds: assertions are accepted or rejected on the basis of whether they reflect the correct distinctions between kinds.

Having it oneself . . . others: a basic rule of consistency and fairness.

Some is not all . . . it: this section introduces three concepts relevant to disputation. 'Some' and 'all' refer to quantification. 'Supposing' probably refers to giving conditional or counterfactual examples. 'Emulating' a model determines whether something is 'this/right' or not.

Analogy is mentioning . . . it: these are four typical methods used to support one's claims in disputation: giving analogies; drawing syntactic parallels; adducing a case the opponent affirms and challenging the opponent to explain how the case at hand is different; and asserting that the case at hand is indeed the same as a case the opponent accepts. The aim is to show that the case under consideration is indeed similar to an accepted model.

Things have respects . . . side: compare §44.27. The four methods of disputation introduced in §45.1d are all based on analogical reasoning and judgement. (1) Analogy is grounded in similarities between things. (2) 'Paralleling' is based on syntactic similarities between utterances. (3) 'Pulling' is based on similarities between an opponent's previous explanation or assertion and one's own. (4) 'Pushing' is based on similarity between what the opponent accepts and what one now asserts. Since analogical reasoning and judgement are not invariably reliable, there are a plurality of ways in which the methods can break down and yield incorrect results. Disputers must be cautious and carefully examine the various reasons underlying how to distinguish kinds correctly.

177 *As to things . . . but so*: inserting a phrase to designate the type of case corresponding to the examples in §45.2d.

one case not: omitting twenty-two graphs mistakenly inserted here by dittography from the end of §45.1e.

'this and so': in each example, with respect to the more general kind mentioned, the less general kind or the individuals mentioned are 'this', or members of that kind. (White horses are 'this' with respect to horses.) As to the action mentioned, performing that action on the less general kind qualifies as a case of performing it on the more general kind, so the action is 'so' with respect to performing it on the more general kind. (Riding white horses is 'so' with respect to riding horses.) Each example is thus a case of 'this and so'.

serving people: being employed as a servant. Since §20.3 uses 'serving someone' to refer to marriage, an alternative translation is 'Jane's serving her parents isn't getting married'.

Her brother is . . . no people: these examples are cases of 'this but not so' (see the last line of the section). Although the things mentioned are indeed members of the kinds mentioned, performing the action mentioned on those things does not count as a case of performing it on those kinds. Jane's brother is a handsome man, but caring about her brother (fraternal affection) is not a case of caring about a handsome man (sexual attraction). Analogously, the Mohists will argue, although robbers are people, killing them (capital punishment for banditry) is not killing people (murder). Compare B54.

178 *If it's like this . . . fate*: emending these two sentences to be parallel with the preceding lines.

There's no difficulty . . . so: emending the closing description to match the examples and contrast with §45.2b.

in one case comprehensive . . . not comprehensive: to count as inclusively caring about people, one must care about all of them. Excluding even one person from our care entails failing to 'care for people', in the Mohist sense. To count as riding horses, one need ride only one; to count as not riding horses, one mustn't ride any.

PART V: THE DIALOGUES

BOOK 46: GĒNG ZHÙ

This book is named after Gēng Zhù, a disciple of Mòzǐ who figures in two of the anecdotes (omitted here).

183 *Zhì Túyú and Xiàn Zǐshuò*: probably two of Mòzǐ's students.

Wūmǎzǐ: appears in several philosophically important conversations with Mòzǐ. Some commentaries suggest he was an Erudite (Rú), but his comments in §46.6 and §46.7 are inconsistent with their doctrines.

184 *Zǐ Xià*: a disciple of Confucius.

'Do gentlemen have fights?': among some of the ancient Chinese elite, gentlemen or officers—men of social rank—were expected to be prepared to defend their honour in one-on-one fights. Several early texts denounce this custom, including *Mòzǐ*, *Xúnzǐ* (for instance, book 4), and *The Annals of Lü Buwei* (for instance, §16.8).

'Those good at governing . . . renewed': these lines are a version of *Analects* §13.16.

185 *Don't use what . . . them*: Zǐgāo surely already knew that a good ruler forms new relationships with formerly distant people while reinvigorating existing relationships. However, he did not know how to do so. Confucius's answer assumed he already knew how to do this and so did not explain what to do in a way he would understand.

Lǔyáng: a district in the state of Chǔ.

children playing horse: wars of aggression are exhausting and useless, as romping around playing horse is. The children are probably riding a hobby horse. See too §19.7.

Statements adequate . . . regular: alternatively, 'Teachings adequate to repeatedly put into practice, repeat them often. Those inadequate to put into practice, don't repeat them often.' See too §47.5.

Guǎn Qián Aó . . . Gāo Shízǐ: two of Mòzǐ's students.

186 *Qínzǐ*: Mòzǐ's head disciple. He is mentioned again in §50.3.

Gōng Mèngzǐ: the most prominent representative of the Erudites (Rú, 'Confucians') in the *Mòzǐ*. Book 48 is named after him.

'This gentlemen doesn't . . . that's all': a reference to *Analects* §7.1. Compare §39.7.

I am different . . . me: if, as seems plausible, Wūmǎzǐ and Mòzǐ were residents of the same state, this paragraph implies their home was in Lǔ 魯.

187 *norm: yì* 義, used here as in books 11–13 (and in other contexts translated as 'righteous'). Mòzǐ regards the norm of conduct Wūmǎzǐ articulates—sacrificing others to benefit oneself, but not oneself to benefit others—as a proposed conception of what is morally righteous. He tests it to see whether it can be publicized and practised consistently by everyone. He claims it cannot: if it is publicized, those who affirm it will seek to kill Wūmǎ to benefit themselves, while those who reject it will seek to punish him for spreading a vile teaching. Publicizing his norm would bring harmful, self-defeating consequences, in Mòzǐ's view, thus disqualifying it as a defensible norm.

pleased with you: that is, pleased or persuaded by your statement, which the person then puts into practice.

187 *inauspicious statement*: alternatively, an inauspicious saying or teaching. Wūmǎzǐ's norm is expressed as a statement, which functions as a maxim in guiding action.

    kleptomania: compare §50.2.

BOOK 47: VALUING RIGHTEOUSNESS

188 *single statement*: such a statement (*yán* 言, also 'saying' or 'teaching') might express a norm or conception of righteousness that someone sees as worth fighting for, or it might be an insult, which prompts the target to defend his honour.

    '*Statements adequate . . . jabbering*': alternatively, teachings or sayings that help to reform conduct should be repeated often. Compare §46.12. On 'empty jabbering', see too §46.18.

189 *Now the blind . . . selecting*: the blind can make correct statements using the names 'white' and 'black'. However, since they are unable to distinguish white from black objects, the writers consider them not to know white or black. Compare §19.1b.

190 *Gōngliáng Huánzǐ*: a high minister of Wèi.

191 *This produces doubling . . . calculation*: increasing participation in discussions of righteousness would multiply the benefits to society beyond calculation.

    Using others' statements . . . wrong: alternatively, using others' teachings to negate or refute my teachings or pronouncements.

BOOK 48: GŌNG MÈNG

The book begins with a collection of conversations between Mòzǐ and Gōng Mèngzǐ, whom it is named after. Gōng Mèngzǐ is the chief spokesman for the Erudites (Confucians) in the 'Dialogues'.

192 *These four rulers . . . same*: each of the four governed his state while clothed in different local dress, yet all four were the same in governing well and achieving good order.

    '*The gentleman must . . . benevolent*': the same saying is criticized in §39.6.

    speech: *yán* 言, the same word elsewhere translated as 'statements', referring to teachings, assertions, or what one says. Here it may refer to the three men using the same ancient pronunciation or manner of speaking.

193 *you emulate the Zhōu . . . ancient*: the Erudites modelled themselves on the high culture of the Western Zhōu dynasty (1046–771 BC). The Mohists admired the founding rulers of the Zhōu but also exalted supposedly earlier rulers, including the mythical sage-king Yǔ, founder of the even earlier Xià dynasty (*c*.2100–1600 BC). (The historicity of the Xià is uncertain.)

    wisdom: or, equivalently, knowledge.

    This is counting . . . wealthy: tallies were paired strips of wood or bamboo used to record contracts. Amounts were recorded by carving notches across the two strips, forming 'teeth' that fitted together when the two halves were joined. The text seems to allude to the story of a fool who picked up one half of a used, discarded tally, counted the teeth, and concluded he had become rich. Learning the odes, documents, and ceremonies is analogous to counting the teeth on someone else's used tally—it doesn't show Confucius himself is competent.

'Poverty or wealth . . . increased': compare §39.4, §48.14, and books 35–7.

wrap up their hair . . . hat: hair was worn long and wrapped into a bun to fit inside a hat. As this passage and §§48.8, 48.9, and 48.10 illustrate, a common way of criticizing a view perceived to be inconsistent or perverse was to give an analogy to an action regarded as absurdly contradictory or confused.

if we use your statements: if we apply the Erudites' pronouncements or teachings.

194 *order*: since 'order' (*zhì* 治) can also be interpreted here as 'govern', an alternative reading is 'as to the state's being well-governed, we govern it and so it is well-governed'.

'Three years of mourning . . . parents': some Erudites held that the three-year mourning rite symbolically reflects children's special reliance on and attachment to their parents in the first three years of life. See *Analects* §17.21.

Chéngzǐ: this may be the same person as Chéng Fán in book 7.

enough to ruin the world: since the phrase *tiān xià* 天下 refers specifically to the social world, not the natural world, plausible alternative interpretations include 'enough to destroy society' or 'enough to lose the realm'.

195 *poverty or wealth . . . increased*: compare §§39.4 and 48.6.

You deem the Erudites wrong: alternatively, you condemn or reject the Erudites.

even if the sage-kings . . . anything: even the sage-kings could not plan better tactics for these creatures to avoid the hazards.

seeing and knowing: that is, sentient and sapient.

196 *you're committing a heavy crime*: the implication is that many others are more worthy of blessings, and so in seeking blessings for himself rather than praising others, the man is concealing others' good conduct. He thus commits an ethical transgression analogous to concealing a fugitive.

a robber has no way in: compare §49.15.

the wise: alternatively, the knowledgeable.

Even the finest . . . up: that is, they cannot do two things at once.

BOOK 49: THE QUESTIONS OF LǓ

The Lǔ in the title of this book refers to the state of Lǔ, the most likely candidate for Mòzǐ's home state. The Lord of Lǔ mentioned in the first anecdote is the ruler of Lǔ, a different person from Lord Wén of Lǔ Yáng mentioned in §46.11, §46.19, and several passages in this book. Lǔ Yáng was a district in the state of Chǔ.

197 *lǐ*: a unit of measurement of roughly 400 metres. Presumably the text is referring to a block of territory 100 *lǐ* on each side.

they gained the world: they became rulers of all the world.

198 *Now suppose commoners...clothing*: compare §17.2 and §28.5a.

'*The gentlemen ... to*': on black and white, compare §§17.2 and 28.5c. On the little things versus the big things, compare §§9.5b, 26.1, 27.2a, 28.1a, and 28.5b.

when the eldest son ... custom: compare §25.7.

199 *Killing the father ... son*: perhaps a reference to the practice of compensating families for the loss of their father in a military campaign.

What's the use ... it: what is the point of gathering followers and travelling about offering teachings or making pronouncements about righteousness, as Mòzǐ does?

201 "*Where do robbers come in*": compare §48.19.

Before I saw ... Sòng: Gōngshū was employed by the King of Chǔ to attack the city of Sòng. See §50.1.

BOOK 50: GŌNGSHŪ

Gōngshū Bān was a famous ancient engineer and inventor, also known as Lǔ Bān. In later centuries, he came to be revered as China's patron saint of carpenters and builders.

202 *cloud-ladder machines*: siege engines for scaling city walls.

Chǔ ... Sòng: Chǔ was a large, powerful southern state, Sòng a small, weak central state.

Qí: a powerful northeastern state far from Chǔ.

Yǐng: the capital of Chǔ.

what commands ... out: a polite greeting, similar to 'What can I do for you?'

Jǐng: another name for Chǔ.

wisdom: alternatively, 'knowledge'. Compare §§18.3 and 19.4.

loyalty: (*zhōng* 忠) also covers integrity.

knowing kinds: a technical term in early Chinese logic for distinguishing and responding to different kinds of things correctly and consistently. Mòzǐ is alluding to an analogical argument familiar from §17.1, §49.6, and other passages. Gōngshū knows well enough that the 'little' crime of murdering one person is wrong, but doesn't acknowledge that the 'big' crime of attacking another state and killing its inhabitants is an even more serious wrong of the same kind. Failing to recognize that such large-scale cases are of the same kind as commonsense small-scale cases is failing to 'know kinds'. Gōngshū is guilty of inconsistency in cognition and in conduct. See too §19.5.

203 *he is a kleptomaniac*: compare §46.19.

rhinoceroses and milu deer: both were rare and exotic animals.

to be of the same kind as this: to be of the same kind as the well-off person stealing his neighbour's inferior cart, clothing, and food.

untied his belt . . . machines: he improvised a model of a city wall and defence machines using his belt and some small sticks.

'Those who handle . . . them': a version of a proverb to the effect that the sage manages things or achieves good order through unseen, preternatural influence, as spirits do, and thus goes unrecognized, while fools struggle in the open light where all can see.

GLOSSARY

aggression. See *gōng* 攻.

ài 愛 (care, concern). For the Mohists, care is the attitude of taking others' welfare into consideration in determining our course of action. The concept of care is paired with that of benefit; other things being equal, to care about others is to be disposed to benefit them. Care contrasts with detesting or despising others (*wù* 惡) and so disregarding their welfare. Detesting and harming form a concept pair that contrasts with care and benefit; to detest others is to be disposed to harm them. Sinologists in the past commonly translated *ài* as 'love'. Although in some contexts *ài* may indeed refer to parents' affection for children or to sexual affection, in classical texts it is more commonly used to refer to care or concern, which is its chief connotation in the *Mòzǐ*. In §46.18, for example, Mòzǐ's interlocutor Wūmǎzǐ, a native of the state of Lǔ, remarks that he has greater *ài* for the people of Zōu, a neighbouring state with a similar culture, than for the people of Yuè, a distant, foreign state. Wūmǎ is not referring to how much he loves the people of Zōu or Yuè, but to how much he cares about or is concerned about them. Similarly, when canon A7 speaks of having *ài* for a horse, it is not referring to feeling love for the horse but to caring about it, since it is a valuable asset.

altars of soil and grain. See *shè jì* 社稷.

assert. See *wèi* 謂.

bèi 誖 (perverse, contradictory, fallacious). In later Mohist logic, an assertion is perverse when it runs contrary to logical, semantic, or pragmatic norms. Canon B71 explains that 'perverse' refers to a statement's being impermissible and thus having no circumstances in which it can be correct. A logical contradiction is perverse, but not all claims that are perverse are logical contradictions. (See canons B34 and B76 for examples of claims rejected as perverse that are not obviously contradictory.)

benefit. See *lì* 利.

benevolence. See *rén* 仁.

biàn 辨 (distinction, distinguish). As a verb, *biàn* refers to the cognitive function of distinguishing between similar and different things or kinds of things. As a noun, it refers to the differences between things that we seek to recognize correctly. Distinguishing is closely related to knowledge: in many contexts, to know is to be able to distinguish things correctly. Early Chinese thinkers regard distinguishing as the fundamental cognitive function and the basis for explaining knowledge, language, reasoning, and action.

biàn 辯 (disputation, distinction-drawing, debate, dialectics, argumentation). The activity, often public and sometimes competitive or adversarial, of examining and disputing how to distinguish between similar and different things, typically by citing analogical models for comparison and offering explanations (*shuō* 說) that give reasons to support drawing distinctions one way or another. Since the subject of disputation (*biàn* 辯) is how to draw distinctions (*biàn* 辨), the two concepts are not always clearly distinguished and in some texts the graphs 辨 and 辯 are used interchangeably. As an adjective, *biàn* 辯 refers to being quick-witted or intelligent—that is, skilled at drawing distinctions.

bié 別 (difference, separate, exclude, exclusion). In some contexts, *bié* is a difference between things that must be distinguished properly. It is also used to refer to differentiating or separating things. By extension, in 'Inclusive Care (III)', it is used as a technical term to refer to the opposite of inclusive care, namely separating others from those one cares about and thus excluding them from care. A common misinterpretation is that *bié* refers to distinguishing different degrees of care according to others' relation to us. This is not how the Mohists use it, however. For them, *bié* refers to not caring about others at all. Another common interpretation is that *bié* refers to partiality. However, *bié* as used in the text is not merely a bias or preference for a favoured person or group but complete disregard for the disfavoured person or group.

call. See *wèi* 謂.

care. See *ài* 愛.

ceremony, ceremonial propriety. See *lǐ* 禮.

cí 慈 (paternal kindness). The relational virtue manifested by ethically admirable fathers toward their children. (In a few contexts, virtuous conduct toward political subordinates is also referred to as 'paternal kindness'.)

cí 辭 (expressions, phrasings, rhetoric). A series of 'names' (words) linked together to express an intention or thought (*yì* 意); in some contexts a near synonym for 'statement' (*yán* 言). Expressions (*cí*) are understood in terms of their function, not their structure, and so have no specific grammatical composition. They may consist of a phrase, a sentence, or several sentences. Any series of names that expresses intentions or thoughts can be considered an expression.

conduct. See *xíng* 行.

Confucian. See Rú 儒.

consequentialism. A family of ethical theories according to which what is ethically or morally right or wrong is determined by what has better or worse consequences. The Mohists clearly advocate consequentialist norms of action, as their writings repeatedly claim that the right way (*dào*) is one that promotes the benefit of all and eliminates harm to all. (See, for example, §32.1.) A more controversial question is whether this consequentialist stance is fundamental for the Mohists or whether it rests on a non-consequentialist foundation, such as Heaven's intent.

dàng 當 (fit, accord, coincide, fit the facts, on the mark). In later Mohist logic and semantics, *dàng* refers to an asserted term or phrase properly fitting the thing or situation it is asserted of and thus being semantically correct. Along with *rán* 然 (so), it plays a role overlapping that of truth. *Dàng* is also used to express approval of conduct or judgement as ethically fitting and of praise or blame and rewards or punishments as going to fitting recipients.

dào 道 (way, path). A fundamental structural and normative concept in Mohist thought. In their own conceptual framework, the Mohists understand themselves not as seeking the truth about reality, proposing a correct ethical and political theory, or fighting for justice, but as working to identify, follow, and promulgate the proper way—the way of benevolence and righteousness, of the sage-kings, and of good order. A way is a set of norms, practices, and policies governing how we do something, including both the content of what is done and the manner in which it is performed. Throughout the translation all instances of '*dào*' are rendered as 'way'.

dà rén 大人 (great men). Many of the Triads are addressed to 'kings, dukes, and great men'. Kings and dukes are the highest-ranking members of the aristocracy. 'Great men' refers to other aristocrats, high officials, and powerful men.

disputation. See *biàn* 辯.

detest. See *wù* 惡.

Dí 翟. Mòzǐ's given name.

disorder. See *luàn* 亂.

distinctions, distinguishing. See *biàn* 辨.

doctrine. See *shuō* 說.

Erudite. See Rú 儒.

exclusion. See *bié* 別.

explain, explanation. See *shuō* 說.

fǎ 法 (model, standard, law, prototype legal judgement, to emulate, to model on, to take as a standard). Models are standards, norms, or exemplars by which to guide and check conduct, judgements, and policies. The Mohists' chief metaphor for understanding models is that they are like measuring tools, such as the wheelwright's compass or the carpenter's square, which guide and confirm production of round wheels and square corners. Concrete exemplars, action-guiding intentions, ethical guidelines or maxims, instructions, and laws are all regarded as varieties of models. Models guide action by providing an example to emulate. Rather than speaking of rules to follow or principles to apply, the Mohists speak of emulating models. For example, the Mohist ethical ideal of inclusive care is considered a model. To clarify the prominent role of the concept of models in Mohist thought, the translation consistently renders all instances of *fǎ* as 'model' or 'to take as a model'.

fate. See *mìng* 命.

fēi 非 (not, wrong, not this, condemn, reject). *Fēi* expresses negation. Along with *shì* 是 (this, right), it forms a pair of terms expressing basic pro/con attitudes. In ethical contexts, *fēi* has the connotation of 'wrong'; in semantic and logical contexts, it has the connotation of 'not this', or not the correct referent of a term under discussion. Used as a verb, *fēi* refers to deeming something wrong and, in some contexts, thereby condemning or rejecting it. To reflect the connections between the various uses of *fēi*, with the exception of the titles of the Triads on aggression, music, and fatalism, the translation consistently renders the verbal use as 'to deem wrong'. Readers should keep in mind that for the Mohists 'deeming wrong' often also carries the sense of 'condemn' or 'reject'.

filial devotion, filial piety. See *xiào* 孝.

generous. See *huì* 惠.

gentlemen. See *jūnzǐ* 君子.

ghosts. See *guǐ* 鬼.

gōng 攻 (aggression, attack). As the Mohists use it, *gōng* refers to unjustified military aggression against another city or state. For clarity, the translation consistently renders *gōng* as 'aggression' or 'wars of aggression'. Aggression contrasts with defensive warfare in support of an innocent state, which the Mohists consider justified, and with punitive war against a rogue ruler or state, which they hold can be justified in certain circumstances.

government policy. See *zhèng* 政.

great men. See *dà rén* 大人.

guǐ 鬼 (ghosts). A cornerstone of the Mohist worldview is that humans share the cosmos with a variety of sentient deities, ghosts, and spirits, who are ethically good, have higher social status than humans, and possess greater powers than we do and thus should be respected and obeyed. The *Mòzǐ* mentions three kinds of ghosts: ghosts of the sky, ghosts of deceased human ancestors, and ghosts and spirits of mountains and rivers. When the Mohists speak of promoting the benefit of all the world, they have in mind the benefit not only of humans but also of these other entities.

hài 害 (harm). The Mohists typically articulate their values through pairs of opposing concepts. Their ethics thus focuses not only on promoting benefit but removing harm, which they understand as a list of evils that are the opposite of their list of basic goods. The 'Greater Selection' discusses how in circumstances in which some harm is inevitable, selecting the lesser of two harms counts as promoting benefit.

harm. See *hài* 害.

Heaven. See Tiān 天.

huì 惠 (generosity). The relational virtue manifested by ethically admirable rulers toward their subjects.

intent. See *zhì* 志.

jiān 兼 (inclusion, whole, aggregate). The core connotation of *jiān* is to include or combine two or more things together, as when §47.9 speaks of collecting (*jiān*) white and black things together or §19.1b speaks of merging and annexing (*jiān*) territories. In Mohist ethics, *jiān* refers to including everyone together as the object of our ethical care or concern. The connotation of *jiān* in ethical contexts is not impartiality, as some translations suggest, but all-inclusiveness. (The Mohist term for impartiality is *wú sī* 無私.) In later Mohist ontology, *jiān* is a whole or an aggregate, of which the parts are *tǐ* 體 (units, parts, individuals).

jiān ài 兼愛 (inclusive care). A core Mohist ethical model that people are to emulate. We are to care all-inclusively about everyone and so take their welfare into consideration in determining courses of action. Accordingly, we are to be committed to promoting the benefit of all, including ourselves. As stated in the text (§15.1c), the model is for everyone to include one another within the scope of those we care about while interacting with one another in ways beneficial to both sides. This seems to imply that inclusive care is a standing attitude that is manifested in mutually beneficial conduct when we interact with each other. Since the benefits are mutual, inclusive care is not purely altruistic.

Jié 桀 (1818?–1766? BC). One of the four tyrants. According to tradition, the cruel last ruler of the Xià dynasty.

jié 節 (moderate, moderation). Although their rhetoric implies an austere lifestyle, officially the Mohists advocate not parsimony but moderation, which they understand as a mean between the excessive and the meagre.

jì sì 祭祀 (sacrifice, sacrificial rites or ceremonies). Although the Mohists reject excessively elaborate norms of ceremonial propriety, they are deeply committed to observing regular sacrificial rituals in honour of Heaven, the ghosts and spirits, and deceased ancestors. These rites include large-scale state rituals performed at the city altars of soil and grain and small-scale rituals performed in the home to express devotion to deceased kin.

jǔ 舉 (mention, cite, bring up, raise). In later Mohist semantic theory, *jǔ* refers to using a name (a spoken word) to talk about something. In the Mohists' view, the name functions like a model that informs listeners what the thing is like.

jūnzǐ 君子 (gentleman, princeling). Originally referring to the son of a prince or lord, by the Mohists' time *jūnzǐ* had come to have a connotation roughly like that of the English 'gentleman'. For the Erudites, being a gentleman is an ethically exemplary status that students of the way can realistically hope to achieve. For the Mohists, 'gentleman' is a descriptive rather than a normative term, designating a social status, not an ethical ideal. The gentlemen are socially prominent men with a status above that of the common people and the masses but below that of rulers and high officials. They are either holders of government posts or potential candidates for such posts and may include landholders, military officers, merchants, scholars, ritual priests, and others of similar status. Along with rulers, ministers, and officers, the gentleman is among the main audience to which many of the Triads are addressed.

kě 可 (acceptable, permissible, feasible, possible). In ethical contexts, *kě* refers to what is normatively acceptable or permissible. In other contexts, it can refer to what is possible or practically feasible. In semantic and logical contexts, it refers to an assertion being permissible according to semantic, logical, and pragmatic norms. *Kě* can also be used as a verb for deeming something acceptable, permissible, and so on.

kind. See *lèi* 類.

lèi 類 (kind). Distinguishing and disputation aim to draw distinctions between things correctly according to the kinds of which they are parts. Different kinds are associated with different reasons or bases (*gù* 故), which determine whether things are similar in relevant respects and so whether they belong to that kind. When the Mohists criticize others for being confused about how to draw distinctions, their explanation is that those they criticize fail to understand the relevant kind relations. See, for example, §19.5.

lǐ 禮 (ceremony, ritual, propriety, etiquette). Ceremonial or ritual propriety refers to norms of etiquette for circumstances ranging from everyday greetings and dining customs to wedding and funeral rites to large-scale state ceremonies. In Ruism, ceremonial or ritual propriety provides norms of conduct, outward forms by which to express attitudes, and a means of ethical development. The Mohists reject what they regard as excessively elaborate and wasteful practices of ceremonial propriety (§§21.3, 39.12, 48.8). They also reject customary etiquette as a fundamental guide to action (§25.7). They do not reject ceremonial propriety entirely (§12.1), however, and they invest great importance in the observance of regular sacrificial rituals in honour of Heaven, ghosts, and spirits. See *jì sì* 祭祀.

lǐ 里 (unit of distance). An ancient unit of distance slightly longer than 400 metres.

lì 利 (benefit, welfare). The core good in Mohist ethics. Right and wrong are determined by what increases the benefit of all the world and reduces its opposite, harm (*hài* 害), to all the world. Mohist ethics is consequentialist because it holds that the way lies in practices and policies that produce beneficial consequences for all. As the Mohists understand it, benefit is a complex, composite good consisting of material wealth, a large population, and social order.

Lì 厲 (*c.*878 BC). A cruel tyrant of the Zhōu dynasty.

Lord on High. See *Shàng Dì* 上帝.

loyal. See *zhōng* 忠.

luàn 亂 (disorder, chaos). The antithesis of order. A society in disorder is ethically and politically unsatisfactory. Incorrect cognition and judgement result from disorder in one's ability to draw distinctions properly.

mandate. See *mìng* 命.

mandate of Heaven. See *Tiān mìng* 天命.

Miáo 苗. A group of purportedly cruel and disorderly tribes conquered in the sage-king Yǔ's punitive wars. Their lands were to the south, between modern Húnán and Jiāngxī.

míng 名 (names). In Mohist semantics, all spoken words are considered names, which are used to mention objects, or 'stuff'. Names are 'that by which we assert/say' (A80). The Mohists understand them to refer at three levels of generality (A78): all-reaching names, which refer to everything; kind names, which refer to all the similar things that form a kind; and personal names, which refer to only one thing. Another use of *míng* (name) is refer to one's reputation.

mìng 命 (fate, destiny, mandate, command). A label or explanation for events that are beyond human control; the doctrine that people's fate is mandated by factors or forces beyond their control. The Mohists accuse some of their contemporaries, including the Erudites, of holding that fate determines what happens regardless of anything agents do. The Mohists deny that any such force or factor exists. See too *Tiān mìng* (the mandate of Heaven).

model. See *fǎ* 法.

Mò Dí 墨翟. Mòzǐ's surname and given name. Mòzǐ refers to himself as 'Dí'.

Mòzǐ 墨子 (Master Mò). How Mòzǐ is addressed.

names. See *míng* 名.

objects, reality. See *shí* 實.

officer. See *shì* 士.

order. See *zhì* 治.

paternal kindness. See *cí* 慈.

penal code. See *xíng* 刑.

permissible. See *kě* 可.

perverse. See *bèi* 誖.

punishments. See *xíng* 刑.

rán 然 (so, like this). *Rán* can indicate that something is like what has been said, that a statement is like the facts, or that something is like a model for the use of some term and thus the term correctly applies to it. In certain technical contexts, it is used specifically to affirm that a verbal predicate applies to something, but in other contexts it is used of noun predication as well. It can be used to affirm that something is indeed the case or that an assertion is indeed fitting. As such, its role sometimes overlaps that of 'true'.

relational virtues. The Mohists regard (male) social life as structured by three core relationships: those between rulers and subjects, fathers and sons, and elder and younger brothers. Each of the six roles involved in these relationships is associated with a relational virtue manifested in ethically appropriate attitudes and conduct for a person in that role to direct toward the other partner in the relationship. The Mohists consider the relational virtues to be elements of social order (*zhì* 治). An orderly society is one in which rulers, subjects, fathers, sons, and brothers manifest these virtues toward each other. See *cí* 慈, *huì* 惠, *tì* 悌, *xiào* 孝, and *zhōng* 忠.

rén 仁 (benevolence, kindness, humaneness). A core virtue for the Mohists, referring to an ethically exemplary status. The benevolent person is among the Mohists' fundamental ethical models (§§16.1, 32.1), someone who is concerned for all the world as a filially devoted son is concerned for his parents (§25.1). Benevolence seems a more demanding ethical standard than righteousness. Righteousness represents the minimal norms of conduct that, if jointly followed, tend to promote the benefit of everyone. Benevolence may involve acting more directly to promote the benefit of all. Canon A7 seems to indicate that benevolence is care for each individual, not merely for humanity as a whole.

righteousness. See *yì* 義.

Rú 儒 (erudite, scholar, Confucian). At the height of the Mohist movement—probably during the fourth century BC—the other most prominent self-identified ethical and cultural group was the Rú ('Erudites'), often referred to in English as the Confucians. (The word 'Rú' in Chinese has the connotation of 'erudite' or 'classicist' and does not explicitly refer to Confucius.) Although the Mohists' core ethical, political, and religious doctrines—such as inclusive care, identifying upward, condemning aggression, and respecting Heaven—were not motivated by opposition to the Rú, the Mohists did regard the Rú as embracing practices and doctrines they rejected, such as disrespect to Heaven, fatalism, costly but useless musical entertainment, and recklessly wasteful burial and mourning rituals. Hence the Rú are targets of criticism in book 39 and in the dialogues, especially book 48.

sacrifice. See *jì sì* 祭祀.

sage-kings. See *shèngwáng* 聖王.

same, similar. See *tóng* 同.

say. See *wèi* 謂.

Shāng 商 **dynasty,** *c.*1766–1122 BC. One of the three dynasties.

shàng 上 (above, upper, superior) and *xià* 下 (below, lower, subordinate). The *Mòzǐ* often refers to those occupying higher positions in the social and political hierarchy as 'those above' or 'above' and those occupying lower positions as 'those below' or 'below'. (A similar English formulation might be to speak of the 'higher-ups' and the 'underlings'.) The translation consistently renders such locutions as 'superiors' and 'subordinates'.

Shàng Dì 上帝 (the Lord on High, the Lord above). The high ancestor deity worshipped by the Shāng dynasty nobility, which the Mohists partially incorporate into their conception of Tiān (Heaven), the Zhōu dynasty deity. In the *Mòzǐ*, Dì and Tiān sometimes seem to be distinct entities, with distinct names, and Dì but not Tiān is frequently grouped together with the 'ghosts and spirits' or the 'ghosts and spirits of mountains and rivers', suggesting it ranks below Tiān in the cosmic hierarchy. At the same time, offering sacrifices to Dì and the ghosts and spirits counts as paying reverence to Tiān, so in some respect Dì is incorporated within or can represent Tiān.

shè jì 社稷 (altars of soil and grain). Along with the ancestral shrine of the rulers, the altars for paying reverence to the spirits of soil and grain were central sites in civic religious practices, symbols of a city's identity, and core elements of the city's physical design. By synecdoche, they represent the state and its sovereignty. To secure the altars is to secure the state; to overturn them is to overthrow the state.

shèngrén 聖人 (sage). An ideal figure who epitomizes ethical values and the practice of the way. Mohist writings sometimes appeal to the sage as a paragon to emulate, sometimes as an authority figure to justify their doctrines. §47.6 urges its audience to become sages.

shèngwáng 聖王 (sage-kings). The *Mòzǐ* regularly cites as moral and political exemplars six purportedly historical ancient sage-kings: Yáo, Shùn, Yǔ, Tāng, Wén, and Wǔ. (See the glossary entries for each king.)

shì 士 (officer, gentry, scholar-knight, men of service). Like the English 'knight', *shì* originally referred to a military rank but later came to denote a broad social class ranking above commoners but below the nobility, ministers, and high officials. This educated elite included minor aristocrats, landowners, gentry, military officers, and scholars. Commoners such as Mòzǐ could move into the *shì* class through education and meritorious service. The *shì* formed the main pool of talent for appointment to government office. Since many of the *shì* either were or aspired to become military or civil service officers, the translation consistently renders *shì* as 'officer'.

shì 是 (right, this). *Shì* expresses affirmation. Along with *fēi* (not, wrong), it forms a pair of terms for basic pro/con attitudes. In ethical contexts, *shì* has the connotation of 'right'; in semantic and logical contexts, it has the connotation of 'this', or the correct referent of a term under discussion. Used as a verb, *shì* refers to deeming something right and, in some contexts, thereby approving or endorsing it. To reflect the connections between the various uses of *shì*, the translation consistently renders the verbal use as 'to deem right'.

shí 實 (objects, stuff, facts, reality, in fact). In later Mohist semantics, *shí* are what names mention. They may be objects or things, including animate and inanimate things, as well as facts or situations. *Shí* refers to what actually exists, so by extension the word is also used to refer to what is indeed or in fact the case. *Shí* connotes a solid or full region and may be used as either a count noun or a mass noun. *Shí* is also used as an adverb with the sense of 'really' or 'sincerely'.

Shùn 舜 (reigned 2255?–2205? BC). Mythical ruler, second of the six sage-kings.

shuō 說 (explanation, doctrine, account). A piece of discourse that clarifies something (A72), typically by presenting the reasons for it (§45.1b). In Mohist logic, *shuō* refers to an account or a justification to support what one asserts. More generally, *shuō* can be any form of account or explanation. By extension, in some contexts it is plausibly interpreted as a doctrine or teaching. Pronounced *shuì*, the same graph refers to persuading, recommending, or presenting a case for something.

so. See *rán* 然.

Son of Heaven. See *Tiānzǐ* 天子.

statements. See *yán* 言.

superior and subordinate. See *shàng* 上 and *xià* 下.

Glossary 267

Tāng 湯 (reigned 1766?–1753? BC). The fourth of the six sage-kings. Defeated the tyrant Jié to topple the Xià dynasty and found the Shāng dynasty.

three dynasties. The Xià, Shāng, and Zhōu dynasties, three successive lineages of rule in ancient history as the Mohists understand it. The Mohists frequently cite examples from the three dynasties as historical precedents to support their doctrines.

three models (*sān fǎ* 三法), also three markers (*sān biǎo* 三表). The core doctrine in early Mohist epistemology and logic. Evaluating statements is a matter of distinguishing whether they are right or wrong and yield benefit or harm. To do so, we check to see whether they conform to three models or standards. In the first of the three versions of the doctrine, the models are the 'foundation' (the sage-kings' precedent), the 'source' (what the common people observe), and the 'use' (whether the doctrine proves beneficial in practice). See books 35–7.

tì 悌 (brotherliness, fraternal devotion to older brothers). The relational virtue manifested by ethically admirable younger brothers toward elder brothers, involving respect and obedience. The corresponding fraternal attitude of older brothers to younger ones is variously described as amicable, respectful, good, and peaceful or harmonious.

tǐ 體 (unit, part, body, individual). In later Mohist ontology, a thing considered as a unit or as part of a larger whole. The whole is *jiān* 兼. What counts as *tǐ* or *jiān* is relative to context. The same object can be regarded as *jiān* in one context—as a hand can be considered a whole that includes the fingers and thumb—and *tǐ* in another context—as a hand can be considered a part of the body.

Tiān 天 (Heaven, nature, sky). The Zhōu dynasty high deity, revered by the Mohists as the wisest, noblest, and most powerful entity in the cosmic sociopolitical and ontological order, which embodies moral norms by rewarding virtue and punishing viciousness. Since for the Mohists Heaven amounts to a deified conception of nature as a whole, other suprahuman entities, such as the Lord on High and various ghosts and spirits, are not fully distinct from it. Paying reverence to them counts as revering Heaven and their actions are by extension Heaven's actions.

Tiān mìng 天命 (the mandate of Heaven, Heaven's mandate, fated by Heaven). Heaven's sanction for a ruler on the grounds of his worthiness and competence. Heaven may withdraw its mandate from a vicious, corrupt ruler and mandate or command (*mìng*) another leader to overthrow him. Although the Mohists reject *mìng*, the doctrine that people's fate is mandated by forces beyond their control, in some contexts they affirm the traditional belief in Heaven's *mìng*, or mandate (see §19.5). Presumably, in such contexts, they see this belief as consistent with rejecting fatalism, since Heaven's mandate is earned or lost through actions that are within agents' control.

tiān xià 天下 (all the world, all under Heaven). The entire social world and everyone within it. (The social world is conceptually distinct from the natural world, which is referred to as *tiān dì* 天地.) In Mohist ethics, righteousness requires acting by a way (*dào*) that, if practised by everyone, will promote the benefit of all the world—not only one's own state, clan, town, or self, but everyone's. The benevolent person seeks to promote the benefit of all the world. Inclusive care is care directed at all the world.

Tiān zhì 天志 (Heaven's intent), *Tiān yì* 天意 (Heaven's intention). What Heaven intends to do; what it intends for humanity to do. See *yì* 意 and *zhì* 志. The Mohists hold that since Heaven is the wisest and noblest agent in the cosmos, its intention can serve as a model or standard of what is righteous.

Tiānzǐ 天子 (Son of Heaven). A title for the emperor, who rules over all under Heaven and answers to Heaven.

tóng 同 (same, similar). A pivotal concept in later Mohist semantics. Whether a name applies to something is determined by whether that thing is relevantly the same as what normally takes that name. All horses are parts of the same kind (*lèi* 類) and take the name 'horse' because they are all relevantly the same or similar. Things that are not the same are different (*yì* 異). Disputation (*biàn* 辯) and distinguishing (*biàn* 辨) are concerned with identifying relevant points of sameness or difference.

tyrants. The Mohists regularly cite four vicious historical tyrants as negative exemplars: Jié, Zhòu, Yōu, and Lì. The tyrants contrast with the sage-kings, who are paragons of wisdom and virtue. (See the entries for each tyrant.)

use. See *yòng* 用.

various lords. See *zhū hóu* 諸侯.

way. See *dào* 道.

wèi 謂 (say, assert, call). In later Mohist semantics and logic, to say something, to assert a name of something, or to mention something by name (see canon A79). A distinction-drawing disputation (*biàn* 辯) concerns which of two contradictory terms, such as 'ox' and 'non-ox', to *wèi* of something (to call it, to assert of it or say of it; see A74). Names are what speakers use to *wèi* (say things, make assertions); what speakers *wèi* (call by various names, say things of, make assertions about) is objects or stuff (see A80). When a speaker does not know a name *x* or what *x* refers to, the speaker asks either '*x*, what does it *wèi*?' (what does *x* refer to?) or 'what *wèi* *x*?' (what is called *x*?). In Mohist semantics, *wèi* is an extensional concept, making no reference to intensions or meanings.

Wén 文. One of the six sage-kings. A feudal lord loyal to the vicious tyrant Zhòu, last of the Shàng dynasty rulers. Father of the sage-king Wǔ.

wise. See *zhī zhě* 知者.

worthy. See *xián* 賢.

Wǔ 武 (reigned *c*.1122–1115 BC). One of the six sage-kings, son of Wén. Overthrew the tyrant Zhòu 紂 to found the Zhōu 周 dynasty, the third of the three dynasties.

wù 惡 (detest, despise, dislike). The opposite of care (*ài* 愛). Just as caring about others is associated with a disposition to benefit them, detesting them is associated with a disposition to harm or injure them.

Xià 夏 dynasty, *c*.2205–1766 BC. Semi-mythical dynasty considered the first of the three dynasties.

xián 賢 (worthy, worthies). As an adjective, a combination of competence and ethical excellence; as a noun, a competent, ethically excellent person, usually a *shì* (officer). A dedicated officer could realistically aspire to become a worthy. Being worthy contrasts with being unworthy or worthless (*bù xiào* 不肖) and with being vicious or cruel (*bào* 暴).

xiào 孝 (filial devotion, filial piety, familial devotion). The relational virtue manifested by ethically admirable children toward their parents, involving respect, obedience, and seeing to parents' welfare. (In a few contexts, virtuous conduct toward one's superiors is also referred to as 'filial devotion'.) Filial devotion is a cornerstone of the Mohist value system, as the Mohists take it to be a basic component of social order and treat the attitudes and conduct of filially devoted sons as a model for those of the benevolent person toward all the world. See §25.1.

xíng 行 (conduct, practice, actions). A term for conduct or practices, usually referring to patterns or habits of conduct, not individual acts. Conduct is closely associated with *yán* 言 (statements). The Mohists assume that the statements people hear and endorse will tend to guide their conduct. An agent's conduct and statements are expected to coincide and are open to criticism if they do not (see §16.2).

xíng 刑 (punishments, penal code, legal system). *Xíng* refers to criminal punishment or the penal code and by extension to the content and administration of the legal system. The *Mòzǐ* frequently uses the phrase *xíng zhèng* 刑政 to refer jointly to the legal system and government administration, or, roughly, laws and administration. The translation renders this phrase as 'punishments and government'. In a few passages where *xíng* refers specifically to a legal code, the translation uses 'penal code'.

yán 言 (sayings, statements, pronouncements, teachings, speech). *Yán* refers to any string of 'names' (*míng* 名, words) that states an intention or a point. Statements are understood functionally, not structurally; a statement may consist of a phrase, a sentence, or several sentences. Moreover, since pluralization is usually not marked in classical Chinese, references to a speaker's *yán* could denote one or several statements. (The *yán* of the fatalists quoted in §35.1, for example, consists of several sentences, which could constitute a single extended statement or a series of several statements.) Statements can function as teachings or maxims that direct conduct. Proper statements can express and guide practice of the way; improper ones can corrupt and mislead. Hence the Mohists regard promulgating appropriate statements and refuting misleading ones as crucial to their ethical and political aims. One means of social and ethical reform is for subordinates to model themselves on the exemplary statements and conduct—the words and deeds—of worthy superiors (see §11.4, for example). The statements agents endorse are normally expected to be consistent with their conduct, and inconsistency between the two is grounds for criticism (see §16.2). To reflect the pivotal role of *yán* in Mohist thought, the translation consistently renders it as 'statements' or 'to state'. It is worth keeping in mind that in various contexts the Mohists may understand statements to be functioning as teachings, assertions, or maxims.

Yáo 堯 (reigned 2356?–2255? BC). Mythical ruler, first of the six sage-kings. Passed over his own unworthy son to transmit the throne to Shùn, a farmer renowned for filial devotion.

yì 意 (thought, intention). What one has in mind or the aim of what one says or does. In the text of the 'Heaven's Intent' triad, Heaven's attitudes are more frequently referred to as Heaven's intentions (*yì*) or what Heaven wants or desires (*yù* 欲) than as Heaven's intent (*zhì* 志). In later Mohist semantics, *yì* is what a speaker is thinking of or intending, which the speaker aims to communicate. *Yì* refers not to the meaning of words but to the speaker's point; grasping the speaker's *yì* is the outcome of successful communication, not an explanation of how language enables communication. In some contexts, it may have a role similar to the Gricean notion of speaker's meaning.

yì 義 (righteousness, norm, rightness, appropriate). Along with benevolence (*rén* 仁), one of the Mohists' two core values, to which they are dedicated above all else. A widely cited ancient gloss explains *yì* as what is appropriate or fitting, given one's role and situation. By extension, it refers to what is appropriate generally and thus what is right or is the correct norm. The translation adopts 'righteous' as an English counterpart for *yì*, partly to distinguish it from *shì* 是 (right), partly to highlight its connection to specifically ethical or moral norms.

yòng 用 (use, apply, put into practice). The third of the three models for evaluating statements: using the statements to guide practice so as to determine whether they produce beneficial results. As ethical consequentialists, the Mohists are especially concerned with utility and frequently discuss the practical application of statements or policies. In such contexts, the translation consistently renders the word *yòng* as 'use'. It is worth keeping in mind various senses of the word, such as 'apply', 'employ', or 'practise'. Mohist economic texts also frequently discuss moderation in use—that is, in using up or expending resources. For consistency, in these contexts *yòng* is also rendered 'use'. Again, it is worth keeping in mind a range of senses, such as 'utilize', 'expend', and 'consume'.

Yōu 幽 (*c*.781 BC). Vicious tyrant who ruled during the Zhōu dynasty.

Yǔ 禹 (reigned 2205?–2197? BC). Third of the six sage-kings, mythical founder of the Xià dynasty. According to legend (see §15.3), he carried out vast flood-control projects across much of the known world, dedicating himself to benefiting others. The 'All Under Heaven' essay in the *Zhuāngzǐ* reports that Yǔ's extensive labours on behalf of all the world won him special admiration from Mohists of later generations, who saw Mohism as dedicated to 'the way of Yǔ'.

zhèng 政 (government, administration, policy). Many *Mòzǐ* passages mention adopting doctrines as a basis for *zhèng*—governing, government administration, or state policy. Applying a doctrine as state policy to see whether it proves beneficial is one aspect of the third of the three models for evaluating statements as right or wrong (see §35.1). To ensure such references are obvious to readers, the translation consistently renders them as adopting or taking something 'as government policy', although in some contexts simply 'as a policy' would produce more natural English. The *Mòzǐ* also frequently uses the phrase *xíng zhèng* 刑政 to refer jointly to the legal system and government administration. The translation consistently renders this phrase as 'punishments and government'.

zhì 志 (intent, aim, ambition). Used in the title of the 'Heaven's Intent' triad, which presents the doctrine that humanity should follow the intentions of Tiān (Heaven). *Zhì* refers to having one's heart set on, directed toward, or determined to pursue something. Unlike the English noun 'will', *zhì* does not refer to a psychological faculty that decides on or directs action.

zhì 治 (good order, put in order, govern, control, manage). A basic good of Mohist ethics. For the Mohists, what is right is determined by what promotes the benefit of all, and benefit consists in what increases wealth, population, and social order. Order in turn lies in the absence of war, crime, feuding, intimidation, exploitation, and other harms; the exercise of the relational virtues; rule by the virtuous and wise; appropriate distribution of rewards and punishments; and neighbourly sharing of resources. Besides its use as a noun to refer to good order, *zhì* is used as a verb to mean 'put in good order', 'govern', and in some contexts 'control' or 'manage'. To reflect the conceptual connections between all of these contexts and the crucial role of order in the Mohist value system, the translation consistently renders *zhì* as either 'order', 'put in order', or 'bring order to'. It is worth keeping in mind that for the Mohists *zhì* also connotes 'govern', 'control', and 'manage'.

zhì zhě 智者 or *zhī zhě* 知者 (knowledgeable, knowing, wise). In most contexts this phrase has been translated as 'the wise', but it could equally well be interpreted as 'the knowing' or 'the knowledgeable'. For the Mohists, a person of wisdom is a person of extensive knowledge or know-how.

zhōng 忠 (loyalty, integrity). The relational virtue manifested by ethically admirable political subjects toward their ruler.

Zhōu 周 (1122–771 BC). The third of the three dynasties, founded by the sage-king Wǔ.

Zhòu 紂 (reigned 1154–1122 BC). Vicious tyrant, last ruler of the Shāng dynasty.

zhū hóu 諸侯 (various lords, feudal lords, nobles). A general term for the enfeoffed rulers of various states, cities, and regions in the Chinese *fēngjiàn* 封建 (semi-feudal) social structure.

APPENDIX

THE CHRONOLOGY OF THE TRIADS

THE Mohist 'core chapters' or 'Triads'—books 8–37 of the *Mòzǐ*—present from one to three versions of each of the ten core doctrines that the Mohists eventually assembled into an explicit platform representing their movement.[1] One influential view of the Triads—first proposed by the Qīng dynasty scholar Yú Yuè 俞樾 (1821–1907)—is that the three books in each triad represent the views of three roughly contemporaneous Mohist sects, who according to the *Hánfēizǐ* 韓非子 squabbled with each other over doctrinal issues.[2] A modified version of this view was defended by A. C. Graham, who contended that once several misplaced books were removed, the books in each triad could be classified into three doctrinally distinct groups, corresponding to the positions of three quarrelling factions.[3] Other early sources, such as the *Zhuāngzǐ* 莊子 and *The Annals of Lǚ Bùwéi* 呂氏春秋, indicate that by the late Warring States period, the Mohist movement indeed included several geographically dispersed branches. There were almost certainly more than three, however, and nothing in the texts themselves ties them to exactly three rival factions. Moreover, the divergences in content between the books of each triad seem better explained as the product of doctrinal evolution than three opposing, potentially antagonistic stances. For this reason, the 'three factions' theory is no longer considered an adequate explanation for why there are up to three books on each doctrine or what the relationship between the three might be.[4]

Instead, in recent years a fairly broad scholarly consensus has formed according to which the three books in each triad are probably best explained as presenting Mohist doctrines at different stages in the movement's development.[5] In complete triads, such as the 'Inclusive Care' triad, many

[1] See §49.14.

[2] Yú's suggestion appears in his preface to Sūn Yíràng's edition of the *Mòzǐ*.

[3] A. C. Graham, *Divisions in Early Mohism Reflected in the Core Chapters of Mo-tzu* (Singapore: National University of Singapore, Institute of East Asian Philosophies, 1985). Graham's view is summarized in his *Disputers of the Tao* (La Salle, IL: Open Court, 1989), 36.

[4] C. Defoort and N. Standaert (eds), *The Mozi as an Evolving Text* (Leiden: Brill, 2013), 12. See too C. Fraser, 'Significance and Chronology of the Triads', supplement to 'Mohism', *The Stanford Encyclopedia of Philosophy*, E. Zalta (ed.), http://plato.stanford.edu/entries/mohism/triads.html (original publication 2002).

[5] Defoort and Standaert, *The Mozi as an Evolving Text*, 12–19. This consensus developed from research by Watanabe Takashi 渡邊卓 and A. Taeko Brooks. See Watanabe, 古代中國思想の研究 [*Research on Ancient Chinese Thought*] (Tokyo: Sōbunsha, 1973), and Brooks, 'The Mician Ethical Chapters', *Warring States Papers* 1 (2010), 100–18.

features of the three books seem explained well by the hypothesis that one (in this case, book 14) represents the views of Mohists writing at a relatively early date, another (here book 15) presents more elaborate and polished views written somewhat later, and a third (book 16) records still more thoroughly developed views written last. This pattern of sequential development plausibly explains the growth in the length of the books, their increased rhetorical and theoretical sophistication, their more thorough arguments, their expansion to include sections addressing objections to Mohist doctrines, and their practice of citing the deeds of the sage-kings and later also ancient documents to support their claims. Sequential development also plausibly explains thematic shifts from one book to another as the result of new problems and social conditions superseding older ones. For example, book 8, 'Promoting the Worthy (I)', is framed around the problem of attracting an adequate pool of competent government administrators. The second and third books in the same triad focus instead on denouncing cronyism and nepotism, contending that effective rule requires that only genuinely qualified candidates be appointed to office. A reasonable explanation of this thematic shift might be that between the time books 8 and 9 were written, population growth, social mobility, and increased educational opportunities had resolved the problem of attracting talented personnel. The more pressing issue was then to persuade rulers to employ competent candidates rather than favouring their kin and associates.

Of course, a sequential development theory is consistent with the possibility that different sets of books could have been produced by distinct Mohist factions, possibly based in different regions. The point is that the existence of three different books carrying the same title is not adequately explained merely by attributing them to different factions. There must be more to the story.

As it turns out, besides features suggestive of doctrinal evolution, the triad books also have structural, thematic, and linguistic features that divide them into at least four groups.[6] Several characteristics of these groups seem best explained by taking them to represent sequential stages in the evolution of Mohist doctrines. A hypothesis worth considering, then, is that the grouping might represent both different origins or

---

[6] This classification is based on the findings of Stephen Durrant, A. C. Graham, and A. Taeko Brooks. See Durrant, 'A Consideration of Differences in the Grammar of the Mo Tzu "Essays" and "Dialogues"', *Monumenta Serica* 33 (1977–8), 248–67; Graham, *Divisions in Early Mohism Reflected in the Core Chapters of Mo-tzu* (Singapore: National University of Singapore, 1985); and Brooks, 'The Mician Ethical Chapters', *Warring States Papers* 1 (2010), 100–18.

TABLE 1 Stratification of the Mohist Triads (*Mòzǐ*, books 8–37)

Stage	Group	賢	同	兼	攻	用	葬	天	鬼	樂	命
Earliest	P			14	17	20	(23)		(29)		
Early	M	8	11	15	18	21	(24)	26	(30)		35?
Middle	H	9*	12*	16	19	(22)	25	27*	31	32	37?
Later	R	10*	13*					28*		(33, 34)	36?

affiliations of the books and different historical stages or strata in the accretional development of the Triads.

The first of the four groups comprises the three short books—one each from the 'Inclusive Care', 'Condemning Aggression', and 'Moderation in Use' triads—that do not begin with the incipit phrase 'Our master Mòzǐ stated'. One of these books does not quote Mòzǐ at all; two quote him only once, in their concluding lines. The rhetoric and doctrines in these books are conspicuously simpler and less elaborate than those in other books, and so many scholars tentatively consider these the earliest of the triad writings. Let me call these books the 'P' series, as they seem to form a precursor layer within the Triads. (See the first row of Table 1.)

The second group contains seven books that do begin with the incipit 'Our master Mòzǐ stated' but do not cite ancient documents and do not share linguistic features associated with the third group. These books include one from each of seven triads, 'Promoting the Worthy' (book 8), 'Identifying Upward' (11), 'Inclusive Care' (15), 'Condemning Aggression' (18), 'Moderation in Use' (21), 'Heaven's Intent' (26), and 'Condemning Fatalism' (35). (See the second row of Table 1.) Because these books seem rhetorically and doctrinally more complex than the precursor group but less so than the third group, many scholars consider them to fall chronologically between the two. Let me refer to this as the 'M' group, because they introduce the convention of starting each book with the 'our master Mòzǐ' formula. These books appear to reflect Mohist thought in an early stage of development, the writers seeking to clarify their doctrines, ground them in the purported deeds of the sage-kings, and in some cases formulate responses to critics. Most likely there is some time depth within this layer—for example, book 11, 'Identifying Upward (I)', seems a rougher, earlier work than book 15, 'Inclusive Care (II)', which is longer, uses more polished rhetoric, and includes replies to objections.

Like the books in the 'M' layer, the third group has an incipit quotation from Mòzǐ and references to the sage-kings. All but two of the books in this group also include citations from ancient documents. What identifies the group as a whole is a distinctive linguistic trait along with certain terminological and rhetorical features. Let me call this the 'H' group, since its identifying feature is an unusual postverbal use of the word *hū* 乎. (See the third line in Table 1.) The 'H' group includes one book from each of the Triads except for 'Moderation in Use', which is missing its third book. The 'H' group seems to represent a distinct chronological layer in the evolution of the Triads. The arguments and doctrines in this group tend to be the most subtle, detailed, and sophisticated among the triad books and probably represent Mohist doctrines during mature stages of the movement's development. Again, the various books in the 'H' group probably range in date, but as a set they seem to form a stratum from a later time than the 'P' and 'M' books. Since their distinguishing feature is an unusual linguistic usage, they could reflect the speech habits of Mohists from a distinct region. Their shared linguistic and rhetorical features make it likely they were produced by the same or closely related writers or editors, probably within a relatively narrow timeframe.

The fourth group includes only four books. These are the third books in the 'Promoting the Worthy', 'Identifying Upward', and 'Heaven's Intent' triads, along with one book from the 'Condemning Fatalism' triad. This group shares the opening Mòzǐ quotation and references to ancient documents but is notable for two linguistic peculiarities, use of the particle *rán* 然 when citing from ancient documents and, in three books, the locution *kě ér* 可而. I will call this the 'R' group, after the particle *rán*. (See the last line in Table 1.) With the exception of the fatalism book, thematically the 'R' books are each noticeably different from the others in their triad, as I will explain momentarily. Like the 'H' books, then, they seem to form a set whose features may be best explained by attributing them to a distinct team of writers or editors, again possibly from a different Mohist faction. One of these books—'Heaven's Intent (III)'—mentions an analogy based on the kings of the southern states of Chǔ and Yuè, which might suggest the text was written for an audience in those regions.

If we combine the above observations and provisionally suppose the 'R' books may be of later date than the 'H' books, the result is a rough, four-stage picture of the sequential development of the Triads,[7] as shown in Table 1. (Books indicated in parentheses are missing from the extant Mòzǐ.)

The three books on fatalism—marked in Table 1 with question marks—are a special case, as they appear to have suffered extensive textual corruption. Some paragraphs seem to have been switched between the three, while others may be missing. For these reasons, I will set these books aside without further discussion.

---

[7] The proposal that these observations about the Triads provide the basis for a sequential theory of their development is due to Taeko Brooks.

As we saw in the example of books 8 and 15, comparing books within each of the four rough strata may yield plausible grounds for subdividing the strata further to produce a more fine-grained theory of the Triads' development.[8] For the purposes of this discussion, however, I will stop with this simple four-stage model.

A potential source of complications is that some of the books are highly likely to be composite texts themselves, and so some of their sections could be earlier or later than others. Unfortunately, given the data currently available, our ability to investigate this possibility is limited.

At present, there are two main rival sequential development theories for the Triads, those of Watanabe Takashi and A. Taeko Brooks. The theories agree on the sequence of development within six of the ten triads. (Three of these have only a single extant book, so there is no sequence to disagree about.) This leaves three triads about which they disagree: 'Promoting the Worthy' (books 8–10), 'Identifying Upward' (books 11–13), and 'Heaven's Intent' (books 26–8). Brooks proposes that the chronological order in which the books in these triads were composed is the order in which they appear in the *Mòzǐ* and in Table 1: 8–9–10, 11–12–13, and 26–27–28. Watanabe argues instead that in these triads, the third of the three books was written before the second. The order of composition was 8–10–9, 11–13–12, and 26–28–27. Thus, the difference between the two theories comes down to the relative dating of the books marked with an asterisk in Table 1: 9 versus 10, 12 versus 13, and 27 versus 28.

Without presuming to settle this complex issue, let me offer several reasons why Brooks's proposal for the relative chronology of these three pairs of books may be more justified.[9] The following remarks bear only on the relative sequence of the books, not on the historical dates that either Watanabe or Brooks assigns to them.

The first point is that book 28, 'Heaven's Intent (III)', appears to borrow several lines in §28.1b from book 27, 'Heaven's Intent (II)'.[10] There are three reasons for thinking the direction of borrowing is likely to have been from 27 to 28, not the other way around. First, in 27 the material is part of a coherent discussion, while in §28.1b it abruptly changes the subject of the

---

[8] Brooks, 'The Mician Ethical Chapters', undertakes research along these lines.

[9] Here I part from Defoort and Standaert, who favour Watanabe's ordering. See Defoort and Standaert, *The* Mozi *as an Evolving Text*, 16. Their conclusions rest partly on the findings of K. Desmet, 'The Growth of Compounds in the Core Chapters of the *Mozi*', *Oriens Extremus* 45.6 (2005–6), 99–118. See too J. Knoblock and J. Riegel, *Mozi: A Study and Translation of the Ethical and Political Writings*, China Research Monograph 68 (Berkeley, CA: Institute of East Asian Studies, 2013), 33, who accept Watanabe's view except for the ordering of books 12 and 13.

[10] The borrowed material appears at 28/16–18 in the Harvard–Yenching concordance text, which appears to be imitating 27/5–6.

paragraph and introduces a conclusion that is a non sequitur.[11] Second, the same section, §28.1b, appears to blend material, not fully coherently, from two further sections of 'Heaven's Intent (I)',[12] so it is likely that the entire section is based on other sources. Third, although many triad books appear to be composite texts, book 28 stands out for its extensive yet clumsy borrowing from other books. §28.4 adopts the analogy between Heaven's intent and the craftsmen's compass and square from §26.7 (and perhaps §27.3a) but confuses it, stating that the tools are used to distinguish between square and round, rather than square and non-square, round and non-round. §28.5a then jumps without explanation to the conclusion that the gentlemen of the world are far from righteousness, a claim presented clearly and logically in §26.7. Unlike 26 or 27, book 28 includes an extended criticism of aggression based on material from the 'Condemning Aggression' triad. §28.5a seems to use phrasing from §19.3 and ideas from §17.1; §28.5b is a rewritten version of §17.1; and §28.5c reworks material from §17.2 but garbles its analogy about seeing black and white or tasting sweet and bitter. This extensive, uneven mixing of material suggests that book 28 is a late, syncretic text. Moreover, were 28 earlier than 27, we might expect 27 to follow it in including an extended argument against aggression, but it does not.

If books 10, 13, and 28 indeed form a set with similar origins, and if 28 is indeed later than 27, an 'H' layer book, and 19, another 'H' layer book with which it shares phrasing, then we have *prima facie* grounds to think the 'R' group books 10 and 13 may be chronologically later than the 'H' layer books 9 and 12. I suggest that they may indeed be later because of how 10 and 13 develop themes broached in their respective 'H' series books.[13] A pivotal topic in books 10 and 13 is the integrity of society's system of rewards and punishments, which for the Mohists was the key means by which rulers governed the populace. The reward and punishment system amounted to a combination of a legal system and a social and career ladder. The Mohists who produced books 9 and 12 had become concerned with how social order depended on effective functioning of this system, which in turn depended on reliable, consistent application of norms shared by rulers and the ruled (and, accordingly, on eliminating arbitrary cronyism and nepotism). These issues are presented in §9.5a and §12.7c, after the initial presentation of each book's theme. They are foregrounded in §10.1

[11] Of course, it is possible that books 27 and 28 might both draw on a third text as a shared source. In that case, however, the fact that the source material appears as part of a coherent, well-wrought discussion in 27 but not in 28 suggests that the relevant sections of 27 may present an earlier, unconfused version of the material.

[12] For details, see the notes to §28.1b in the translation.

[13] This point was first argued in C. Fraser, 'Thematic Relationships in MZ 8–10 and 11–13', *Warring States Papers* 1 (2010), 139–40.

and mentioned again in §10.5c. In §13.1, they are framed as the main topic of book 13, which proposes an approach—grasping the actual situation among subordinates—that seems to develop ideas from §12.8. In both triads, then, the 'H' book seems to raise a practical problem in the administration of rewards and punishments, which is treated more prominently and addressed further in the 'R' books. A plausible explanation of this pattern is that the 'R' books were composed later. Moreover, the approach to unifying society's norms proposed in §13.4 combines the norm of inclusive care with the doctrine of identifying upward, thus ensuring that the norms promulgated by leaders will be ones people can identify with. This is an intriguing, potentially compelling modification of the doctrine of identifying upward. If book 12 were later than 13, we might expect it to follow 13 in mentioning inclusive care, but it does not. Hence 13 may be the later of the two. The best explanation for all of these features seems to be that the 'R' layer as a whole was composed after the 'H' layer and thus that the chronological development of the Triads followed the pattern shown in Table 1.

The
Oxford
World's
Classics
Website

www.worldsclassics.co.uk

- Browse the full range of Oxford World's Classics online

- Sign up for our monthly e-alert to receive information on new titles

- Read extracts from the Introductions

- Listen to our editors and translators talk about the world's greatest literature with our Oxford World's Classics audio guides

- Join the conversation, follow us on Twitter at OWC_Oxford

- Teachers and lecturers can order inspection copies quickly and simply via our website

www.worldsclassics.co.uk

American Literature

British and Irish Literature

Children's Literature

Classics and Ancient Literature

Colonial Literature

Eastern Literature

European Literature

Gothic Literature

History

Medieval Literature

Oxford English Drama

Philosophy

Poetry

Politics

Religion

The Oxford Shakespeare

A complete list of Oxford World's Classics, including Authors in Context, Oxford English Drama, and the Oxford Shakespeare, is available in the UK from the Marketing Services Department, Oxford University Press, Great Clarendon Street, Oxford OX2 6DP, or visit the website at www.oup.com/uk/worldsclassics.

In the USA, visit www.oup.com/us/owc for a complete title list.

Oxford World's Classics are available from all good bookshops. In case of difficulty, customers in the UK should contact Oxford University Press Bookshop, 116 High Street, Oxford OX1 4BR.

Classical Literary Criticism
The First Philosophers: The Presocrats
   and the Sophists
Greek Lyric Poetry
Myths from Mesopotamia

APOLLODORUS   **The Library of Greek Mythology**

APOLLONIUS OF RHODES   **Jason and the Golden Fleece**

APULEIUS   **The Golden Ass**

ARISTOPHANES   **Birds and Other Plays**

ARISTOTLE   **The Nicomachean Ethics**
Politics

ARRIAN   **Alexander the Great**

BOETHIUS   **The Consolation of Philosophy**

CAESAR   **The Civil War**
The Gallic War

CATULLUS   **The Poems of Catullus**

CICERO   **Defence Speeches**
The Nature of the Gods
On Obligations
Political Speeches
The Republic and The Laws

EURIPIDES   **Bacchae and Other Plays**
Heracles and Other Plays
Medea and Other Plays
Orestes and Other Plays
The Trojan Women and Other Plays

HERODOTUS   **The Histories**

HOMER   **The Iliad**
The Odyssey

A SELECTION OF   **OXFORD WORLD'S CLASSICS**

HORACE	**The Complete Odes and Epodes**
JUVENAL	**The Satires**
LIVY	**The Dawn of the Roman Empire**
	Hannibal's War
	The Rise of Rome
MARCUS AURELIUS	**The Meditations**
OVID	**The Love Poems**
	Metamorphoses
PETRONIUS	**The Satyricon**
PLATO	**Defence of Socrates, Euthyphro, and Crito**
	Gorgias
	Meno and Other Dialogues
	Phaedo
	Republic
	Symposium
PLAUTUS	**Four Comedies**
PLUTARCH	**Greek Lives**
	Roman Lives
	Selected Essays and Dialogues
PROPERTIUS	**The Poems**
SOPHOCLES	**Antigone, Oedipus the King, and Electra**
SUETONIUS	**Lives of the Caesars**
TACITUS	**The Annals**
	The Histories
THUCYDIDES	**The Peloponnesian War**
VIRGIL	**The Aeneid**
	The Eclogues and Georgics
XENOPHON	**The Expedition of Cyrus**

A SELECTION OF   **OXFORD WORLD'S CLASSICS**

THOMAS AQUINAS	**Selected Philosophical Writings**
FRANCIS BACON	**The Major Works**
WALTER BAGEHOT	**The English Constitution**
GEORGE BERKELEY	**Principles of Human Knowledge and Three Dialogues**
EDMUND BURKE	**A Philosophical Enquiry into the Sublime and Beautiful** **Reflections on the Revolution in France**
CONFUCIUS	**The Analects**
RENÉ DESCARTES	**A Discourse on the Method** **Meditations on First Philosophy**
ÉMILE DURKHEIM	**The Elementary Forms of Religious Life**
FRIEDRICH ENGELS	**The Condition of the Working Class in England**
JAMES GEORGE FRAZER	**The Golden Bough**
SIGMUND FREUD	**The Interpretation of Dreams**
G. W. E. HEGEL	**Outlines of the Philosophy of Right**
THOMAS HOBBES	**Human Nature and De Corpore Politico** **Leviathan**
DAVID HUME	**An Enquiry concerning Human Understanding** **Selected Essays**
IMMANUEL KANT	**Critique of Judgement**
SØREN KIERKEGAARD	**Repetition and Philosophical Crumbs**
JOHN LOCKE	**An Essay concerning Human Understanding**

A SELECTION OF   **OXFORD WORLD'S CLASSICS**

NICCOLÒ MACHIAVELLI   **The Prince**

THOMAS MALTHUS   **An Essay on the Principle of Population**

KARL MARX   **Capital**
The Communist Manifesto

J. S. MILL   **On Liberty and Other Essays**
Principles of Political Economy and
Chapters on Socialism

FRIEDRICH NIETZSCHE   **Beyond Good and Evil**
The Birth of Tragedy
On the Genealogy of Morals
Thus Spoke Zarathustra
Twilight of the Idols

THOMAS PAINE   **Rights of Man, Common Sense, and**
Other Political Writings

JEAN-JACQUES ROUSSEAU   **The Social Contract**
Discourse on the Origin of Inequality

ARTHUR SCHOPENHAUER   **The Two Fundamental Problems of**
Ethics

ADAM SMITH   **An Inquiry into the Nature and Causes**
of the Wealth of Nations

MARY WOLLSTONECRAFT   **A Vindication of the Rights of Woman**

A SELECTION OF   **OXFORD WORLD'S CLASSICS**

Bhagavad Gita

The Bible Authorized King James Version
With Apocrypha

The Book of Common Prayer

Dhammapada

The Gospels

The Koran

The Pañcatantra

**The Sauptikaparvan (from the
Mahabharata)**

**The Tale of Sinuhe and Other Ancient
Egyptian Poems**

The Qur'an

Upanisads

ANSELM OF CANTERBURY   **The Major Works**

THOMAS AQUINAS   **Selected Philosophical Writings**

AUGUSTINE   **The Confessions**
    On Christian Teaching

BEDE   **The Ecclesiastical History**

KĀLIDĀSA   **The Recognition of Śakuntalā**

LAOZI   **Daodejing**

RUMI   **The Masnavi**

ŚĀNTIDEVA   **The Bodhicaryāvatāra**

A SELECTION OF   **OXFORD WORLD'S CLASSICS**

The Anglo-Saxon World

Beowulf

Lancelot of the Lake

The Paston Letters

Sir Gawain and the Green Knight

The Poetic Edda

The Mabinogion

Tales of the Elders of Ireland

York Mystery Plays

GEOFFREY CHAUCER   **The Canterbury Tales**
                             Troilus and Criseyde

GUILLAUME DE LORRIS   **The Romance of the Rose**
and JEAN DE MEUN

HENRY OF HUNTINGDON   **The History of the English People**
                             1000–1154

JOCELIN OF BRAKELOND   **Chronicle of the Abbey of Bury**
                             St Edmunds

WILLIAM LANGLAND   **Piers Plowman**

SIR JOHN MANDEVILLE   **The Book of Marvels and Travels**

SIR THOMAS MALORY   **Le Morte Darthur**

A SELECTION OF **OXFORD WORLD'S CLASSICS**

An Anthology of Elizabethan Prose
Fiction

Early Modern Women's Writing

Three Early Modern Utopias (Utopia;
New Atlantis; The Isle of Pines)

FRANCIS BACON Essays
The Major Works

APHRA BEHN Oroonoko and Other Writings
The Rover and Other Plays

JOHN BUNYAN Grace Abounding
The Pilgrim's Progress

JOHN DONNE The Major Works
Selected Poetry

JOHN FOXE Book of Martyrs

BEN JONSON The Alchemist and Other Plays
The Devil is an Ass and Other Plays
Five Plays

JOHN MILTON The Major Works
Paradise Lost
Selected Poetry

EARL OF ROCHESTER Selected Poems

SIR PHILIP SIDNEY The Old Arcadia
The Major Works

SIR PHILIP and The Sidney Psalter
MARY SIDNEY

IZAAK WALTON The Compleat Angler

Travel Writing 1700–1830

Women's Writing 1778–1838

WILLIAM BECKFORD   Vathek

JAMES BOSWELL   Life of Johnson

FRANCES BURNEY   Camilla
                     Cecilia
                     Evelina

ROBERT BURNS   Selected Poems and Songs

LORD CHESTERFIELD   Lord Chesterfield's Letters

JOHN CLELAND   Memoirs of a Woman of Pleasure

DANIEL DEFOE   A Journal of the Plague Year
                     Moll Flanders
                     Robinson Crusoe
                     Roxana

HENRY FIELDING   Jonathan Wild
                     Joseph Andrews and Shamela
                     Tom Jones

JOHN GAY   The Beggar's Opera and Polly

WILLIAM GODWIN   Caleb Williams

OLIVER GOLDSMITH   The Vicar of Wakefield

MARY HAYS   Memoirs of Emma Courtney

ELIZABETH INCHBALD   A Simple Story

SAMUEL JOHNSON   The History of Rasselas
                     Lives of the Poets
                     The Major Works

CHARLOTTE LENNOX   The Female Quixote

MATTHEW LEWIS   The Monk

A SELECTION OF   **OXFORD WORLD'S CLASSICS**

HENRY MACKENZIE	**The Man of Feeling**
ALEXANDER POPE	**Selected Poetry**
ANN RADCLIFFE	**The Italian** **The Mysteries of Udolpho** **The Romance of the Forest** **A Sicilian Romance**
CLARA REEVE	**The Old English Baron**
SAMUEL RICHARDSON	**Pamela**
RICHARD BRINSLEY SHERIDAN	**The School for Scandal and Other Plays**
TOBIAS SMOLLETT	**The Adventures of Roderick Random** **The Expedition of Humphry Clinker**
LAURENCE STERNE	**The Life and Opinions of Tristram Shandy, Gentleman** **A Sentimental Journey**
JONATHAN SWIFT	**Gulliver's Travels** **Major Works** **A Tale of a Tub and Other Works**
JOHN VANBRUGH	**The Relapse and Other Plays**
HORACE WALPOLE	**The Castle of Otranto**
MARY WOLLSTONECRAFT	**Letters written in Sweden, Norway, and Denmark** **Mary and The Wrongs of Woman** **A Vindication of the Rights of Woman**

	Late Victorian Gothic Tales
	Literature and Science in the
	Nineteenth Century
JANE AUSTEN	**Emma**
	Mansfield Park
	Persuasion
	Pride and Prejudice
	Selected Letters
	Sense and Sensibility
MRS BEETON	**Book of Household Management**
MARY ELIZABETH BRADDON	**Lady Audley's Secret**
ANNE BRONTË	**The Tenant of Wildfell Hall**
CHARLOTTE BRONTË	**Jane Eyre**
	Shirley
	Villette
EMILY BRONTË	**Wuthering Heights**
ROBERT BROWNING	**The Major Works**
JOHN CLARE	**The Major Works**
SAMUEL TAYLOR COLERIDGE	**The Major Works**
WILKIE COLLINS	**The Moonstone**
	No Name
	The Woman in White
CHARLES DARWIN	**The Origin of Species**
THOMAS DE QUINCEY	**The Confessions of an English**
	Opium-Eater
	On Murder
CHARLES DICKENS	**The Adventures of Oliver Twist**
	Barnaby Rudge
	Bleak House
	David Copperfield
	Great Expectations
	Nicholas Nickleby

A SELECTION OF   **OXFORD WORLD'S CLASSICS**

CHARLES DICKENS   **The Old Curiosity Shop**
     Our Mutual Friend
     The Pickwick Papers

GEORGE DU MAURIER   **Trilby**

MARIA EDGEWORTH   **Castle Rackrent**

GEORGE ELIOT   **Daniel Deronda**
     The Lifted Veil and Brother Jacob
     Middlemarch
     The Mill on the Floss
     Silas Marner

EDWARD FITZGERALD   **The Rubáiyát of Omar Khayyám**

ELIZABETH GASKELL   **Cranford**
     The Life of Charlotte Brontë
     Mary Barton
     North and South
     Wives and Daughters

GEORGE GISSING   **New Grub Street**
     The Nether World
     The Odd Women

EDMUND GOSSE   **Father and Son**

THOMAS HARDY   **Far from the Madding Crowd**
     Jude the Obscure
     The Mayor of Casterbridge
     The Return of the Native
     Tess of the d'Urbervilles
     The Woodlanders

JAMES HOGG   **The Private Memoirs and Confessions
     of a Justified Sinner**

JOHN KEATS   **The Major Works**
     Selected Letters

CHARLES MATURIN   **Melmoth the Wanderer**

HENRY MAYHEW   **London Labour and the London Poor**

A SELECTION OF OXFORD WORLD'S CLASSICS

WILLIAM MORRIS **News from Nowhere**

JOHN RUSKIN **Praeterita**
Selected Writings

WALTER SCOTT **Ivanhoe**
Rob Roy
Waverley

MARY SHELLEY **Frankenstein**
The Last Man

ROBERT LOUIS STEVENSON **Strange Case of Dr Jekyll and Mr Hyde**
and Other Tales
Treasure Island

BRAM STOKER **Dracula**

W. M. THACKERAY **Vanity Fair**

FRANCES TROLLOPE **Domestic Manners of the Americans**

OSCAR WILDE **The Importance of Being Earnest**
and Other Plays
The Major Works
The Picture of Dorian Gray

ELLEN WOOD **East Lynne**

DOROTHY WORDSWORTH **The Grasmere and Alfoxden Journals**

WILLIAM WORDSWORTH **The Major Works**

WORDSWORTH and **Lyrical Ballads**
COLERIDGE

A SELECTION OF   **OXFORD WORLD'S CLASSICS**

LUDOVICO ARIOSTO	**Orlando Furioso**
GIOVANNI BOCCACCIO	**The Decameron**
LUÍS VAZ DE CAMÕES	**The Lusíads**
MIGUEL DE CERVANTES	**Don Quixote de la Mancha** **Exemplary Stories**
CARLO COLLODI	**The Adventures of Pinocchio**
DANTE ALIGHIERI	**The Divine Comedy** **Vita Nuova**
GALILEO	**Selected Writings**
J. W. VON GOETHE	**Faust: Part One and Part Two**
FRANZ KAFKA	**The Metamorphosis and Other Stories** **The Trial**
LEONARDO DA VINCI	**Selections from the Notebooks**
LOPE DE VEGA	**Three Major Plays**
FEDERICO GARCIA LORCA	**Four Major Plays** **Selected Poems**
NICCOLÒ MACHIAVELLI	**Discourses on Livy** **The Prince**
MICHELANGELO	**Life, Letters, and Poetry**
PETRARCH	**Selections from the Canzoniere and** **Other Works**
LUIGI PIRANDELLO	**Three Plays**
RAINER MARIA RILKE	**Selected Poems**
GIORGIO VASARI	**The Lives of the Artists**

A SELECTION OF OXFORD WORLD'S CLASSICS

Ludovico Ariosto	Orlando Furioso
Giovanni Boccaccio	The Decameron
Baldassare Castiglione	The Book of the Courtier
Miguel de Cervantes	Don Quixote de la Mancha
	Exemplary Stories
Carlo Collodi	The Adventures of Pinocchio
Dante Alighieri	The Divine Comedy
	Vita Nuova
	Selected Poetry
J. W. von Goethe	Faust: Part One and Part Two
Franz Kafka	The Metamorphosis and Other Stories
	The Trial
Leonardo da Vinci	Selections from the Notebooks
Lope de Vega	Three Major Plays
Federico García Lorca	Four Major Plays
	Selected Poems
Niccolò Machiavelli	Discourses on Livy
	The Prince
Michelangelo	Life, Letters, and Poetry
Petrarch	Selections from the Canzoniere and
	Other Works
Luigi Pirandello	Three Plays
Rainer Maria Rilke	Selected Poems
Giorgio Vasari	The Lives of the Artists